Better Homes and Gardens®

SIMPLE EVERYDAY

diabetic

MEALS

Meredith® Books
Des Moines, Iowa

Simple Everyday Diabetic Meals
Editor: Stephanie Karpinske, R.D.
Contributing Editor: Janet Figg
Contributing Writers: Alice Lesch Kelly, Heidi McIndoo, R.D.
Senior Associate Design Director: Ken Carlson
Contributing Designer: Terry Hall
Copy Chief: Terri Fredrickson
Publishing Operations Manager: Karen Schirm
Edit and Design Production Coordinator: Mary Lee Gavin
Book Production Managers: Pam Kvitne, Marjorie J. Schenkelberg,
   Rick von Holdt, Mark Weaver
Contributing Copy Editor: Kim Catanzarite
Contributing Proofreaders: Jodie Littleton, Elise Marton, Gretchen Kauffman
Photographers: Pete Krumhardt, Blaine Moats
Food Stylists: Paige Boyle, Charles Worthington
Indexer: Spectrum Communications Services, Inc.
Editorial Assistant: Cheryl Eckert

Test Kitchen Director: Lynn Blanchard
Test Kitchen Product Supervisor: Jennifer Kalinowski, R.D.
Test Kitchen Home Economists: Marilyn Cornelius; Juliana Hale; Laura Harms, R.D.;
   Maryellyn Krantz; Jill Moberly; Dianna Nolin; Colleen Weeden; Lori Wilson

Meredith® Books
Editor in Chief: Linda Raglan Cunningham
Design Director: Matt Strelecki
Managing Editor: Gregory H. Kayko
Executive Editor: Jennifer Dorland Darling

Publisher: James D. Blume
Executive Director, Marketing: Jeffrey Myers
Executive Director, New Business Development: Todd M. Davis
Executive Director, Sales: Ken Zagor
Director, Operations: George A. Susral
Director, Production: Douglas M. Johnston
Business Director: Jim Leonard

Vice President and General Manager: Douglas J. Guendel

Better Homes and Gardens® Magazine
Editor in Chief: Karol DeWulf Nickell
Deputy Editor, Food and Entertaining: Nancy Hopkins

Meredith Publishing Group
President, Publishing Group: Stephen M. Lacy
Vice President-Publishing Director: Bob Mate

Meredith Corporation
Chairman and Chief Executive Officer: William T. Kerr

In Memoriam: E.T. Meredith III (1933-2003)

All of us at Meredith® Books are dedicated to providing you with the information and ideas
you need to create delicious foods. We welcome your comments and suggestions.
Write to us at: Meredith Books, Cookbook Editorial Department, 1716 Locust St.,
Des Moines, IA 50309-3023.

If you would like to purchase any of our cooking, crafts, gardening, home improvement, or
home decorating and design books, check wherever quality books are sold.
Or visit us at: bhgbooks.com

Pictured on front cover: Pizza with Red Pepper Sauce (see recipe, page 213)

Our seal assures you that every
recipe in *Simple Everyday
Diabetic Meals* has been tested
in the Better Homes and
Gardens® Test Kitchen. This
means that each recipe is
practical and reliable, and meets
our high standards of taste
appeal. We guarantee your
satisfaction with this book for as
long as you own it.

contents

LESS THAN 10 GRAMS OF CARBS

Counting carbs? Look for this symbol on recipes that contain less than 10 grams total carbohydrate per serving.

GREAT FOR KIDS

Find this symbol on recipes that are sure to be hits with diabetic kids and teens.

diabetes today

If you're reading this book, you probably have diabetes or know someone who does. In fact, most people today have at least one friend or family member with the disease. That's because diabetes is fast becoming an epidemic; it currently affects 18 million people in America, or 6.3 percent of the population. Amazingly, almost a third of them don't even know they have it.

The number of Americans with diabetes has risen by more than 32 percent since 1990. Even more distressing, Americans are developing diabetes at earlier ages. Doctors used to think of type 2 diabetes, also known as adult-onset diabetes, as something that happened to people in their forties, fifties, and sixties. Increasingly, however, people in their thirties, twenties, and even teens are developing it.

These statistics are alarming because diabetes can cause a number of health problems, including high blood pressure, blindness, kidney disease, and nervous system disorders, as well as amputations, dental problems, and pregnancy complications. People with diabetes are also more susceptible to ailments such as pneumonia and influenza.

Fortunately diabetes is a disease that responds well to lifestyle improvements. As a diabetic you actually have the power to make yourself healthier. By making smart choices regarding diet, exercise, blood glucose testing, and stress management, you can feel better, help keep your diabetes in control, and reduce your risk of some of the potential complications of the disease.

You'll have to watch your diet, of course, but you can still eat delicious foods that are simple to prepare and appropriate for the whole family. As a matter of fact, foods in a diabetic diet can be sensational crowd-pleasers that are bursting with flavor and satisfying to everyone at the table.

know THE FACTS

Diabetes is a disease in which the body does not produce or properly use insulin. Insulin is a hormone that helps the body convert sugar, starches, and other food into the energy needed for daily life. Both genetics and environmental factors such as obesity and lack of exercise play roles in the development of diabetes.

There are four major types of diabetes. The following chart, based on information from the American Diabetes Association, explains what they are, why they occur, and how common they are.

What Are the Symptoms?

All forms of diabetes have similar symptoms, including the following:

- Unusual thirst
- Frequent need to urinate
- Blurred vision
- Unexplained fatigue
- Unexplained weight loss
- Increased hunger and food intake
- Irritability

Type of Diabetes	Description	Incidence
Type 1 diabetes (also known as immune-mediated diabetes mellitus)	Occurs when the body fails to produce insulin, a hormone that enables glucose to enter the cells and give them fuel.	5% to 10% of Americans with diabetes have type 1 (1.2 million). About half of all cases of type 1 diabetes appear in childhood or teen years.
Type 2 diabetes (also known as insulin-resistant diabetes mellitus)	Occurs when the body becomes resistant to and deficient in insulin.	90% to 95% of Americans with diabetes have type 2 (17 million).
Gestational diabetes	Appears during pregnancy and goes away after pregnancy in 90% to 95% of all cases. However, women who develop gestational diabetes have a 20% to 50% chance of developing type 2 diabetes in the five to 10 years after pregnancy. A woman who had gestational diabetes has a 90% chance of having it again during subsequent pregnancies.	Each year there are about 135,000 cases in the U.S. It affects about 4% of all pregnant women.
Pre-diabetes	This is a condition in which a person has blood glucose levels that are higher than normal, but not high enough to merit a diagnosis of type 2 diabetes.	At least 20.1 million Americans are believed to have pre-diabetes.

Treatment Options

Several approaches are used to treat and manage diabetes, including the following:

1. **A healthy diet** can help control weight and blood glucose levels.
2. **Exercise** can lower blood glucose levels, control weight, and increase your body's ability to use medication effectively.
3. **Oral medications** can reduce blood glucose levels by boosting the release of insulin, reducing the amount of glucose available to your cells, and/or decreasing your body's resistance to insulin.
4. **Insulin injections** can give your body the extra insulin it needs to use glucose.

Did You Know? Diabetics and Genetics

Genetics plays an important part in diabetes, but simply having the genes for diabetes doesn't mean you'll automatically develop the disease. Diabetes genes are usually "turned on," so to speak, when a person engages in high-risk behaviors such as becoming overweight, eating a diet rich in processed starches, and leading a sedentary lifestyle.

How can you minimize your chances of developing diabetes? You can't do anything about the genes you were born with, but you can change the way you live. If you have diabetes in your family, develop healthy eating and living habits to reduce your risk.

Not everyone with diabetes requires this four pronged approach so talk to your doctor to decide what's best for you. All diabetics benefit from a healthy diet and exercise program. In some cases diet and exercise are enough to control diabetes. But some diabetics also need to take oral medications; still others need to combine diet, exercise, oral medications, and insulin.

Weighing Your Risks

Excess weight is a particularly strong risk factor for type 2 diabetes: Approximately 90 percent of people with newly diagnosed diabetes are overweight or obese. In fact, many diabetes experts believe that the major cause of the increase of diabetes is the increase of obesity in people who have a genetic predisposition for type 2 diabetes. Excess weight can trigger development of the disease.

Overweight and obese people have large amounts of body fat. Although researchers aren't exactly sure why, excess body fat can contribute to the body's resistance to the action of insulin. In addition, many overweight and obese people get little exercise, and exercise helps the body use glucose. If someone is overweight or obese people and also sedentary, their muscles use much less of the glucose in their blood as fuel than during exercise.

Luckily, you don't have to be reed thin to diminish your risk of diabetes. According to the results of the Diabetes Prevention Program, a study of 3,234 people with pre-diabetes, losing just 5 to 7 percent of body weight sharply lowered the participants' risk of developing diabetes. If you weigh 240 pounds, for example, losing even 12 to 17 pounds can help.

For those who already have diabetes, losing weight can help improve blood glucose levels and reduce the risk of developing complications such as heart disease—which is very common in diabetics. In some cases, diabetics who lose weight can reduce or even eliminate their need for medications or insulin.

diet COUNTS

What you eat, when you eat, and how much you eat all impact the levels of glucose in your blood. After diagnosing you with diabetes, your doctor will probably refer you to a registered dietitian who can design a meal plan that's right for you. The plan will take into account whether you take insulin, whether you need to lose weight, and whether you have other health problems such as high blood pressure or heart disease.

Choose the Best Foods

In general, dietary guidelines for diabetics are similar to those for people who don't have diabetes. The focus is on eating a wide variety of fruits and vegetables, high-fiber whole grains, lean protein, and fat-free dairy products while reducing consumption of foods that are high in heart-harming fats and cholesterol. However, diabetics must go a few steps further to ensure that the foods they eat keep blood glucose levels stable. In particular they have to pay close attention to their intake of carbohydrates, which along with protein and fats are the main nutrients in foods.

Here's a quick primer on these nutrients:

Carbohydrates provide immediate energy. There are three types of carbohydrates: complex carbohydrates, simple carbohydrates (sugars), and fiber. Complex carbohydrates include foods such as whole grain breads and cereals, fruits, vegetables, and legumes. Simple carbohydrates include white breads, table sugar, and soft drinks such as cola or sweetened iced tea. Foods that are rich in fiber include fruits, vegetables, whole grains, and legumes.

Fats offer a concentrated source of energy, but they have other jobs as well. Fats transport fat-soluble vitamins through the blood, help maintain healthy skin, assist in maintaining cell structure, help manufacture hormones, and insulate body tissues. The fats in food are made of different types of fatty acids, including saturated, polyunsaturated, monounsaturated, and trans fatty acids.

Protein supplies amino acids, the building blocks that erect, repair, and maintain body tissues. It transports vitamins and minerals in the blood and helps build muscle. Protein also can provide energy when your body's supply of carbohydrates and fat is low.

Count Carbs or Track Exchanges

Two main eating plans are recommended for diabetics. The first is the exchange system. In this system, people design their diet based on a series of exchanges. Each food is assigned to a category (starch, fruit, milk, and so on), and you are permitted a certain number of food exchanges for each meal. People using this system work with a registered dietitian to determine how many of each exchange they should eat each day.

The second eating plan, called carbohydrate counting, is used by diabetics but has also gained popularity as a weight-loss tool for nondiabetics. In this system you are permitted a certain amount of carbohydrates per day and per meal. Diabetics work with a registered dietitian to determine how many grams of carbohydrates they should eat at each meal and snack to keep blood glucose levels within a normal range. Many people, expecially children and teens, find it easier to count carbohydrates than to use the exchange system.

If you and your dietitian decide that a low-carbohydrate diet is best for you, be sure that when you do choose carbohydrates, you're picking ones that deliver the best nutritional value. Whenever possible, choose high-fiber fresh fruits and vegetables, whole grain breads and cereals, and other high-quality carbohydrates.

Fiber is important because it slows the rate at which carbohydrates are broken down into glucose and absorbed into the blood. (It also promotes proper bowel function and reduces the risk of cardiovascular disease and cancer.) Since the body doesn't break down fiber, fiber doesn't contribute calories or glucose to the blood. If you are using the carbohydrate counting method for meal planning, you can subtract the grams of fiber in a particular food from the total grams of carbohydrates you are eating. For example, if you eat a serving of cereal that has 24 grams of total carbohydrates and 3 grams of fiber, you would count only 21 grams of carbohydrates. High-fiber foods include fruits and vegetables (especially those with edible skins left on), nuts, beans, whole grain breads, and cereals.

Diabetics can also use the diabetic food pyramid to help them make daily food choices. The pyramid offers daily recommendations of two to three servings of milk; two to three servings of meat, fish, nuts, or meat substitutes; three to five servings of vegetables; two to four servings of fruits; and six or more servings of grains, beans, and starchy vegetables. It also allows small amounts of fats, sweets, and alcohol.

Eat to Your Heart's Content

Many diabetics don't realize that they are two to four times more likely than nondiabetics to develop heart

Artificial Sweeteners

Artificial sweeteners, which contain no carbohydrates, give food a sweet taste without raising blood glucose. You may see them listed on the labels of "sugar-free" or "low-sugar" foods. These artificial sweeteners have been approved by the U.S. Food and Drug Administration and are widely used in food products.

Name	Also listed on food labels as...	Concerns	Uses
Saccharin	Sweet 'n Low	Large amounts of saccharin have caused cancer in lab rats, but no evidence proves that it causes cancer in people. However, pregnant and breastfeeding women are advised not to use saccharin.	To sweeten both hot and cold foods.
Aspartame	NutraSweet, Equal	Shouldn't be used by people with phenylketonuria, a genetic metabolic disorder.	Ingredient in diet sodas and other beverages, candy, drink mixes, frozen desserts, yogurt, and puddings. Loses sweetness if used in cooking or baking.
Acesulfame potassium	Sweet One or acesulfame-K	None	Can be used in all baking and cooking.
Sucralose	Splenda Note: In this book, Splenda sweetener is listed generically as no-calorie, heat-stable granular sugar substitute.	None	Used in baked goods, beverages, gum, frozen dairy desserts, fruit juices, and gelatins. Can be used in baking and cooking.

disease or have a stroke. That's why it's important to watch fat intake, but remember that not all fats are bad for the heart. Monounsaturated fats, which are found in olive oil, canola oil, avocados, and nuts, help to lower levels of harmful LDL cholesterol, which is good for heart health. Saturated fat, on the other hand, contributes to the formation of artery-clogging plaque. Foods such as fatty meats, full-fat dairy products, butter, palm oil, and coconut oil are high in saturated fats. Polyunsaturated fats, found in corn, soybean, sunflower, and safflower oils, lower overall cholesterol levels, although they do so by reducing helpful HDL cholesterol as well as harmful LDL cholesterol. Omega-3 fatty acids, which are found in fish such as salmon and tuna, are believed to help the heart by preventing blood cells from sticking to the insides of blood vessels. Trans fats, which are hydrogenated and are used in many processed foods, are believed to be as dangerous to the heart as saturated fats.

If you have high blood pressure, your registered dietitian or doctor may recommend that you reduce levels of sodium and salt in your diet. The easiest way to do this is to avoid processed foods such as bacon, ham, canned soups and vegetables, as well as fast foods.

Get Moving!

Think of exercise as a sponge that soaks up excess glucose in your blood. Not only does exercise help your body use glucose more effectively and help you maintain a healthy weight, but it also improves your body's sensitivity to insulin. That's why you should always let your doctor know if you're exercising since it can affect how your diabetes is treated.

In addition to lowering blood glucose levels, exercise can do the following:
- **Reduce stress** and improve mood.
- **Lower blood pressure.**
- **Strengthen your heart**, which reduces your risk of heart disease and stroke.

Did You Know? Diet Colas and Bone Health

Drinking artificially sweetened beverages is a way for diabetics to enjoy sweet-tasting drinks without sabotaging their blood glucose levels. However, drinking too many diet soft drinks can impact bone health, particularly among women, who are more susceptible to osteoporosis. Diet drinks affect the bones in two ways:

1. People who replace most or all of the milk in their diets with soft drinks miss out on a valuable source of calcium and vitamin D, which are crucial for bone health.
2. Diet colas contain phosphorous in the form of phosphoric acid. Phosphorous is believed to interfere with calcium absorption. Drinking large amounts of diet colas could impact the body's ability to get adequate amounts of calcium from the diet.

The bottom line? Don't go overboard with diet sodas. Try these substitutions: diet fruit drinks, fresh fruit juice mixed with unsweetened soda water, unsweetened iced tea with a splash of orange juice, and iced decaffeinated coffee sweetened with artificial sweetener.

- **Strengthen your lungs** and respiratory system.
- **Build muscle**, which helps your body use glucose more effectively and makes you stronger and better able to function on a daily basis.
- **Improve your circulation**, lowering your risk of circulatory disease and impairment.
- **Build strength** and flexibility.
- **Play a part in heart health** by increasing HDL cholesterol, the "good" cholesterol, and lowering levels of triglycerides, blood fats that at high levels can contribute to heart disease.

Of course, making exercise part of your daily routine can be a challenge. Most experts recommend that people exercise for a minimum of 30 minutes a day,

It's hard to motivate yourself to exercise regularly. Having built-in goals, rewards, and habits can make it much easier. Try these suggestions:

1. Set very specific weekly goals and reward your successes. Specify what you'll do when and for how long—and what you'll give yourself when you meet that goal. For example, set a goal of walking 30 minutes a day five days a week, and whenever you meet your weekly goal, reward yourself with a new CD for your portable CD player.

2. Set long-term goals such as completing a fundraiser walk. Give yourself long-term rewards, such as a mini vacation, new outfit, or a professional massage.

3. Keep things interesting. Don't do the same workout day after day. Walk a new route, swim a different stroke, hike an unfamiliar trail.

4. Have the proper equipment and clothing for your activity so you're comfortable while doing it.

5. Join a team or club, especially in the winter. Or exercise with a friend—your time spent walking or jogging flies by when you have someone to talk to.

6. Post notes around your house or office reminding yourself to exercise.

7. Decide when you'll exercise each day and write it in your date book in pen. Plan the rest of your day around it.

8. Use a logbook to keep track of when and for how long you exercise each day.

9. Be sure to choose activities you enjoy. If you think of exercise as fun rather than a chore, you're more likely to stay committed to it.

10. If at first you don't succeed, try, try again. Even elite athletes miss a workout once in a while. If you do, don't worry about it. Just start again tomorrow.

Add a swim on Saturday mornings or a hike on Sunday afternoons. Gradual lifestyle shifts—not dramatic changes—are more likely to turn into lifetime habits.

Remember that you don't have to do all of your day's exercise at once. Not everyone has time to exercise for 30 minutes a day, but most everyone can fit a few 10-minute spurts of activity into their daily routine. Walk the dog, play tag with your children or grandchildren, rake leaves, walk to the post office, ride your bike to the corner store for milk, talk to a friend on the phone while you're walking on the treadmill, or go dancing with your spouse rather than out to dinner. The activity you do all day adds up. The trick is to find ways to make exercise enjoyable so you'll make it into a daily, lifelong habit. Then it will become as natural to you as brushing your teeth.

When you exercise keep in mind these important tips: Wear shoes and socks that fit properly and are activity appropriate. Protect your feet by making sure shoes and socks fit properly. Drink plenty of water before, during, and after exercising. Test your blood glucose before and after exercising. If it is too high (above 300), do not exercise. If it is too low (below 100), have a small snack before beginning your workout. Have hard candy or glucose tablets with you while you exercise in case you feel your blood glucose levels drop too low.

five days a week. However, if you go from doing nothing to doing hours of exercise, you're destined to fail. Your goal is not to become a weekend warrior who exercises like crazy on Saturday and Sunday and can't get off the couch on Monday. Your goal is to build a habit of lifelong exercise, and that takes time.

Begin by taking a 10-minute walk a few evenings a week after dinner, and then build up from there. Walk 15 minutes instead of 10 and gradually build to more.

meal PLANNING

It's important for people with diabetes to eat small meals and snacks throughout the day. It helps keep glucose levels at a healthy, relatively stable level. Try to eat meals and snacks at about the same time every day and don't skip meals or snacks. Take your medications at the same times each day and stick to a regular exercise time. Your registered dietitian can help you decide how many meals and snacks to eat and how much you should eat at each meal and snack.

Cooking for the Family

Meal planning can, at first, be tricky for diabetics, especially those who are preparing foods for nondiabetic family members too. Ideally your family would be happy to eat the same foods you eat, but that's not always the case. Try to bring your family onboard by sitting down with them and explaining your new eating plan. Ask them to help you out by making some of the changes you are making: choosing healthier foods, eating smaller portion sizes, and reducing the portion size of certain foods. Explain that by eating better they, too, can be healthier.

If that doesn't work and your family continues to demand the usual heavy dishes they're used to, try some different strategies. Analyze your family's favorite recipes to see if you can prepare them in ways that fit into your eating plan. Look for ways to shave calories and carbohydrates and replace full-fat ingredients with low-fat or fat-free ingredients. Experiment with recipes. Make your famous macaroni and cheese with low-fat cheese or your chicken cacciatore with skinless chicken.

Either way, you can and should make fresh fruits and vegetables a major part of the menu. Serve cut-up carrots, celery, cucumbers, broccoli, and other vegetables before dinner. Accompany meals with a large salad and serve fresh fruit for dessert. Whenever possible avoid take-out food, which tends to be high in calories and fat. As much as possible keep your kitchen free of tempting sweets and sugary drinks. If your family must have these foods, store them out of sight so you won't be tempted to indulge.

Grocery Shopping

You can only eat what you have in the house, so thoughtful grocery shopping—choosing the raw ingredients of your diet—is an important part of healthful meal planning. Here are some tips to help you shop smart:

- **Take time to prepare a list.** When you shop without a list, you come home without the foods you want and with foods you don't want. Use a master list (computers are great for this) and check off what you need.
- **Plan a week's worth of menus.** Then you'll know exactly what you need and you won't have to run to the store for forgotten items.
- **Shop alone.** It's much easier to shop smart when you leave the impatient toddler or grumpy 7-year-old at home. Shopping alone also makes it easier to read food labels for nutrition information.
- **Don't hurry.** Try to carve out at least an hour to shop, especially when you're just getting started with a new eating strategy.
- **Shop when the store isn't busy.** Crowds can be distracting.
- **Read food labels.** This is crucial, particularly when you are first making changes to your eating plan. Food labels give information about serving sizes, fat, added sugars, carbohydrates, fiber, saturated fat, cholesterol, sodium, and other nutrients. Familiarize yourself with food labels before you shop and ask your registered dietitian for explanations if you need them.

- **Read ingredient lists.** Ingredients are listed in order of weight, so choose foods whose first few ingredients are ones you are trying to eat more of, such as whole grains. Avoid foods that list sugars and fats as first ingredients.
- **Be skeptical about health claims.** Read the fine print to see if claims are true. Don't assume that because a food label says "lite" or "reduced sugar," the food is right for your eating plan.
- **Try new produce.** Eating lots of fruits and vegetables can get boring if all you eat are apples and celery. Make it a policy to try a new fruit or vegetable every week in an effort to expand your food choices.
- **Choose treats that fit your meal plan.** If you can't live without ice cream, go ahead and buy it—but read labels and choose a low-fat or low-sugar variety, and select a quart rather than a half-gallon.

Eating in Restaurants

You might have diabetes but you can still eat out. Here are some tips on how to enjoy dining out while keeping an eye on your carbohydrates and calories:

- **Choose wisely.** Pick a restaurant whose menu revolves around something other than breads, pasta, cheese, or other foods you're trying to avoid. A seafood restaurant is an excellent choice.
- **Start with a salad.** Request low-fat or fat-free dressing, or sprinkle your salad with olive oil and balsamic vinegar. Order it without cheese, croutons, or other high-fat, high-carbohydrate garnishes.
- **Try to eat at your normal dining time.** Eating much later than usual can knock blood glucose levels off kilter.
- **Ask for what you want.** When you place your order, don't be afraid to ask for your food to be served without a bun, without added oils or butter, or with dressings or sauces on the side. If you don't know what's in a dish, ask the waiter.
- **Order extra vegetables instead of potatoes.** Ask that they be steamed and made without butter or oil.
- **Choose healthfully cooked foods.** Select broiled, baked, poached, or grilled meat and fish instead of fried. If fried foods are your only option, scrape off the breading.
- **Watch portions.** Try to eat moderate portion sizes. Bring leftovers home to eat the next day or share an entrée with a friend.
- **Go for a walk.** Instead of lingering over dessert and coffee, invite your dining companions on an after-dinner stroll.
- **Select your restaurant companions carefully.** If you find that certain friends or family members push you to overeat or to indulge in foods you'd rather avoid, don't eat out with them. Instead enjoy restaurant dinners with people who support you in your quest for good health.

diabetes
IN CHILDREN

The number of children, teens, and young adults diagnosed with type 2 diabetes each year in the United States is skyrocketing. The prevalence of type 2 diabetes among children has increased as much as tenfold over the past 20 years.

As with adults, type 2 diabetes in children is strongly associated with obesity. A recent study found that 92 percent of children newly diagnosed with type 2 diabetes were obese. The number of overweight children has climbed dramatically over the past 20 years—researchers estimate that 25 percent of American children are overweight—and as children get heavier, their risk of developing type 2 diabetes increases.

It's plain to see what's at the root of the problem: Many American kids eat too much and don't get enough exercise. From a young age, children have access to high-calorie, high-fat foods. Many grow up eating sugary cereals and greasy fast foods, quenching their thirst with large quantities of sugar-laden soft drinks. Making matters worse, they are spending less time playing active sports or games and more time watching TV or play video games. That's why it's so important for parents to make exercise a family activity. If your kids see you being active, they're more likely to participate. Not sure what to do? Check out the sidebar on page 15, "Let's Play! Fun Ways to Get Kids Active."

In addition to obesity, other risk factors for type 2 diabetes include ethnicity, gender, sedentary lifestyle, family history, and birth weight. Type 2 diabetes is more common in American Indian, African American, Latino, and Hispanic children than in the general population. Girls are three times more likely than boys to develop type 2 diabetes, and children who don't exercise are at higher risk than those who do. The most common ages for diagnosis are 12 to 16. Risk is also higher for children with a family history of type 2

Did You Know? The Rise in Type 2 Diabetes

In the past, children diagnosed with diabetes were most likely to have type 1 diabetes, an autoimmune disorder in which the immune system attacks the beta cells in the pancreas that make insulin. These days, however, more and more children and teens are being diagnosed with type 2 diabetes, which in the past was called adult-onset diabetes. The beta cells in children with type 2 diabetes still produce insulin, but either the body's cells don't respond properly to the insulin or the insulin produced naturally is not enough to meet the needs of the body. This means insulin is usually still present in a person with type 2 diabetes, but it doesn't work as well as it should.

Doctors must determine whether a child has type 1 or type 2 diabetes because treatment plans differ for the two. A doctor may perform several medical tests to determine which kind of diabetes a child or teen has. A child with type 1 diabetes must inject insulin several times a day because his or her pancreas produces little or no insulin. Treatment for type 2 diabetes includes diet control, exercise, blood glucose monitoring, and in some cases, oral drugs or insulin.

diabetes and in children with very low or very high birth weight. Researchers suspect that undernutrition or overnutrition in the uterus may cause permanent metabolic and hormonal changes that later promote obesity, insulin resistance, and dysfunction in the pancreatic cells that produce insulin.

Children with type 2 diabetes are at risk for the same kinds of complications diabetic adults are, including heart disease, kidney failure, blindness, and nerve damage. Glucose control is crucial for these children because the longer an individual has type 2 diabetes, the greater his or her risk of developing complications. Unfortunately type 2 diabetes sometimes goes undiagnosed in children and teens.

The symptoms of diabetes (both type 1 and type 2) in children and teens match those in adults: extreme thirst, unusual hunger, weight loss, fatigue, weakness, and blurry vision. Some children, however, have mild symptoms or no symptoms at all.

A Kid's Menu That Works

Children and teens with diabetes need to follow the same kind of healthy eating plan as diabetic adults do. A perfect diet for a diabetic child doesn't exist, but you, your child, and a registered dietitian can put together one that best fits your child.

Diabetes presents some unique issues for young people. They must check their blood sugar several times a day and may need to take oral medication or injected insulin. They also may have to avoid some foods that their friends eat.

Children with diabetes should eat meals and snacks at regular intervals and at approximately the same times each day. Missing meals or delaying snacks can lead to hypoglycemia. Dietitians usually recommend three meals and two to three snacks per day for diabetic children.

Once an eating plan has been designed, work with your child to help him or her understand why it's important to stick with it. Over time children usually come to realize that they feel better when they follow their diet.

questions & ANSWERS

As a parent of a diabetic child, you probably have many questions about what your child should eat, especially in social situations. Following are some commonly asked questions about kids and teens with diabetes.

Q How can I help my child follow his diabetic eating plan?

A The best thing to do is to have your family eat many of the same healthy foods your diabetic child eats. To avoid tempting your child, keep junk food, fattening snacks, and sweets out of the house; serve them for special occasions only. Everyone in the family can benefit from eating a healthy diet, and children find it easier to follow their food plan when they're not tempted by a house filled with snacks that are off-limits only to them.

Q Can my child still have sweet snacks at parties, like cake or ice cream?

A Yes. Years ago doctors forbade kids with diabetes to eat any sugar. Now diabetes experts know that people with diabetes can sometimes eat sugary snacks, provided they are part of a healthy eating plan. Kids with diabetes can have cake at birthdays, candy on Halloween, or ice cream at a picnic. However, they and their parents have to work together and, if necessary, with a registered dietitian to fit snacks into the child's prescribed meal plan. Also, sugary snacks such as birthday cake are best eaten with a meal, if possible.

Q How can I make sure my child eats a healthy lunch at school?

A The best way to keep control is to pack your child's lunch. Involve your child in making lunch so that he or she can choose favorite foods. Even young children can help prepare foods. Have a wide selection of healthy foods available for the lunch bag, including a variety of fresh fruits and vegetables. Use healthy, low-fat foods whenever possible, such as whole wheat bread, low-salt meats, and low-fat cheeses. If your child likes dessert, choose cookies or snacks made for diabetics with artificial sweeteners. If your child would rather buy lunch at school, compromise and let him or her eat school lunch once a week. Be sure your child understands what foods are best and why it's important to stick with the prescribed meal plan.

Q Do kids with diabetes have to avoid fast food?

A Fresh, whole foods are certainly better than fast foods. But kids like to go to fast-food places with their friends and should be allowed to go along with the crowd sometimes. Kids with diabetes must choose smaller portions, however—a single hamburger rather than the double burger; a small order of fries rather than the super size, etc. Some fast-food restaurants offer excellent salads with

Let's Play! Fun Ways to Get Kids Active

Kids who aren't used to being active may not warm up easily to the idea of taking part in fitness activities. The best way to get them interested is to make it fun—and for parents and other family members to get involved too. Here are some ways to get your whole family involved in fitness:

- **Go out and play together.** Play tag, toss a Frisbee, ride bikes to the park, have a family basketball or badminton game.
- **Dance.** This is a great indoor activity that you can do anytime—just turn on the radio and get moving.
- **Focus on noncompetitive activities.** Losing can be discouraging to a child who's just getting started.
- **Go for a family swim.** Many community pools and recreation centers have family swim times on weekends. Swimming is an excellent fitness activity, and for an overweight child it's an easier exercise than some other activities.
- **Do exercise videos together.** Buy them, rent them, or borrow them from the public library. Try a variety of activities—aerobics, yoga, calisthenics, Pilates—to see what your child enjoys most.
- **Work fitness into daily activities.** Walk to school, to friends' houses, to stores. Do errands on bicycles.

- **Make an activity such as volleyball the theme of your next picnic.** Focus on the activity rather than the food.
- **Make family walks a habit.** Go for a walk every night after dinner.
- **Do things you've never done before.** Go on a hike, participate in a walk for charity, go bowling, play pool, go climbing at an indoor gym, take a karate class.
- **Turn off the TV and the computer.** The less time kids spend watching, the more time they'll spend doing.
- **Set goals and offer rewards.** When your child has accomplished a goal, reward him or her with a nonfood prize such as a sleepover with a friend. For a child or teen, life with diabetes presents some challenges. But once children adjust to an eating and exercise plan, they can live happy, normal lives.

nonfat dressing, low-fat chili, grilled chicken sandwiches, and diet sodas, which can all fit into a healthy eating plan. However, it's best to make fast food a special treat rather than a regular habit.

Q What can I do when my child "cheats" on his diabetic diet?

A It's normal for children—teens in particular—to test their limits and rebel against the rules. Try not to react angrily. Instead sit down with your child and explain why it's so important that he follow his diet. (For some children, setting up a meeting with the child and an authority figure such as a dietitian is more effective.) You can also reward your child's good eating behavior with nonfood rewards such as a toy or trip to an amusement park. If your child is older, he might benefit from a support group with other diabetic kids or a summer camp for diabetic children. These camps serve appropriate food, have medical personnel on staff, and offer peer support and physical activities that are just right for diabetic kids.

Sources for More Information

The American Diabetes Association
1701 North Beauregard St.
Alexandria, VA 22311
800/DIABETES
www.diabetes.org

The American Dietetic Association
120 South Riverside Plaza, Suite 2000
Chicago, IL 60606-6995
800/877-1600
www.eatright.org

The American Heart Association
National Center
7272 Greenville Ave.
Dallas, TX 75231
800/242-8721
www.americanheart.org

The American Association of Diabetes Educators
100 W. Monroe, Suite 400
Chicago, IL 60603
800/338-3633
www.aadenet.org

The Canadian Diabetes Association
National Office
15 Toronto Street, Suite 800
Toronto, Ontario M5C 2E3
416/363-3373
www.diabetes.ca

The Juvenile Diabetes Research Foundation International
120 Wall St.
New York, NY 10005-4001
800/533-CURE (2873)
www.jdf.org

The National Diabetes Information Clearinghouse
1 Information Way
Bethesda, MD 20892-3560
800/860-8747 or 301/654-3327
www.diabetes.niddk.nih.gov

Joslin Diabetes Center
1 Joslin Place
Boston, MA 02215
617/732-2400
www.joslin.org

diabetes GLOSSARY

Adult-onset diabetes: The former name for type 2 diabetes.

Blood glucose: The main sugar found in the blood. Glucose is the main fuel source of the body and is created when the body breaks down carbohydrates. Also known as blood sugar.

Carbohydrate: A major nutrient and source of energy in foods. Sugars and starches are the most common carbohydrates. Food sources include sugars, breads, cereals, vegetables, fruit, and milk. One gram of carbohydrate equals four calories.

Fiber: An indigestible part of foods that adds bulk but not calories to the diet. Fiber is found in fruits, vegetables, whole grains, dried beans, and cereals.

Fructose: A simple carbohydrate that is naturally found in fruit and honey. Added to various foods in the form of crystalline fructose or high-fructose corn syrup. It's one and a half times sweeter than table sugar (sucrose).

Glucose: One of the simplest forms of sugar.

Glycemic index: A ranking of foods that contain carbohydrates. The ranking is based on each food's effect on blood glucose in comparison to a reference food. Low-glycemic-index foods raise blood glucose less than high-glycemic-index foods.

Hyperglycemia: A condition that indicates high blood glucose (sugar) levels.

Hypoglycemia: A condition that indicates low blood glucose (sugar) levels.

Insulin: A hormone produced by the pancreas that ushers glucose from the blood into the body's cells.

Juvenile-onset diabetes: The former name for type 1 diabetes.

Pancreas: An organ that makes insulin and enzymes for digestion.

Starch: One of the two major types of carbohydrates. (The other is sugar.) Starch is found in breads, pastas, starchy fruits such as bananas, and baked goods that contain white flour.

Sugar alcohols: Sweeteners such as sorbitol, mannitol, and xylitol, which are often used as substitues for sugar. These sugars do not contain ethanol, which is found in alcoholic beverages. They are found naturally in many fruits and vegetables and used to sweeten sugarless gums, candies, jams, and jellies. For some people sorbitol and mannitol cause a laxative effect when eaten in large amounts.

Sugars: One of the two major types of carbohydrates. (The other is starch.) Sugars include table sugar and sugar alcohols. Sugar also can be found in milk, fruit, and some processed foods.

Trans fats: A type of fat that is hydrogenated or chemically altered to make it solid at room temperature. Trans fats are used in many processed foods such as fast-food french fries, commercially baked cookies, and many fried snack foods. Some researchers believe they are as dangerous to the heart as saturated fats.

Triglycerides: A type of fat that is normally found in the blood. These fats are made from foods. Being overweight or eating too much fat, alcohol, or sugar can increase triglycerides, which contribute to heart disease.

breakfast
& BRUNCH

Greet the day with a delicious breakfast that will keep you going all morning long. When time is short, choose an on-the-go meal, like a Berry-Banana Smoothie or a Breakfast Tortilla Wrap. Or, for more relaxed a.m. fare, try the Ham and Cheese Frittata or Pancakes with Berry Sauce.

Breakfast Bread Pudding, *recipe page 20*

BREAD PUDDING

If you love bread pudding, here's a great way to start the day. Cubes of cinnamon-swirl bread nestle in a custard made with protein-packed egg product and fat-free milk.

Prep: 25 minutes
Bake: 35 minutes
Stand: 15 minutes
Oven: 325°F
Makes: 6 servings

- **6 slices cinnamon-swirl bread or cinnamon-raisin bread**
- **Nonstick cooking spray**
- **1½ cups fat-free milk**
- **¾ cup refrigerated or frozen egg product, thawed**
- **3 tablespoons sugar**
- **1 teaspoon vanilla**
- **¼ teaspoon ground nutmeg**
- **1 5½-ounce can apricot or peach nectar (⅔ cup)**
- **2 teaspoons cornstarch**

Exchanges: 1 Milk, 1 Starch

1 To dry bread, place slices in a single layer on a baking sheet. Bake in a 325° oven for 10 minutes, turning once. Cool on a wire rack. Cut slices into ½-inch cubes (you should have about 4 cups).

2 Lightly coat six 6-ounce soufflé dishes or custard cups with nonstick cooking spray. Divide bread cubes among the prepared dishes. In a medium bowl combine milk, egg product, sugar, vanilla, and nutmeg. Use a rotary beater or wire whisk to beat until mixed. Pour milk mixture evenly over bread cubes. Press lightly with the back of a spoon to thoroughly moisten bread.

3 Place dishes in a 13×9×2-inch baking pan. Place baking pan on oven rack. Carefully pour the hottest tap water available into the baking pan around dishes to a depth of 1 inch.

4 Bake in the 325° oven for 35 to 40 minutes or until a knife inserted near centers comes out clean. Transfer dishes to a wire rack. Let stand for 15 to 20 minutes.

5 Meanwhile, for sauce, in a small saucepan gradually stir apricot nectar into cornstarch. Cook and stir over medium heat until thickened and bubbly. Reduce heat. Cook and stir for 2 minutes more. Spoon sauce over warm puddings.

Nutrition Facts per serving: 164 cal., 2 g total fat (1 g sat. fat), 1 mg chol., 189 mg sodium, 28 g carbo., 0 g fiber, 8 g pro.
Daily Values: 13% vit. A, 15% vit. C, 9% calcium, 10% iron

blueberry BREAKFAST SCONES

Spread good morning cheer with these orange-glazed scones served warm with a dab of butter.

breakfast & brunch

Prep: 25 minutes
Bake: 15 minutes
Oven: 400°F
Makes: 10 scones

- 2 **cups all-purpose flour**
- ¼ **cup sugar**
- 1 **tablespoon baking powder**
- 1 **tablespoon finely shredded orange peel**
- ¼ **teaspoon salt**
- ¼ **teaspoon baking soda**
- ¼ **cup butter**
- ½ **cup buttermilk or sour milk***
- ¼ **cup refrigerated or frozen egg product, thawed**
- 1 **teaspoon vanilla**
- 1 **cup fresh or frozen blueberries**
- **Nonstick cooking spray**
- 1 **recipe Orange Powdered Sugar Icing**

Exchanges: 2 Starch, 1 Fat

1 In a large bowl stir together flour, sugar, baking powder, orange peel, salt, and baking soda. Using a pastry blender, cut in butter until mixture resembles coarse crumbs. Make a well in the center of the flour mixture. Combine buttermilk, egg product, and vanilla. Add to flour mixture all at once, stirring just until moistened. Gently stir in blueberries. Lightly coat a baking sheet with nonstick cooking spray; set aside.

2 Turn dough out onto a lightly floured surface. Quickly knead dough by folding and pressing gently for 12 to 15 strokes or until nearly smooth. Pat dough into a 7-inch circle on the prepared baking sheet. Cut dough into 10 wedges.

3 Bake in a 400° oven for 15 to 20 minutes or until golden brown. Cool slightly on a wire rack. Drizzle Orange Powdered Sugar Icing over tops of scones.

Orange Powdered Sugar Icing: In a small bowl stir together ¾ cup sifted powdered sugar and ¼ teaspoon finely shredded orange peel. Stir in enough orange juice or fat-free milk (3 to 4 teaspoons) to make an icing of drizzling consistency.

***Note:** To make ½ cup sour milk, place 1½ teaspoons lemon juice or vinegar in a glass measuring cup. Add enough fat-free milk to make ½ cup total liquid; stir. Let stand for 5 minutes before using.

Nutrition Facts per scone: 194 cal., 5 g total fat (3 g sat. fat), 13 mg chol., 273 mg sodium, 34 g carbo., 1 g fiber, 4 g pro.
Daily Values: 7% vit. A, 6% vit. C, 10% calcium, 9% iron

Fruit Picking

Fruits are an excellent source of vitamins, minerals, and fiber and contain virtually no fat. That's true whether you're using fresh, frozen, or canned fruit. A couple of things to watch out for: When selecting canned fruit read the label carefully and choose those canned in juice, not syrup; check the ingredient list on frozen fruits for added sugars or sauces and buy those without these additions.

pear-almond MUFFINS

Cream cheese laced with ginger and honey complements these fruit-filled muffins. Store the batter in the refrigerator for up to 3 days and bake a few at a time, if you like.

Prep: 20 minutes
Bake: 15 minutes
Stand: 10 minutes
Oven: 400°F
Makes: 7 muffins

Nonstick cooking spray

⅔ **cup all-purpose flour**

⅓ **cup packed brown sugar**

1½ **teaspoons baking powder**

¼ **teaspoon ground ginger**

⅛ **teaspoon salt**

½ **cup whole bran cereal**

½ **cup fat-free milk**

½ **cup chopped, peeled pear**

2 **tablespoons refrigerated or
   frozen egg product, thawed**

2 **tablespoons cooking oil**

1 **tablespoon finely chopped
   almonds**

1 **recipe Ginger-Cream Spread**

Exchanges: 1 Starch, ½ Fat

1 Lightly coat 7 muffin cups with nonstick cooking spray or line with paper baking cups; set aside. In a medium bowl stir together flour, brown sugar, baking powder, ginger, and salt. Make a well in the center of the flour mixture; set aside.

2 In another medium bowl stir together cereal and milk; let cereal mixture stand for 5 minutes. Stir in pear, egg product, and oil. Add cereal mixture all at once to flour mixture. Stir just until moistened (batter should be lumpy). (If desired, cover and refrigerate the batter in an airtight container for up to 3 days. Bake muffins as needed.)

3 Spoon batter into prepared muffin cups, filling each three-fourths full. Sprinkle with nuts.

4 Bake in a 400° oven for 15 to 18 minutes or until a wooden toothpick inserted near centers comes out clean. Cool in muffin cups on a wire rack for 5 minutes. Remove from muffin cups. Serve warm with Ginger-Cream Spread.

Ginger-Cream Spread: In a small bowl stir together one-third of an 8-ounce tub fat-free cream cheese, 1½ teaspoons honey, and 1½ teaspoons finely chopped crystallized ginger or ⅛ teaspoon ground ginger.

Nutrition Facts per muffin: 165 cal., 5 g total fat (1 g sat. fat), 2 mg chol., 157 mg sodium, 28 g carbo., 2 g fiber, 5 g pro.
Daily Values: 3% vit. A, 5% vit. C, 15% calcium, 9% iron

fruity OATMEAL

Make your morning oatmeal even more satisfying by adding fresh and dried fruits.

breakfast & brunch

Start to Finish: 15 minutes
Makes: 4 servings

2 cups water
¼ teaspoon salt
1 cup rolled oats
1 cup chopped peeled peaches
   or chopped apple
¼ cup raisins or snipped pitted
   whole dates
1 teaspoon vanilla
¼ teaspoon ground cinnamon
   Fat-free milk (optional)

Exchanges: ½ Fruit, 1½ Starch

1 In a medium saucepan bring the water and salt to boiling. Stir in oats, peaches, raisins, vanilla, and cinnamon. Reduce heat and simmer, uncovered, for 3 minutes (for quick oats) or 5 minutes (for regular oats), stirring occasionally. Remove from heat. Cover and let stand for 2 minutes.

2 Divide oat mixture among 4 bowls. If desired, serve with fat-free milk.

Nutrition Facts per serving: 143 cal., 2 g total fat (0 g sat. fat), 0 mg chol., 151 mg sodium, 29 g carbo., 4 g fiber, 4 g pro.
Daily Values: 5% vit. A, 5% vit. C, 2% calcium, 7% iron

fruited GRANOLA

This very berry granola starts your day with an appetizing crunch. Bowls of the cinnamon-scented cereal make great snacks too.

Prep: 15 minutes
Bake: 38 minutes
Oven: 325°F
Makes: 5 servings

Nonstick cooking spray

2½ **cups regular rolled oats**

1 **cup whole bran cereal**

½ **cup toasted wheat germ**

¼ **cup sliced almonds**

½ **cup raspberry applesauce**

⅓ **cup honey**

¼ **teaspoon ground cinnamon**

⅓ **cup dried cranberries, blueberries, and/or cherries**

Vanilla low-fat yogurt or fat-free milk (optional)

Exchanges: ½ Fruit, 1½ Starch, ½ Fat

1 Lightly coat a 15×10×1-inch baking pan with nonstick cooking spray; set aside. In a large bowl stir together rolled oats, bran cereal, wheat germ, and almonds. In a small bowl stir together applesauce, honey, and cinnamon. Pour applesauce mixture over cereal mixture; stir until combined.

2 Spread cereal mixture evenly in the prepared baking pan. Bake in a 325° oven for 35 minutes, stirring occasionally. Carefully stir in dried cranberries. Bake for 3 to 5 minutes more or until golden brown.

3 Turn out onto a large piece of foil to cool completely. To store, place in an airtight container for up to 2 weeks. If desired, serve with vanilla yogurt or fat-free milk.

Nutrition Facts per serving: 216 cal., 4 g total fat (1 g sat. fat), 0 mg chol., 18 mg sodium, 41 g carbo., 6 g fiber, 7 g pro.
Daily Values: 4% vit. A, 6% vit. C, 6% calcium, 14% iron

bananas foster OATMEAL

For a breakfast that's quick to make and keeps you going all morning long, add banana slices, toasted pecans, and caramel ice cream topping to a packet of instant oatmeal.

Start to Finish: 10 minutes
Makes: 2 servings

- **2 1-ounce envelopes instant oatmeal (plain)**
- **1 medium banana, sliced**
- **2 tablespoons chopped pecans, toasted**
- **2 to 3 teaspoons caramel ice cream topping**
- **Fat-free milk (optional)**

Exchanges: ½ Fruit, 2 Starch, 1 Fat

1 In 2 microwave-safe bowls prepare oatmeal according to package directions. Top with banana and pecans. Drizzle with caramel topping.

2 If desired, microwave on 100 percent power (high) about 30 seconds or until toppings are warm. If desired, serve with fat-free milk.

Nutrition Facts per serving: 230 cal., 7 g total fat (1 g sat. fat), 0 mg chol., 17 mg sodium, 38 g carbo., 5 g fiber, 6 g pro.
Daily Values: 1% vit. A, 9% vit. C, 3% calcium, 9% iron

breakfast & brunch

no-fry FRENCH TOAST

Crisp French toast makes everyone happy. Sweet orange-cinnamon syrup entices breakfast eaters, and the easy, one-batch preparation pleases the cook.

breakfast & brunch

Prep: 15 minutes
Bake: 11 minutes
Oven: 450°F
Makes: 4 servings

Nonstick cooking spray

1 **slightly beaten egg**

1 **slightly beaten egg white**

¾ **cup fat-free milk**

1 **teaspoon vanilla**

⅛ **teaspoon ground cinnamon**

8 **½-inch slices French bread**

¼ **teaspoon finely shredded orange peel**

½ **cup orange juice**

1 **tablespoon honey**

1 **teaspoon cornstarch**

⅛ **teaspoon ground cinnamon**

Exchanges: 2 Starch

1 Lightly coat a large baking sheet with nonstick cooking spray; set aside. In a pie plate combine egg, egg white, milk, vanilla, and ⅛ teaspoon cinnamon. Soak bread slices in the egg mixture about 1 minute on each side. Place on the prepared baking sheet.

2 Bake in a 450° oven about 6 minutes or until bread is lightly browned. Turn bread; bake for 5 to 8 minutes more or until golden brown.

3 Meanwhile, for orange syrup, in a small saucepan stir together orange peel, orange juice, honey, cornstarch, and ⅛ teaspoon cinnamon. Cook and stir over medium heat until thickened and bubbly. Reduce heat. Cook and stir for 2 minutes more.

4 Serve toast with orange syrup.

Nutrition Facts per serving: 171 cal., 3 g total fat (1 g sat. fat), 54 mg chol., 263 mg sodium, 29 g carbo., 0 g fiber, 7 g pro.
Daily Values: 5% vit. A, 26% vit. C, 7% calcium, 8% iron

Toast Toppers

Choose from a variety of different toppings for your pancakes, waffles, and French toast. Regular syrup contains 52 calories and 13 grams of carbohydrate (12 of which come from sugar) per tablespoon, and reduced-calorie syrups cut those numbers in half. Sugar-free syrups have only 8 calories and 3 grams of carbs per tablespoon. One hundred percent fruit spreads are similar in calorie and sugar counts to regular syrup, but a variety of low-sugar and sugar-free preserves also are available. Per tablespoon, low-sugar preserves have 25 calories, 6 grams of carbs, and 5 grams of sugar, while sugar-free preserves contain 10 calories and 5 grams of carbs.

breakfast BLINTZES

On the weekend, when the pace of life slows, plan a brunch around these ricotta-filled crepes made with the season's fresh berries. You can make the crepes up to 2 days in advance.

Prep: 30 minutes
Bake: 15 minutes
Oven: 350°F
Makes: 15 servings

- **1 egg**
- **1½ cups fat-free milk**
- **1 cup all-purpose flour**
- **Nonstick cooking spray**
- **½ teaspoon shortening**
- **1 15-ounce carton low-fat or light ricotta cheese**
- **2 tablespoons sugar-free orange marmalade**
- **1 tablespoon sugar**
- **⅛ teaspoon ground cinnamon**
- **⅔ cup light dairy sour cream**
- **5 tablespoons sugar-free orange marmalade**
- **½ cup fresh raspberries or blueberries**

Exchanges: 1 Starch, ½ Lean Meat

1 For crepes, in a medium mixing bowl combine egg, milk, and flour; beat with a rotary beater until well mixed. Lightly coat a 6-inch skillet or crepe pan with nonstick cooking spray. Heat skillet over medium heat. Remove skillet from heat and pour in about 2 tablespoons batter. Lift and tilt skillet to spread batter evenly. Return skillet to heat; cook 30 to 60 seconds or until browned on 1 side. Remove from pan. Repeat with remaining batter to make 15 crepes, lightly brushing skillet with shortening between crepes, as needed.

2 Lightly coat a shallow baking pan with nonstick cooking spray. Set aside. For filling, in a bowl combine ricotta cheese, the 2 tablespoons orange marmalade, sugar, and cinnamon. Spoon about 2 tablespoons filling onto the unbrowned side of a crepe; spread out slightly. Fold in half. Fold in half again, forming a wedge. Arrange in prepared pan. Repeat with remaining filling and crepes.

3 Bake in a 350° oven for 15 to 20 minutes or until heated through. To serve, spoon 2 teaspoons sour cream and 1 teaspoon marmalade onto each blintz. Sprinkle with berries.

Nutrition Facts per serving: 99 cal., 3 g total fat (2 g sat. fat), 25 mg chol., 97 mg sodium, 13 g carbo., 1 g fiber, 6 g pro.
Daily Values: 4% vit. A, 2% vit. C, 17% calcium, 3% iron

pancakes WITH BERRY SAUCE

A fresh strawberry sauce drizzled over feathery-light whole wheat pancakes is sure to open sleepy eyes.

Start to Finish: 25 minutes
Makes: 5 (2-pancake) servings

- ½ **cup whole wheat flour**
- ½ **cup all-purpose flour**
- 1 **tablespoon sugar**
- 2 **teaspoons baking powder**
- ¼ **teaspoon salt**
- ¾ **cup fat-free milk**
- 1 **teaspoon cooking oil**
- 2 **egg whites**
  Nonstick cooking spray
- 2 **cups fresh or frozen unsweetened strawberries, thawed**
- 1 **tablespoon sugar**
- 1 **teaspoon vanilla**
  Quartered fresh strawberries (optional)

Exchanges: ½ Fruit, 1½ Starch

1 In a medium bowl combine whole wheat flour, all-purpose flour, sugar, baking powder, and salt. Stir in milk and oil. In another bowl, beat egg whites until stiff (tips stand straight). Fold egg whites into flour mixture.

2 Lightly coat a griddle with nonstick cooking spray. Heat griddle over medium heat. For each pancake pour about ¼ cup batter onto the hot griddle. Cook over medium heat until pancakes are golden brown (1 to 2 minutes per side); turn to second sides when pancakes have bubbly surfaces and slightly dry edges.

3 Meanwhile, in a blender container or food processor bowl combine strawberries, sugar, and vanilla. Cover and blend or process until smooth. In a small saucepan heat sauce until warm. If desired, top pancakes with quartered strawberries. Serve pancakes with sauce.

Nutrition Facts per serving: 148 cal., 2 g total fat, 1 mg chol., 319 mg sodium, 28 g carbo., 3 g fiber, 6 g pro.
Daily Values: 2% vit. A, 55% vit. C, 16% calcium, 7% iron

breakfast & brunch

ham and cheese FRITTATA

A frittata may look intimidating, but it's easy to make. Once the egg mixture is in the pan, run a spatula around the edge of the skillet, lifting the set egg mixture so the uncooked portion flows underneath.

Start to Finish: 25 minutes
Makes: 6 servings

Nonstick cooking spray

1 **cup chopped cooked ham (about 5 ounces)**

½ **cup chopped onion**

½ **cup chopped green or red sweet pepper**

6 **slightly beaten eggs**

¾ **cup low-fat cottage cheese**

⅛ **teaspoon black pepper**

2 **roma tomatoes, thinly sliced**

¼ **cup shredded reduced-fat cheddar cheese (1 ounce)**

Exchanges: 1 Vegetable, 2 Medium-Fat Meat

1 Lightly coat an unheated 10-inch ovenproof skillet with nonstick cooking spray. Heat skillet over medium heat. Cook ham, onion, and sweet pepper in the hot skillet about 4 minutes or until vegetables are tender and ham is lightly browned.

2 Meanwhile, in a medium bowl combine eggs, cottage cheese, and black pepper. Pour over ham mixture in skillet. Cook over medium-low heat. As egg mixture sets, run a spatula around the edge of the skillet, lifting egg mixture so the uncooked portion flows underneath. Continue cooking and lifting edges until egg mixture is almost set but still glossy and moist.

3 Place skillet under broiler 5 inches from heat. Broil for 1 to 2 minutes or until eggs are set. Arrange tomato slices on top of frittata. Sprinkle cheese over tomato. Broil 1 minute more.

Nutrition Facts per serving: 169 cal., 9 g total fat (3 g sat. fat), 232 mg chol., 563 mg sodium, 5 g carbo., 1 g fiber, 17 g pro.
Daily Values: 11% vit. A, 23% vit. C, 8% calcium, 7% iron

breakfast & brunch

egg and potato CASSEROLE

This breakfast casserole is both delicious and convenient—you can assemble it up to 24 hours ahead.

Prep: 15 minutes
Bake: 40 minutes
Stand: 5 minutes
Oven: 350°F
Makes: 6 servings

Nonstick cooking spray

2 **cups frozen loose-pack diced hash brown potatoes with onion and peppers**

1 **cup frozen loose-pack cut broccoli or asparagus**

⅓ **cup finely chopped Canadian-style bacon or lean cooked ham (2 ounces)**

⅓ **cup evaporated fat-free milk**

2 **tablespoons all-purpose flour**

2 **8-ounce cartons refrigerated or frozen egg product, thawed**

½ **cup shredded reduced-fat cheddar cheese (2 ounces)**

1 **tablespoon snipped fresh basil or ½ teaspoon dried basil, crushed**

¼ **teaspoon black pepper**

⅛ **teaspoon salt**

Exchanges: 1 Starch, 2 Very Lean Meat

1 Lightly coat a 2-quart square baking dish with nonstick cooking spray. Arrange hash brown potatoes and broccoli in bottom of baking dish; top with Canadian-style bacon. Set aside.

2 In a medium bowl gradually stir evaporated milk into flour. Stir in egg product, half of the cheese, the basil, pepper, and salt. Pour mixture over vegetables.

3 Bake in a 350° oven for 40 to 45 minutes or until a knife inserted near center comes out clean. Sprinkle with remaining cheese. Let stand for 5 minutes before serving.

Make-ahead directions: Prepare as directed through Step 2. Cover and chill for at least 4 hours or up to 24 hours. To serve, uncover and bake as directed in Step 3.

Nutrition Facts per serving: 142 cal., 3 g total fat (1 g sat. fat), 12 mg chol., 423 mg sodium, 14 g carbo., 2 g fiber, 15 g pro.
Daily Values: 31% vit. A, 31% vit. C, 15% calcium, 11% iron

Eggscellent Nutrition

Considered a no-no for a long time, eggs are making a comeback. With only 75 calories and 5 grams of fat, eggs are a terrific, lean source of protein. In addition they contain nutrients such as choline, which may enhance memory, and lutein, which may help prevent both heart disease and age-related macular degeneration, the leading cause of blindness in older Americans. So go ahead and enjoy a few eggs a week as a healthy way to add protein to breakfast or lunch.

breakfast TORTILLA WRAP

This bacon and egg burrito makes a tidy on-the-go breakfast that you can wrap up in about 10 minutes.

Start to Finish: 10 minutes
Makes: 1 serving

- **1 strip turkey bacon, chopped**
- **2 tablespoons chopped green sweet pepper**
- **⅛ teaspoon ground cumin**
- **⅛ teaspoon salt (optional)**
- **⅛ teaspoon crushed red pepper (optional)**
- **¼ cup refrigerated egg product or 2 slightly beaten egg whites**
- **2 tablespoons chopped tomato**
- **3 dashes bottled hot pepper sauce (optional)**
- **1 8-inch fat-free flour tortilla, warmed**

Exchanges: ½ Vegetable, 1½ Starch, 1 Very Lean Meat, ½ Fat

1 In a medium nonstick skillet cook bacon until crisp. Add green pepper, cumin, and, if desired, salt and crushed red pepper. Cook for 3 minutes. Add egg product; cook for 2 minutes. Stir in tomato and, if desired, hot pepper sauce. Spoon onto tortilla and roll up.

Nutrition Facts per serving: 185 cal., 3 g total fat (1 g sat. fat), 10 mg chol., 643 mg sodium, 27 g carbo., 2 g fiber, 11 g pro.
Daily Values: 5% vit. A, 31% vit. C, 1% calcium, 6% iron

breakfast & brunch

breakfast BAKE

Put all your eggs in one basket (or dish, in this case) along with ham and your favorite cheese such as cheddar, Swiss, American, or Monterey Jack with jalapeño peppers.

Prep: 15 minutes
Bake: 30 minutes
Stand: 10 minutes
Chill: 2 hours
Oven: 325°F
Makes: 4 servings

Nonstick cooking spray

4 **slices bread**

½ **cup diced cooked lean ham**

⅓ **cup reduced-fat shredded cheddar cheese**

4 **eggs**

⅔ **cup fat-free milk**

⅛ **teaspoon black pepper**

Exchanges: 1 Starch, 2 Medium-Fat Meat

❶ Lightly coat two 16- to 20-ounce casseroles with nonstick cooking spray. Tear bread into bite-size pieces; place half of the bread in the prepared dishes. Sprinkle ham and cheese over bread. Top with remaining torn bread.

❷ In a medium mixing bowl beat together eggs, milk, and pepper with a rotary beater or a fork. Pour egg mixture evenly over bread; press lightly with the back of a spoon to thoroughly moisten bread. Cover and chill for 2 to 24 hours.

❸ Bake in a 325° oven about 30 minutes or until a knife inserted near centers comes out clean. Let stand for 10 minutes before serving.

Nutrition Facts per serving: 235 cal., 12 g total fat (5 g sat. fat), 237 mg chol., 546 mg sodium, 15 g carbo., 1 g fiber, 16 g pro.
Daily Values: 10% vit. A, 1% vit. C, 18% calcium, 10% iron

eggs and more PITA POCKETS

Creamy scrambled eggs and Canadian bacon pack these pita breads with protein. It's the ideal breakfast to eat at home or on the go.

Start to Finish: 15 minutes
Makes: 4 servings

- 2 **eggs**
- 4 **egg whites**
- 3 **ounces Canadian-style bacon, finely chopped**
- 3 **tablespoons water**
- 2 **tablespoons snipped fresh chives (optional)**
- ⅛ **teaspoon salt**
  Nonstick cooking spray
- 2 **large pita bread rounds**
- ½ **cup shredded cheddar cheese (2 ounces)**

breakfast & brunch

Exchanges: 1 Starch, 2 Medium-Fat Meat

1 In a medium mixing bowl beat together eggs, egg whites, Canadian-style bacon, water, chives (if desired), and salt with a rotary beater or a fork.

2 Lightly coat a large nonstick skillet with cooking spray. Heat skillet over medium heat. Add egg mixture to skillet. Cook without stirring until egg mixture begins to set. Run a spatula around the edge of the skillet, lifting egg mixture so the uncooked portion flows underneath. Continue cooking until egg mixture is cooked through but is still glossy and moist.

3 Cut pita rounds in half crosswise. Fill pita halves with egg mixture. Sprinkle with cheese.

Nutrition Facts per serving: 233 cal., 9 g total fat (4 g sat. fat), 133 mg chol., 734 mg sodium, 18 g carbo., 1 g fiber, 18 g pro.
Daily Values: 6% vit. A, 14% calcium, 8% iron

the casual OMELET

The indulgence of breakfast in bed is yours to savor with a ready-in-minutes omelet. If you like, round out the meal with fresh fruit.

Start to Finish: 18 minutes
Makes: 2 servings

Nonstick cooking spray

8 **ounces refrigerated or frozen egg product, thawed**

1 **tablespoon snipped fresh chives, Italian parsley, or chervil**

Dash salt

Dash cayenne pepper

¼ **cup shredded reduced-fat sharp cheddar cheese (1 ounce)**

1 **cup spinach leaves**

1 **recipe Red Pepper Relish**

Fresh fruit (optional)

Exchanges: 1½ Vegetable, 2 Very Lean Meat, ½ Fat

❶ Lightly coat an 8-inch nonstick skillet with flared sides or a crepe pan with nonstick cooking spray. Heat skillet over medium heat.

❷ In a mixing bowl combine egg product, chives, salt, and cayenne pepper. Beat with an electric mixer on medium speed or a rotary beater until frothy.

❸ Pour mixture into the prepared skillet. Cook over medium heat. As egg mixture sets, run a spatula around edge of skillet, lifting eggs so uncooked portion flows underneath. When eggs are set but still shiny, sprinkle with cheese. Top with ¾ cup spinach and 2 tablespoons Red Pepper Relish. Fold one side of omelet partially over filling. Top with remaining spinach and 1 tablespoon Red Pepper Relish. Reserve remaining relish for another use. Cut omelet in half; transfer omelet halves to plates. If desired, serve with fresh fruit.

Red Pepper Relish: In a bowl combine ⅔ cup chopped red sweet pepper, 2 tablespoons finely chopped onion, 1 tablespoon cider vinegar, and ¼ teaspoon black pepper.

Nutrition Facts per serving: 122 cal., 3 g total fat (2 g sat. fat), 10 mg chol., 404 mg sodium, 7 g carbo., 3 g fiber, 16 g pro.
Daily Values: 103% vit. A, 167% vit. C, 16% calcium, 19% iron

breakfast & brunch

banana CRUNCH POPS

Remember the frozen bananas of your childhood? These cinnamon-spiced bananas with a crisp coating taste even better.

Prep: 15 minutes
Freeze: 2 hours
Stand: 10 minutes
Makes: 4 servings

- ⅔ **cup fat-free yogurt (any flavor)**
- ¼ **teaspoon ground cinnamon**
- 1 **cup crisp rice cereal or chocolate-flavor crisp rice cereal**
- 2 **bananas, cut in half crosswise**
- 4 **wooden sticks**

Exchanges: 1 Fruit, ½ Starch

1 Place yogurt in a small shallow dish; stir in cinnamon. Place cereal in another small shallow dish. Insert a wooden stick into each banana piece. Roll banana pieces in yogurt mixture, covering the entire piece of banana. Roll in cereal to coat. Place on a baking sheet lined with waxed paper. Freeze about 2 hours or until firm.

2 When frozen, wrap each banana pop in freezer wrap. Store pops in the freezer. Before serving, let stand at room temperature for 10 to 15 minutes.

Nutrition Facts per serving: 99 cal., 0 g total fat (0 g sat. fat), 1 mg chol., 94 mg sodium, 23 g carbo., 2 g fiber, 3 g pro.
Daily Values: 4% vit. A, 21% vit. C, 7% calcium, 4% iron

breakfast & brunch

iced ESPRESSO

Pour tall glasses of this refreshing, low-fat coffee drink for brunch or in place of dessert.

Prep: 20 minutes
Chill: 3 hours
Makes: 6 (6-ounce) servings

½ **cup ground espresso coffee or French roast coffee**

1 **teaspoon finely shredded orange peel**

4 **cups water**

3 **tablespoons sugar**

1½ **cups fat-free milk**

Ice cubes

Orange peel strips (optional)

1 **teaspoon grated semisweet chocolate (optional)**

Exchanges: ½ Other Carbo.

1 In a drip coffee maker or percolator prepare coffee with shredded orange peel and water according to manufacturer's directions. Pour coffee into a heatproof pitcher; stir in sugar and milk. Chill at least 3 hours or until serving time.

2 To serve, fill 6 glasses with ice cubes; pour coffee mixture over ice. If desired, garnish with orange peel strips and grated chocolate.

Nutrition Facts per serving: 48 cal., 0 g total fat (0 g sat. fat), 1 mg chol., 36 mg sodium, 10 g carbo., 0 g fiber, 2 g pro.
Daily Values: 2% vit. A, 1% vit. C, 8% calcium, 1% iron

breakfast & brunch

fruit and soy SMOOTHIES

Whip up a grab-and-go smoothie. To keep it interesting play around with fruit combos such as mango-blueberry, banana-grape, or other duets that suit your personal taste.

breakfast & brunch

Start to Finish: 5 minutes
Makes: 3 (1-cup) servings

- 1 **cup vanilla-flavor soy milk**
- ½ **cup orange juice**
- 1 **cup chopped papaya**
- ½ **cup frozen unsweetened whole strawberries**
- 2 **tablespoons soy protein powder (optional)**
- 1 **tablespoon honey (optional)**

Exchanges: ½ Milk, 1 Fruit

❶ In a blender container combine soy milk, orange juice, fruit, and, if desired, protein powder and honey. Cover and blend until mixture is smooth. Immediately pour into glasses.

Nutrition Facts per serving: 97 cal., 1 g total fat (0 g sat. fat), 0 mg chol., 47 mg sodium, 18 g carbo., 2 g fiber, 3 g pro.
Daily Values: 8% vit. A, 108% vit. C, 12% calcium, 5% iron

berry-banana SMOOTHIES

Keep the ingredients for this recipe on hand to make healthful after-school snacks.

Start to Finish: 10 minutes
Makes: 2 servings

1 cup orange juice

1 small banana, peeled, cut up, and frozen

¼ cup assorted fresh or frozen berries, such as raspberries, blackberries, and/or strawberries

3 tablespoons vanilla low-fat yogurt

Fresh mint (optional)

Fresh berries (optional)

Exchanges: 2 Fruit

1 In a blender container combine orange juice, frozen banana pieces, desired berries, and yogurt. Cover and blend until smooth.

2 To serve, pour into 2 glasses. If desired, garnish with fresh mint and additional fresh berries.

Nutrition Facts per serving: 123 cal., 1 g total fat (0 g sat. fat), 2 mg chol., 19 mg sodium, 28 g carbo., 2 g fiber, 3 g pro.
Daily Values: 6% vit. A, 116% vit. C, 6% calcium, 3% iron

breakfast & brunch

To Caffeine or Not to Caffeine

Several studies have looked at caffeine intake and its effect, or lack thereof, on health. So far there has been little evidence that moderate amounts of caffeine increase the risk of any diseases or conditions. However, excessive caffeine intake could cause jitters and insomnia. How much is too much varies from person to person based on usual caffeine habits and individual sensitivity. In general 200 to 300 milligrams, the amount of caffeine in about two to three cups of coffee, is a safe daily amount.

snacks & APPETIZERS

Looking for a satisfying snack that's also good for you? How about party foods that fill your guests up but not out? Here you'll find something for every occasion. From snack mixes to dips and chicken fingers to milk shakes, these fun munchies really hit the spot.

(clockwise from top right) **Hot and Spicy Walnuts,** *recipe page 50*
Fruit and Peanut Snack Mix, *recipe page 46*
Oriental Trail Mix, *recipe page 47*

fruit and PEANUT SNACK MIX

For a snack kids will go for, add a 6-ounce package of fish-shape crackers to this three-ingredient mix.

Start to Finish: 10 minutes
Makes: about 12 (½-cup)
    servings

1 6-ounce package dried cranberries (1½ cups)

1 7-ounce package dried pears, snipped (1⅓ cups)

1 cup cocktail peanuts

Exchanges: 1 Fruit, 1½ Starch, 1 Fat

1 In a medium bowl stir together all ingredients. Serve immediately.

Nutrition Facts per serving: 212 cal., 8 g total fat (2 g sat. fat), 5 mg chol., 139 mg sodium, 34 g carbo., 3 g fiber, 5 g pro.
Daily Values: 1% vit. A, 2% vit. C, 2% calcium, 6% iron

snacks & appetizers

Nutty Nutrition

The combination of protein from the peanuts and carbohydrate from the fruit makes this an ideal snack. While carbohydrates provide energy, they increase blood sugar levels quickly and are metabolized rapidly, often leaving you feeling hungry again soon. Foods high in protein provide a more lasting feeling of fullness and slow the absorption of the sugars in the carbohydrates. Eating the two together results in an energy-packed snack that stays with you.

oriental TRAIL MIX

Quick to put together, this perfect trail mix features the concentrated nutrition of nuts and dried fruits with crisp rice crackers and the enticing bite of ginger.

Start to Finish: 10 minutes
Makes: 16 (⅓-cup) servings

4 cups assorted oriental rice crackers

¾ cup dried apricots, halved lengthwise

¾ cup lightly salted cashews

¼ cup chopped crystallized ginger and/or golden raisins

Exchanges: 1 Starch, ½ Fat

1 In a medium bowl stir together all ingredients. Serve immediately.

Nutrition Facts per serving: 102 cal., 3 g total fat (1 g sat. fat), 0 mg chol., 78 mg sodium, 17 g carbo., 1 g fiber, 2 g pro.
Daily Values: 9% vit. A, 6% iron

honey-mustard SNACK MIX

Crunchy, spicy, and high in protein, this mix has it all. Take it to the office for a fun midafternoon treat or make it for an at-home movie night instead of plain popcorn.

Prep: 10 minutes
Bake: 20 minutes
Oven: 300°F
Makes: 15 (½-cup) servings

1½ **cups crispy corn-and-rice cereal**

1 **cup bite-size shredded wheat biscuits**

¾ **cup unblanched whole almonds**

½ **cup peanuts**

2 **tablespoons butter**

3 **tablespoons honey mustard**

1 **teaspoon Worcestershire sauce**

¼ **teaspoon garlic powder**

⅛ **teaspoon cayenne pepper**

4 **cups plain popped popcorn**

Exchanges: ½ Starch, ½ High-Fat Meat, ½ Fat

1 In a foil-lined 13×9×2-inch baking pan place cereal, wheat biscuits, almonds, and peanuts; set aside. In a small saucepan melt butter. Remove saucepan from heat; stir in mustard, Worcestershire sauce, garlic powder, and cayenne pepper until combined. Drizzle over cereal and nut mixture in pan, tossing gently to coat.

2 Bake mixture, uncovered, in a 300° oven for 20 minutes, gently stirring after 10 minutes. Stir in popcorn. Lift foil to remove baked mixture from pan; cool completely. Serve immediately.

Nutrition Facts per serving: 113 cal., 8 g total fat (2 g sat. fat), 4 mg chol., 87 mg sodium, 9 g carbo., 2 g fiber, 3 g pro.
Daily Values: 2% vit. A, 1% vit. C, 2% calcium, 8% iron

snacks & appetizers

hot and SPICY WALNUTS

Nuts hit the spot as a snack, and this snack is loaded with them. Walnuts have more heart-healthy omega-3 fat than other nuts. Use canola oil in the recipe to boost its omega-3 content even more.

Prep: 10 minutes
Bake: 20 minutes
Cool: 15 minutes
Oven: 300°F
Makes: 8 (¼-cup) servings

1 **teaspoon ground coriander**
1 **teaspoon ground cumin**
½ **teaspoon salt**
¼ **teaspoon freshly ground black pepper**
⅛ **teaspoon cayenne pepper**
2 **cups walnut halves**
1 **tablespoon cooking oil**

Exchanges: ½ Starch, ½ High-Fat Meat, 3 Fat

1 In a small bowl stir together coriander, cumin, salt, black pepper, and cayenne pepper; set aside. Place nuts in a 13×9×2-inch baking pan. Drizzle with the oil, stirring to coat. Sprinkle with spice mixture; toss lightly.

2 Bake in a 300° oven for 20 minutes or until nuts are lightly toasted, stirring once or twice. Cool in pan for 15 minutes. Turn out onto paper towels; cool completely. Store, covered, in a cool place.

Nutrition Facts per serving: 214 cal., 21 g total fat (2 g sat. fat), 0 mg chol., 147 mg sodium, 4 g carbo., 2 g fiber, 5 g pro.
Daily Values: 1% vit. C, 3% calcium, 5% iron

snacks & appetizers

spiced chili NUTS AND SEEDS

Pick your favorite nuts and seeds for this snack recipe. Orange juice concentrate spiked with piquant spices gives the mixture a burst of flavor.

Prep: 10 minutes
Bake: 15 minutes
Oven: 300°F
Makes: 16 (¼-cup) servings

2 **tablespoons frozen orange juice concentrate, thawed**

2 **teaspoons Worcestershire sauce**

1 **teaspoon garlic powder**

1 **teaspoon ground cumin**

1 **teaspoon chili powder**

½ **teaspoon cayenne pepper**

¼ **teaspoon salt**

¼ **teaspoon ground allspice**

¼ **teaspoon black pepper**

⅛ **teaspoon onion salt**

2 **cups unsalted peanuts, hazelnuts, and/or Brazil nuts**

1 **cup pecan halves**

6 **tablespoons unsalted shelled sunflower seeds**

2 **tablespoons sesame seeds**

Nonstick cooking spray

Exchanges: ½ Starch, 1 High-Fat Meat, 1 Fat

❶ In a large bowl combine orange juice concentrate, Worcestershire sauce, garlic powder, cumin, chili powder, cayenne pepper, salt, allspice, black pepper, and onion salt. Stir in nuts and seeds; toss to coat.

❷ Line a 15×10×1-inch baking pan with foil; lightly coat with nonstick cooking spray. Spread nuts and seeds on foil. Bake in a 300° oven for 15 to 20 minutes or until toasted, stirring once. Cool. Store in an airtight container at room temperature for up to 1 week.

Nutrition Facts per serving: 183 cal., 16 g total fat (2 g sat. fat), 0 mg chol., 59 mg sodium, 7 g carbo., 3 g fiber, 6 g pro.
Daily Values: 2% vit. A, 6% vit. C, 2% calcium, 5% iron

snacks & appetizers

chunky GUACAMOLE

Guacamole is a party favorite any time of year. Lime juice keeps the avocados green and provides a zesty zing.

Prep: 20 minutes
Chill: 1 hour
Makes: 16 (2-tablespoon) servings

- 2 **medium roma tomatoes, seeded and cut up**
- ¼ **cup coarsely chopped red onion**
- 1 **to 2 tablespoons lime juice**
- 1 **tablespoon olive oil**
- ¼ **teaspoon salt**
- ⅛ **teaspoon black pepper**
- 1 **to 2 cloves garlic, halved**
- 2 **ripe avocados, halved, seeded, peeled, and cut up**
- **Chopped tomato (optional)**
- **Tortilla chips**

Exchanges: ½ Fat

1 In a food processor bowl combine tomatoes, red onion, lime juice, olive oil, salt, pepper, and garlic. Cover and process until mixture is coarsely chopped. Add the avocados. Cover and process just until mixture is chopped. Transfer to a serving bowl; cover surface with plastic wrap. Chill for up to 1 hour. If desired, garnish with chopped tomato. Serve with chips.

Nutrition Facts per 2 tablespoons dip with ½ cup chips: 48 cal., 5 g total fat (1 g sat. fat), 0 mg chol., 40 mg sodium, 2 g carbo., 1 g fiber, 1 g pro.
Daily Values: 4% vit. A, 7% vit. C, 2% iron

snacks & appetizers

layered BEAN DIP

Beans and salsa topped with pureed cottage cheese, chopped tomatoes, and cheddar cheese add a splash of color to your party table.

Prep: 25 minutes
Chill: 4 hours
Makes: 18 (½ cup) servings

- **1 15-ounce can pinto or red kidney beans, drained**
- **¼ cup salsa**
- **1 4-ounce can chopped green chile peppers, drained**
- **½ of a 7-ounce jar roasted red pepper, drained and chopped (about ½ cup), or one 4-ounce jar pimiento, drained and chopped**
- **1 cup low-fat cottage cheese**
- **1 cup chopped tomato**
- **¼ cup shredded low-fat cheddar cheese (1 ounce)**
- **1 recipe Tortilla Crisps**

Exchanges: 1 Starch, ½ Very Lean Meat

1 In a blender container or food processor bowl place beans and salsa. Cover and blend or process until smooth. Spread mixture evenly in a 9-inch pie plate. Sprinkle with chile peppers and roasted red pepper.

2 Wash blender container or food processor bowl. Place cottage cheese in the blender container or food processor bowl. Cover and blend or process until smooth. Carefully spread cottage cheese on top of bean mixture in pie plate. Cover and chill for at least 4 hours or up to 24 hours before serving.

3 Before serving, sprinkle tomato and cheddar cheese on top of cottage cheese layer. Serve with Tortilla Crisps or sliced fresh vegetables.

Tortilla Crisps: Cut twelve 6-inch flour or corn tortillas each into 6 wedges. Place wedges in a single layer on an ungreased baking sheet. Lightly coat with nonstick cooking spray. Bake in a 350°F oven for 5 to 10 minutes or until crisp. Use 4 crisps per serving.

Nutrition Facts per ½ cup dip with 4 crisps: 85 cal., 2 g total fat (1 g sat. fat), 2 mg chol., 203 mg sodium, 13 g carbo., 1 g fiber, 4 g pro.
Daily Values: 2% vit. A, 26% vit. C, 6% calcium, 5% iron

Party Tips

Parties present a challenge in the quest to eat healthfully. Armed with these strategies you can keep your diet in check and enjoy the party too. Skipping meals during the day in an effort to save calories for the party is a bad idea—you'll only overeat at the party. Look over all the food that's being served and make a plan instead of rushing to the buffet table. Then choose two or three splurge items you'd really like to try and fill the rest of your plate with healthier foods like veggies and shrimp.

roasted GARLIC-SPINACH DIP

When garlic is roasted it becomes sweet and mellow in flavor. Use roasted garlic paste to add flavor without fat (and virtually no calories) to soups and salad dressings.

Prep: 15 minutes
Bake: 25 minutes
Oven: 375°F
Makes: 8 (¼-cup) servings

1 whole head garlic
1 teaspoon olive oil
1 10-ounce package frozen chopped spinach
¼ cup fat-free milk
   Dash bottled hot pepper sauce
⅛ teaspoon salt
1 8-ounce package reduced-fat cream cheese (Neufchâtel), cut up
   Chopped tomato (optional)
1 recipe Toasted Pita Wedges

Exchanges: 2½ Starch, ½ Very Lean Meat, 1 Fat

❶ Peel away outer dry leaves from head of garlic, leaving skin of garlic cloves intact. Cut off pointed top portion of head (about ¼ inch) with a knife, leaving the bulb intact. Place on a double-thick, 12-inch square of foil. Drizzle garlic with the oil. Fold foil to enclose garlic. Bake in a 375° oven for 25 to 30 minutes or until garlic is soft. Cool.

❷ Cook spinach according to package directions, except omit salt. Drain well; press out excess liquid.

❸ Squeeze pulp from garlic cloves into food processor bowl, discarding skins. Add drained spinach, milk, hot pepper sauce, and salt. Cover and process until well combined. Add cream cheese. Cover; process until nearly smooth.

❹ Transfer mixture to a saucepan. Cook and stir over medium-low heat until heated through.

❺ To serve, transfer to serving bowl. If desired, sprinkle with tomato. Serve with Toasted Pita Wedges.

Toasted Pita Wedges: Split 8 small pita bread rounds; cut each half into 6 wedges. Place wedges cut side up on an ungreased baking sheet. Bake in batches in a 375° oven for 7 to 9 minutes or until lightly browned. Store in an airtight container.

Nutrition Facts per serving: 261 cal., 8 g total fat (4 g sat. fat), 22 mg chol., 204 mg sodium, 37 g carbo., 2 g fiber, 10 g pro.
Daily Values: 109% vit. A, 6% vit. C, 11% calcium, 10% iron

snacks & appetizers

herbed POTATO WEDGES

You can serve these tasty potato wedges as a snack or a side dish with flavored sour cream, catsup, or both. No matter how you serve them, your kids will eat them up.

Prep: 15 minutes
Bake: 15 minutes
Oven: 425°F
Makes: 8 servings

- 2 teaspoons olive oil
- 2 teaspoons balsamic vinegar
- 1 tablespoon grated Parmesan cheese
- 1 tablespoon fine dry bread crumbs
- ½ teaspoon dried Italian seasoning
- ⅛ teaspoon black pepper
  Nonstick cooking spray
- 2 medium baking potatoes
- ½ cup light dairy sour cream
- 1 tablespoon snipped fresh chives
- ¼ teaspoon garlic powder

Exchanges: 1 Starch

❶ In a small bowl or custard cup combine olive oil and balsamic vinegar. In another small bowl combine Parmesan cheese, bread crumbs, Italian seasoning, and pepper.

❷ Lightly coat a foil-lined baking sheet with nonstick cooking spray; set aside. Cut the potatoes in half lengthwise, then cut each half lengthwise into 4 wedges. Arrange potato wedges skin side down on the prepared baking sheet so they don't touch. Brush with olive oil mixture and coat with Parmesan cheese mixture.

❸ Bake in a 425° oven for 15 to 20 minutes or until potatoes are tender and edges are crisp.

❹ Meanwhile, in a small bowl combine sour cream, chives, and garlic powder. Serve warm potatoes with flavored sour cream mixture.

Nutrition Facts per serving: 79 cal., 3 g total fat (1 g sat. fat), 5 mg chol., 43 mg sodium, 11 g carbo., 1 g fiber, 3 g pro.
Daily Values: 2% vit. A, 15% vit. C, 5% calcium, 5% iron

snacks & appetizers

nutty CHICKEN FINGERS

A satisfying snack is ready in a jiffy when you make these crunchy coated chicken strips.

snacks & appetizers

Prep: 15 minutes
Bake: 7 minutes
Oven: 400°F
Makes: 3 servings

⅓ **cup crushed cornflakes**

½ **cup finely chopped pecans**

1 **tablespoon dried parsley flakes**

⅛ **teaspoon salt**

⅛ **teaspoon garlic powder**

12 **ounces skinless, boneless chicken breasts, cut into 3×1-inch strips**

2 **tablespoons fat-free milk**

Reduced-calorie ranch-style dressing (optional)

Exchanges: ½ Starch, 4 Very Lean Meat, 2½ Fat

1 In a shallow dish combine crushed cornflakes, pecans, parsley, salt, and garlic powder. Dip chicken in milk, then roll in cornflake mixture. Place in a 15×10×1-inch baking pan.

2 Bake in a 400° oven for 7 to 9 minutes or until chicken is tender and no longer pink. If desired, serve chicken with ranch-style dressing.

Nutrition Facts per serving: 279 cal., 15 g total fat (0 g sat. fat), 66 mg chol., 219 mg sodium, 8 g carbo., 2 g fiber, 29 g pro.
Daily Values: 3% vit. A, 3% vit. C, 4% calcium, 9% iron

wrap and ROLL PINWHEELS

If you can't find colorful spinach or jalapeño tortillas, use plain or whole wheat tortillas to wrap these cheese- and meat-filled finger foods.

Prep: 20 minutes
Chill: 2 to 4 hours
Makes: about 12 (2-slice) servings

- **3** **7- to 8-inch spinach and/or jalapeño flour tortillas**
- **1** **5- to 5.2-ounce container semisoft cheese with garlic and herb**
- **12** **large fresh basil leaves**
- **½** **of a 7-ounce jar roasted red sweet peppers, cut into ¼-inch strips (about ½ cup)**
- **4** **ounces thinly sliced cooked roast beef, ham, or turkey**
- **1** **tablespoon light mayonnaise dressing**

Exchanges: ½ Starch, ½ Lean Meat, 1 Fat

1 Spread each tortilla with one-third of the semisoft cheese. Top cheese with a layer of the large basil leaves. Divide roasted red sweet pepper strips among the tortillas, arranging pepper strips over the basil leaves 1 to 2 inches apart. Top with meat slices. Spread 1 teaspoon mayonnaise dressing over the meat on each tortilla. Tightly roll up tortillas. Wrap each roll in plastic wrap. Chill for 2 to 4 hours.

2 To serve, remove the plastic wrap from the tortilla rolls; cut each roll into 1-inch diagonal slices.

Nutrition Facts per serving: 103 cal., 7 g total fat (4 g sat. fat), 8 mg chol., 125 mg sodium, 6 g carbo., 0 g fiber, 4 g pro.
Daily Values: 1% vit. A, 29% vit. C, 2% calcium, 4% iron

snacks & appetizers

incredible QUESADILLAS

Capture a south-of-the-border attitude with these flavorful snacks. Cooking becomes a fun activity when you show the kids how to use a waffle baker.

Prep: 20 minutes
Cook: 3 minutes each
Makes: 8 servings

½ cup shredded reduced-fat Mexican-cheese blend

4 8-inch fat-free flour tortillas

4 low-fat brown-and-serve sausage links, cooked and coarsely chopped

2 tablespoons well-drained pineapple salsa or regular salsa

1 small red onion, sliced and separated into rings

2 tablespoons finely snipped fresh cilantro

½ cup pineapple salsa or regular salsa

Cilantro sprigs (optional)

Exchanges: 1 Starch, ½ Lean Meat

1 Heat a waffle baker on a medium-high heat setting. Sprinkle 2 tablespoons of the cheese over half of each tortilla. Top with sausage, the 2 tablespoons salsa, onion, and cilantro. Fold tortillas in half, pressing gently.

2 Place one quesadilla on preheated waffle baker. Close lid, pressing slightly. Bake for 3 to 6 minutes or until tortilla is lightly browned and cheese is melted. Remove from waffle baker. Cut quesadilla in half. Repeat with remaining quesadillas.

3 Place the ½ cup salsa in a bowl. If desired, garnish quesadilla pieces with cilantro sprigs. Serve with salsa.

Note: Or cook each quesadilla in a 10-inch nonstick skillet over medium heat for 3 to 4 minutes or until golden brown. Using a spatula, turn quesadilla over. Cook for 2 to 3 minutes more or until golden brown. Remove the quesadilla from the skillet.

Nutrition Facts per serving: 104 cal., 2 g total fat (1 g sat. fat), 8 mg chol., 362 mg sodium, 17 g carbo., 2 g fiber, 5 g pro.
Daily Values: 2% vit. A, 1% vit. C, 4% calcium, 2% iron

snacks & appetizers

artichoke-feta TORTILLAS

Three cheeses, roasted peppers, and artichokes melt and mingle in these tortilla-wrapped treats. They're the perfect appetizer for a casual gathering.

snacks & appetizers

Prep: 15 minutes
Bake: 15 minutes
Oven: 350°F
Makes: 24 servings

Nonstick cooking spray

1 **14-ounce can artichoke hearts, drained and finely chopped**

½ **of an 8-ounce tub reduced-fat cream cheese (about ½ cup)**

3 **green onions, thinly sliced**

⅓ **cup grated Parmesan or Romano cheese**

¼ **cup crumbled feta cheese (1 ounce)**

3 **tablespoons reduced-fat basil pesto**

8 **8-inch spinach, tomato, or regular flour tortillas**

1 **7-ounce jar roasted red sweet peppers, drained and cut into strips**

1 **recipe Yogurt-Chive Sauce**

Exchanges: ½ Vegetable, ½ Starch, ½ Fat

❶ Lightly coat a 3-quart rectangular baking dish with nonstick cooking spray; set aside. For filling, in a large bowl stir together artichoke hearts, cream cheese, green onions, Parmesan cheese, feta cheese, and pesto.

❷ Place about ¼ cup filling on each tortilla. Top with red pepper strips; roll up. Arrange tortilla rolls in the prepared baking dish. If desired, lightly coat tortilla rolls with additional cooking spray. Bake, uncovered, in a 350° oven about 15 minutes or until heated through.

❸ Cut each tortilla roll into thirds and arrange on a serving platter. Serve with Yogurt-Chive Sauce.

Yogurt-Chive Sauce: In a small bowl stir together one 8-ounce carton plain fat-free yogurt and 1 tablespoon snipped fresh chives.

Nutrition Facts per serving: 75 cal., 4 g total fat (2 g sat. fat), 8 mg chol., 177 mg sodium, 8 g carbo., 1 g fiber, 3 g pro.
Daily Values: 2% vit. A, 26% vit. C, 7% calcium, 4% iron

mini SPINACH POCKETS

A savory spinach and onion mixture fills these miniature stuffed pizzas. The refrigerated pizza dough makes them incredibly easy to prepare.

Prep: 30 minutes
Bake: 8 minutes
Stand: 5 minutes
Oven: 425°F
Makes: 25 pockets

Nonstick cooking spray

½ **of a 10-ounce package frozen chopped spinach, thawed and well drained**

½ **of an 8-ounce package reduced-fat cream cheese (Neufchâtel), softened**

2 **tablespoons finely chopped green onion**

1 **tablespoon grated Parmesan cheese**

Dash black pepper

1 **10-ounce package refrigerated pizza dough**

1 **tablespoon milk**

Bottled light spaghetti sauce, warmed (optional)

Exchanges: ½ Starch

❶ Line a baking sheet with foil; lightly coat foil with nonstick cooking spray. Set baking sheet aside. For filling, in a medium bowl stir together spinach, cream cheese, green onion, Parmesan cheese, and pepper. Set aside.

❷ Unroll pizza dough on a lightly floured surface; roll dough into a 15-inch square. Cut into twenty-five 3-inch squares. Spoon 1 rounded teaspoon filling onto each square. Brush edges of dough with water. Lift a corner of each square and stretch dough over filling to opposite corner, making a triangle. Press edges with fingers or a fork to seal.

❸ Arrange pockets on the prepared baking sheet. Prick tops of pockets with a fork. Brush with milk. Bake in a 425° oven for 8 to 10 minutes or until golden brown. Let stand for 5 minutes before serving. If desired, serve with spaghetti sauce.

Nutrition Facts per pocket: 38 cal., 2 g total fat (1 g sat. fat), 4 mg chol., 62 mg sodium, 5 g carbo., 0 g fiber, 1 g pro.
Daily Values: 9% vit. A, 1% vit. C, 1% calcium, 2% iron

snacks & appetizers

Nutritional Powerhouse

Popeye may have eaten spinach to make him strong, but the leafy green veggie does a lot more than that. With only about 25 calories in a half pound, spinach is one of the most nutrient-dense vegetables around. That same half pound also contains a whopping 21 grams of fiber as well as more than three times the recommended daily amount of vitamin A and the phytochemicals lutein and indoles, which can help lower one's risk of cancer and maintain healthy vision.

fruit SUNDAE SNACKS

Top these pretty waffle cones with shredded jicama for crunchy sweetness with the look of grated coconut.

Start to Finish: 5 minutes
Makes: 6 servings

¾ **cup cut-up strawberries**

3 **cups cut-up fruit, such as apples, bananas, sweet cherries, seedless red grapes, kiwifruits, and/or peaches**

6 **large waffle cones**

¼ **cup finely shredded jicama**

Exchanges: 1 Fruit, 1 Other Carbo., 1 Fat

❶ Place strawberries in a blender container; cover and puree until smooth. In a medium bowl combine cut-up fruits; gently toss together. Spoon into cones. Drizzle with the strawberry puree. Top with jicama.

Nutrition Facts per serving: 175 cal., 8 g total fat (0 g sat. fat), 0 mg chol., 56 mg sodium, 27 g carbo., 2 g fiber, 2 g pro.
Daily Values: 2% vit. A, 29% vit. C, 1% calcium, 4% iron

snacks & appetizers

fruit WITH CREAMY SAUCE

GREAT FOR
KIDS

This blend of cottage cheese, applesauce, and honey is good with any fruit combination, so choose whatever piques your interest in the produce department.

Start to Finish: 15 minutes
Makes: 6 servings

½ **cup low-fat cream-style cottage cheese**

½ **cup unsweetened applesauce**

1 **tablespoon honey**

1 **cup sliced nectarines; sliced, peeled peaches; orange sections; or sliced strawberries**

1 **cup sliced apple or pear**

½ **cup seedless grapes**

1 **small banana, sliced**

Ground cinnamon or ground nutmeg

Exchanges: 1 Fruit, ½ Very Lean Meat

1 For sauce, in a blender container or food processor bowl combine cottage cheese, applesauce, and honey. Cover and blend or process until smooth.

2 In a large bowl stir together nectarine slices, apple slices, grapes, and banana slices. Divide fruit among 6 dessert dishes. Spoon some of the sauce over each serving and sprinkle with cinnamon.

Nutrition Facts per serving: 77 cal., 1 g total fat (0 g sat. fat), 1 mg chol., 77 mg sodium, 17 g carbo., 2 g fiber, 3 g pro.
Daily Values: 4% vit. A, 9% vit. C, 2% calcium, 1% iron

snacks & appetizers

tropical FRUIT POPS

You may think you're making this treat for the kids, but as soon as the adults taste them you're going to have to make more. Experiment with gelatin flavors to determine which you like best.

Prep: 15 minutes
Freeze: 6 hours
Makes: 8 large or
    12 small pops

½ **cup boiling water**

1 **4-serving-size package sugar-free lemon-, mixed fruit-, or strawberry-flavor gelatin**

1 **15¼-ounce can crushed pineapple (juice pack)**

2 **medium bananas, cut into chunks**

Exchanges: 1 Fruit

❶ In a 1- or 2-cup glass measuring cup stir together the boiling water and the gelatin until gelatin dissolves. Pour into a blender container. Add undrained pineapple and banana chunks. Cover and blend until smooth.

❷ Pour a scant ½ cup of the fruit mixture into each of eight 5- to 6-ounce paper or plastic drink cups. (Or pour a scant ⅓ cup into each of twelve 3-ounce cups.) Cover each cup with foil. Using the tip of a knife, make a small hole in the foil over each cup. Insert a wooden stick into the cup through the hole. Freeze about 6 hours or until firm.

❸ To serve, quickly dip the cups in warm water to slightly soften fruit mixture. Remove foil and loosen sides of pops from drink cups.

Nutrition Facts per large pop: 65 cal., 0 g total fat (0 g sat. fat), 0 mg chol., 29 mg sodium, 15 g carbo., 1 g fiber, 1 g pro.
Daily Values: 1% vit. A, 13% vit. C, 1% calcium, 1% iron

snacks & appetizers

chocolate-mint MILK SHAKES

Even adults swoon for a milk shake. This variation takes a childhood favorite and freshens it with a hint of mint flavor. Low-fat and fat-free ingredients keep the fat and calories much lower than a regular milk shake.

Start to Finish: 10 minutes
Makes: 2 (8-ounce) servings

2 cups chocolate low-fat frozen yogurt

½ cup fat-free milk

Few drops peppermint or mint flavoring

Exchanges: 2½ Other Carbo.

1 In a blender container combine frozen yogurt, milk, and flavoring. Cover and blend until smooth. Serve immediately.

Nutrition Facts per serving: 182 cal., 3 g total fat (2 g sat. fat), 21 mg chol., 162 mg sodium, 35 g carbo., 0 g fiber, 8 g pro.
Daily Values: 2% vit. A, 1% vit. C, 24% calcium,

snacks & appetizers

Watch What You Drink

Many people typically grab whatever is around when thirst hits. Many perceived healthy beverages, such as juices and sports drinks, are high in calories and sugar. Know that liquids register differently from solid foods in our bodies. After eating 400–500 calories, we feel satisfied. However, after drinking 400–500 calories, we can then go on to eat another 400–500 calories. Keep this in mind the next time you are thirsty.

tropical banana MILK SHAKES

Take a tropical vacation from your day—share this midafternoon treat with your kids.

Prep: 10 minutes
Freeze: 1 hour
Makes: 4 (6-ounce) servings

1 small banana

1 cup orange juice

**1 cup vanilla low-fat or light
    ice cream**

¼ teaspoon vanilla

Ground nutmeg

Exchanges: 1 Fruit, ½ Other Carbo.

1 Peel and cut up the banana. Place in a freezer container or bag; freeze until firm.

2 In a blender container combine frozen banana, orange juice, ice cream, and vanilla. Cover and blend until smooth. Sprinkle each serving with nutmeg.

Nutrition Facts per serving: 97 cal., 1 g total fat (1 g sat. fat), 5 mg chol., 21 mg sodium, 20 g carbo., 1 g fiber, 2 g pro.
Daily Values: 3% vit. A, 55% vit. C, 2% calcium, 1% iron

snacks & appetizers

lunches
& LIGHT MEALS

If you're bored by the typical ham-sandwich-and-chips lunch, break out of your rut and try something different, like Peppery Artichoke Pitas or Italian Meatball Soup. Add fresh fruit and sparkling water for a lunch you'll look forward to. These recipes also make a great light dinner.

Lahvosh Roll, *recipe page 72*

lahvosh ROLL

Lahvosh looks and feels like a giant crisp cracker, and you must soften it before using. (You may be able to find the presoftened variety and skip Step 1.)

Prep: 15 minutes
Stand: 1 hour
Chill: 2 hours
Makes: 6 servings

1   15-inch sesame seed lahvosh (Armenian cracker bread) or two 10-inch tortillas

½   of an 8-ounce tub cream cheese with chives and onion

¼   cup chopped, drained marinated artichoke hearts

2   tablespoons diced pimiento

1   teaspoon dried oregano, crushed

6   ounces thinly sliced prosciutto or cooked ham

4   ounces sliced provolone cheese

2   large romaine lettuce leaves, ribs removed

1 Dampen both sides of lahvosh by holding it briefly under gently running cold water. Place lahvosh, seeded side down, between 2 damp, clean kitchen towels. Let stand about 1 hour or until soft.

2 In a bowl stir together cream cheese, artichoke hearts, pimiento, and oregano. Remove top towel from lahvosh. Spread lahvosh with cream cheese filling. Arrange prosciutto over cream cheese. Place provolone slices in center and lettuce next to provolone. Roll from lettuce edge, using the towel to lift and roll the bread. (Or, if using tortillas, spread tortillas with cream cheese mixture. Divide remaining ingredients between the tortillas. Roll up tortillas.)

3 Wrap roll in plastic wrap and chill seam side down for at least 2 hours. To serve, cut roll into 1-inch slices.

Make-ahead directions: Prepare Lahvosh Roll as directed through Step 2. Wrap roll in plastic wrap and chill in the refrigerator seam side down for up to 24 hours. To serve, cut roll into 1-inch slices.

Nutrition Facts per serving: 300 cal., 16 g total fat (8 g sat. fat), 51 mg chol., 1,226 mg sodium, 22 g carbo., 0 g fiber, 17 g pro.
Daily Values: 18% vit. A, 17% vit. C, 18% calcium, 9% iron

lunches

deli GREEK-STYLE PITAS

Pita bread rounds are great for lunches on the go because they make tidy, no-leak sandwiches that stay fresh and dry longer than sliced bread or rolls.

Prep: 10 minutes
Chill: 1 hour
Makes: 2 servings

½ **cup deli creamy cucumber and onion salad or Homemade Creamy Cucumber Salad**

¼ **cup chopped roma tomato**

½ **teaspoon snipped fresh dillweed**

2 **whole wheat or white pita bread rounds**

6 **ounces thinly sliced cooked deli roast beef, turkey, or chicken**

Exchanges: ½ Vegetable, 2 Starch, ½ Other Carbo., 3 Lean Meat, ½ Fat

1 In a bowl combine cucumber and onion salad, tomato, and dill. Cover and chill for 1 hour. Cut pita rounds in half crosswise. Line pita halves with roast beef. Spoon some salad mixture into each pita half.

Homemade Creamy Cucumber Salad: Combine 2 tablespoons plain low-fat yogurt, 1 teaspoon vinegar, ¼ teaspoon sugar, and a dash of salt. Add ½ cup thinly sliced cucumber and one-fourth of a small red onion, thinly sliced. Toss gently to coat.

Nutrition Facts per serving: 400 cal., 15 g total fat (5 g sat. fat), 67 mg chol., 703 mg sodium, 39 g carbo., 6 g fiber, 30 g pro.
Daily Values: 4% vit. A, 10% vit. C, 3% calcium, 27% iron

lunches

seasoned TUNA SANDWICHES

Tired of the same brown-bag lunch? This recipe combines an old favorite—tuna—with fruity olive oil, fresh lemon juice, and capers for a taste of the Mediterranean.

Start to Finish: 15 minutes
Makes: 4 servings

2 **6-ounce cans solid white tuna (water-pack), drained**

2 **tablespoons olive oil**

2 **teaspoons lemon juice**

1 **teaspoon capers, drained**

⅛ **teaspoon freshly ground black pepper**

2 **tablespoons fat-free mayonnaise dressing or salad dressing**

8 **slices whole wheat bread**

4 **lettuce leaves (optional)**

4 **tomato slices**

Exchanges: 2 Starch, 3 Very Lean Meat, 1 Fat

1 In a small bowl combine tuna, oil, lemon juice, capers, and pepper.

2 To assemble each sandwich, spread ½ tablespoon of the mayonnaise dressing on a slice of bread. Top with a lettuce leaf (if desired), tomato slice, and one-fourth of the tuna mixture. Top with a second slice of bread.

Nutrition Facts per serving: 309 cal., 11 g total fat (2 g sat. fat), 36 mg chol., 669 mg sodium, 26 g carbo., 2 g fiber, 25 g pro.
Daily Values: 3% vit. A, 8% vit. C, 7% calcium, 15% iron

lunches

turkey-tomato WRAPS

A cool idea for meals on the move, wraps are easy to pack and neat to eat.

Prep: 20 minutes
Chill: 2 hours
Makes: 6 servings

- 1 7-ounce container prepared hummus
- 3 8- to 10-inch tomato-basil flour tortillas or plain flour tortillas
- 8 ounces thinly sliced, cooked peppered turkey breast
- 6 romaine lettuce leaves, ribs removed
- 3 small tomatoes, thinly sliced
- 3 thin slices red onion, separated into rings

Exchanges: 1 Vegetable, 1½ Starch, 2 Lean Meat

1. Spread hummus evenly over tortillas. Layer turkey breast, romaine, tomatoes, and onion on top of each tortilla. Roll up each tortilla into a spiral. Cut each roll in half and wrap with plastic wrap. Chill for 2 to 4 hours. Tote in an insulated cooler with ice packs.

Nutrition Facts per serving: 236 cal., 6 g total fat (1 g sat. fat), 32 mg chol., 458 mg sodium, 29 g carbo., 4 g fiber, 19 g pro.
Daily Values: 27% vit. A, 35% vit. C, 6% calcium, 13% iron

lunches

Brown-Bagging It

Packing your own lunches for work is an easy way to eat healthier and saves money. Pack your lunch the night before so you can grab-and-go in the a.m. Be creative when putting your midday meal together. Wraps are great alternatives to sandwiches. Or skip the bread altogether and make roll-ups with lean meats and cheese. Try sprinkling dried cranberries into a salad with some slices of smoked turkey. Whatever you choose to put in your brown bag, be sure to use cold packs, if necessary, to keep your lunch at the correct temperature.

egg and vegetable WRAPS

Need a lunchtime energy boost? High-protein eggs wrapped with crisp, refreshing veggies with a light dressing are the perfect solution.

Start to Finish: 30 minutes
Makes: 6 servings

- 4 hard-cooked eggs, chopped
- 1 cup chopped cucumber
- 1 cup chopped zucchini or yellow summer squash
- ½ cup finely chopped red onion
- ½ cup shredded carrot
- ¼ cup fat-free or light mayonnaise dressing or salad dressing
- 2 tablespoons Dijon-style mustard
- 1 tablespoon fat-free milk
- 1 teaspoon snipped fresh tarragon or basil
- ⅛ teaspoon paprika
- 6 lettuce leaves
- 6 10-inch whole wheat, spinach, or vegetable flour tortillas
- 2 roma tomatoes, thinly sliced

Exchanges: 1 Vegetable, 2½ Starch, 1 Fat

1. In a large bowl combine eggs, cucumber, zucchini, red onion, and carrot. For dressing, in a small bowl stir together mayonnaise dressing, Dijon mustard, milk, tarragon, and paprika. Pour dressing over the egg mixture; toss gently to coat.

2. For each sandwich, place a lettuce leaf on a tortilla. Place 3 or 4 tomato slices on top of the lettuce, slightly off center. Spoon about ⅔ cup of the egg mixture on top of the tomato slices. Fold in two opposite sides of the tortilla; roll up from the bottom. Cut the rolls in half diagonally.

Nutrition Facts per serving: 265 cal., 7 g total fat (2 g sat. fat), 141 mg chol., 723 mg sodium, 40 g carbo., 4 g fiber, 11 g pro.
Daily Values: 78% vit. A, 27% vit. C, 8% calcium, 14% iron

lunches

peppery ARTICHOKE PITAS

These pitas are filled with ingredients you can keep on hand: canned artichokes, canned beans, and bottled garlic dressing. Keep the pantry stocked and you'll always have what you need to put a great meal on the table.

Start to Finish: 20 minutes
Makes: 6 servings

1 **15-ounce can black-eyed peas, rinsed and drained**

1 **13¾- to 14-ounce can artichoke hearts, drained and cut up**

1 **cup torn mixed salad greens**

¼ **cup bottled creamy garlic salad dressing**

¼ **teaspoon cracked black pepper**

3 **pita bread rounds, halved crosswise**

1 **small tomato, sliced**

Exchanges: 1 Vegetable, 1½ Starch, ½ Fat

❶ In a medium bowl combine black-eyed peas, artichoke hearts, mixed greens, salad dressing, and pepper. Line pita bread halves with tomato slices. Spoon artichoke mixture into pita bread halves.

Nutrition Facts per serving: 189 cal., 4 g total fat (1 g sat. fat), 0 mg chol., 632 mg sodium, 31 g carbo., 5 g fiber, 7 g pro.
Daily Values: 4% vit. A, 7% vit. C, 7% calcium, 17% iron

lunches

sausage and greens RAGOÛT

Look in your supermarket's produce section for washed, packaged escarole, Swiss chard, kale, or spinach.

Start to Finish: 35 minutes
Makes: 4 servings

- **1 8-ounce package cooked chicken andouille sausage links or cooked smoked turkey sausage links, cut into ½-inch slices**
- **1 medium yellow crookneck squash, cut into ½-inch pieces**
- **1 14-ounce can reduced-sodium chicken broth**
- **1 tablespoon snipped fresh rosemary or 1 teaspoon dried rosemary, crushed**
- **2 cups coarsely chopped fresh escarole, Swiss chard, baby kale, and/or spinach leaves**
- **1 15-ounce can white kidney beans (cannellini beans), rinsed and drained**
- **1 cup carrots cut into thin, bite-size sticks**
- **Freshly ground black pepper**
- **Purchased garlic croutons (optional)**

Exchanges: 1 Vegetable, 1 Starch, 1½ Medium-Fat Meat, 1 Fat

1 In a large saucepan combine sausage, squash, broth, and rosemary. Bring to boiling; reduce heat. Simmer, uncovered, for 5 minutes. Stir in escarole, beans, and carrots. Return to boiling; reduce heat. Cover and simmer about 5 minutes more or until vegetables are tender. Season to taste with pepper. If desired, top each serving with croutons.

Nutrition Facts per serving: 156 cal., 8 g total fat (2 g sat. fat), 20 mg chol., 785 mg sodium, 20 g carbo., 7 g fiber, 16 g pro.
Daily Values: 87% vit. A, 6% vit. C, 4% calcium, 13% iron

lunches

GREAT FOR
KIDS

hamburger-vegetable SOUP

Looking for a new way to serve always easy, always satisfying ground beef? Try this family favorite—it's quick, abundant with colorful vegetables, and low-fat to boot.

Start to Finish: 35 minutes
Makes: 6 servings

1 pound lean ground beef or pork
½ cup chopped onion
½ cup chopped green sweet pepper
4 cups beef broth
1 cup frozen whole kernel corn
1 7½-ounce can tomatoes, undrained and cut up
½ of a 10-ounce package frozen lima beans
½ cup chopped peeled potato or frozen loose-pack hash brown potatoes
1 medium carrot, cut into thin bite-size strips
1 tablespoon snipped fresh basil or 1 teaspoon dried basil, crushed
1 teaspoon Worcestershire sauce
1 bay leaf
⅛ teaspoon black pepper

1 In a large saucepan cook ground beef, onion, and sweet pepper until meat is brown and onion is tender. Drain off fat. Stir in beef broth, corn, undrained tomatoes, lima beans, potato, carrot, basil, Worcestershire sauce, bay leaf, and black pepper.

2 Bring mixture to boiling; reduce heat. Cover and simmer for 15 to 20 minutes or until vegetables are tender. Discard bay leaf.

Nutrition Facts per serving: 215 cal., 8 g total fat (3 g sat. fat), 48 mg chol., 652 mg sodium, 18 g carbo., 3 g fiber, 18 g pro.
Daily Values: 64% vit. A, 38% vit. C, 3% calcium, 15% iron

lunches

italian MEATBALL SOUP

Go Italian with this family-pleasing soup, as easy to make as it is hearty. Another day, partner the second half of the bag of frozen meatballs with prepared pasta sauce for a classic spaghetti-and-meatballs dinner.

Start to Finish: 25 minutes
Makes: 4 servings

- 1   14½-ounce can diced tomatoes with onion and garlic, undrained
- 1   14-ounce can reduced-sodium beef broth
- 1½ cups water
- ½   teaspoon dried Italian seasoning, crushed
- ½   of a 16-ounce package frozen Italian-style cooked meatballs
- ½   cup small dried pasta (such as ditalini or orzo)
- 1   cup frozen loose-pack mixed vegetables
- 1   tablespoon shredded or grated Parmesan cheese (optional)

Exchanges: 1 Vegetable, 1 Starch, 2 Medium-Fat Meat, ½ Fat

1 In a large saucepan stir together undrained tomatoes, beef broth, water, and Italian seasoning. Bring to boiling. Add meatballs, pasta, and frozen vegetables. Return to boiling; reduce heat. Cover and simmer about 10 minutes or until pasta and vegetables are tender. If desired, sprinkle individual servings with cheese.

Nutrition Facts per serving: 275 cal., 13 g total fat (6 g sat. fat), 37 mg chol., 1,113 mg sodium, 25 g carbo., 4 g fiber, 15 g pro.
Daily Values: 37% vit. A, 19% vit. C, 6% calcium, 18% iron

lunches

mexican-style TURKEY SOUP

This spicy soup provides health-protective phytochemicals in every bite. For maximum benefits choose the most vividly colored fruits and veggies.

Start to Finish: 40 minutes
Makes: 5 or 6 servings

- 1 **cup chopped onion**
- 1 **large red sweet pepper, chopped**
- 1 **tablespoon cooking oil**
- 1 **teaspoon ground cumin**
- 1 **teaspoon chili powder**
- ½ **teaspoon paprika**
- 5 **cups reduced-sodium chicken broth**
- 1½ **cups peeled, cubed winter squash**
- 1 **large tomato, chopped**
- ¼ **teaspoon salt**
- ¼ **teaspoon black pepper**
- 2 **cups chopped cooked turkey or chicken**
- 1 **cup frozen whole kernel corn**
- 2 **tablespoons snipped fresh cilantro**

Exchanges: ½ Vegetable, 1 Starch, 2 Very Lean Meat, ½ Fat

1 In a Dutch oven cook onion and sweet pepper in hot oil over medium heat about 5 minutes or until tender, stirring occasionally. Stir in cumin, chili powder, and paprika; cook and stir for 30 seconds.

2 Add broth, squash, tomato, salt, and black pepper. Bring to boiling; reduce heat. Simmer, covered, about 20 minutes or until squash is tender, stirring occasionally. Stir in turkey, corn, and cilantro; heat through.

Nutrition Facts per serving: 205 cal., 6 g total fat (1 g sat. fat), 43 mg chol., 790 mg sodium, 17 g carbo., 3 g fiber, 22 g pro.
Daily Values: 73% vit. A, 102% vit. C, 4% calcium, 10% iron

Phytochemicals

Fruits and vegetables contain vitamins, minerals, and fiber. They also contain unique substances called phytochemicals. These compounds, of which more than 4,000 have been identified, can help promote good health and ward off diseases. They have been shown to play roles in preventing some cancers and maintaining eye health. Phytochemicals are also often responsible for the colors of fruits and vegetables, such as the red in tomatoes, the blue in blueberries, and the green in broccoli. To maximize your phytochemical intake, be sure to choose a variety of colors in the produce department.

curried CHICKEN SOUP

You can use leftover cooked chicken in this quick soup or buy a roasted chicken from your supermarket's deli.

Start to Finish: 20 minutes
Makes: 5 servings

5 cups water

1 3-ounce package chicken-flavor ramen noodles

2 to 3 teaspoons curry powder

1 cup sliced fresh mushrooms

2 cups cubed cooked chicken

1 medium apple, cored and coarsely chopped

½ cup canned sliced water chestnuts

Exchanges: ½ Starch, ½ Other Carbo., 2½ Lean Meat

❶ In a large saucepan combine the water, the flavoring packet from noodles, and curry powder. Bring to boiling.

❷ Break up noodles. Add the noodles and mushrooms to mixture in saucepan; reduce heat. Simmer, uncovered, for 3 minutes. Stir in chicken, apple, and water chestnuts; heat through.

Nutrition Facts per serving: 221 cal., 8 g total fat (1 g sat. fat), 54 mg chol., 362 mg sodium, 17 g carbo., 1 g fiber, 20 g pro.
Daily Values: 1% vit. A, 4% vit. C, 2% calcium, 10% iron

lunches

chicken MINESTRONE SOUP

The Italian word minestrone *means "big soup," and countless variations of the bean-and-vegetable soup are big in American kitchens. This version calls for broth as well as chicken breasts for extra flavor.*

Start to Finish: 45 minutes
Makes: 8 servings

1 **cup sliced carrot**

½ **cup chopped celery**

½ **cup chopped onion**

1 **tablespoon olive oil**

3 **14-ounce cans chicken broth**

2 **15- to 19-ounce cans white kidney beans (cannellini beans), rinsed and drained**

8 **to 10 ounces skinless, boneless chicken breasts, cut into bite-size pieces**

1 **cup fresh green beans, cut into ½-inch pieces (4 ounces)**

¼ **teaspoon black pepper**

1 **cup dried bow tie pasta**

1 **medium zucchini, quartered lengthwise and cut into ½-inch slices**

1 **14½-ounce can diced tomatoes with basil, garlic, and oregano, undrained**

Crackers (optional)

Exchanges: 1 Vegetable, 1½ Starch, 1 Very Lean Meat

❶ In a 5- to 6-quart Dutch oven cook carrots, celery, and onion in hot oil over medium heat for 5 minutes, stirring frequently. Add broth, white kidney beans, chicken, green beans, and pepper. Bring to boiling; add pasta. Reduce heat and simmer, uncovered, for 5 minutes.

❷ Stir in zucchini. Return to boiling; reduce heat. Simmer, uncovered, for 8 to 10 minutes more or until pasta is tender and green beans are crisp-tender. Stir in undrained tomatoes; heat through. If desired, serve with crackers.

Nutrition Facts per serving: 181 cal., 4 g total fat (1 g sat. fat), 16 mg chol., 1,079 mg sodium, 27 g carbo., 7 g fiber, 16 g pro.
Daily Values: 86% vit. A, 15% vit. C, 8% calcium, 14% iron

lunches

clam-corn CHOWDER

For a healthy lunch at work, make this chowder the night before, then cover and refrigerate it. In the morning heat the soup on the stove and pour it into a preheated insulated vacuum bottle.

Start to Finish: 30 minutes
Makes: 4 servings

- ½ **cup chopped celery**
- ¼ **cup chopped onion**
- 1 **tablespoon butter or margarine**
- ¼ **cup all-purpose flour**
- 1½ **teaspoons snipped fresh marjoram or ½ teaspoon dried marjoram, crushed**
- 1½ **teaspoons snipped fresh thyme or ½ teaspoon dried thyme, crushed**
- ½ **teaspoon dry mustard**
- ¼ **teaspoon black pepper**
- 2⅔ **cups fat-free milk**
- 1 **8-ounce bottle clam juice**
- 1 **teaspoon instant chicken bouillon granules**
- 1 **15-ounce can cream-style corn**
- 1 **6½-ounce can minced clams, drained**

  Fresh marjoram or thyme (optional)

1 In a large saucepan cook celery and onion in hot butter until tender. Stir in flour, marjoram, thyme, mustard, and pepper. Add milk, clam juice, and bouillon granules all at once.

2 Cook and stir until thickened and bubbly. Cook and stir for 1 minute more. Stir in corn and clams; heat through. If desired, garnish with additional fresh herbs.

Nutrition Facts per serving: 272 cal., 5 g total fat (1 g sat. fat), 43 mg chol., 870 mg sodium, 36 g carbo., 2 g fiber, 20 g pro.
Daily Values: 18% vit. A, 27% vit. C, 26% calcium, 75% iron

Shellfish for Your Heart

Fish has long been considered a healthy source of protein in the diet. However, shellfish is sometimes given a bad rap because of its high cholesterol content. In actuality, there's no need to avoid shellfish. Foods like lobster, shrimp, scallops, clams, and mussels contain virtually no fat and even less saturated fat, both of which play a greater role in increasing blood cholesterol and one's risk of heart disease than dietary cholesterol alone.

lunches

gazpacho TO GO

Keep this easy-to-tote cold soup in mind for summertime picnics or potlucks. Show off gazpacho's mosaic of bright colors by carrying it in a clear plastic storage container.

Prep: 30 minutes
Chill: 2 hours
Makes: 6 servings

- 1 **15-ounce can chunky Italian- or salsa-style tomatoes, undrained**
- 2 **cups quartered yellow pear-shape and/or halved cherry tomatoes**
- 1 **15-ounce can garbanzo beans (chickpeas), rinsed and drained**
- 1¼ **cups vegetable juice**
- 1 **cup beef broth**
- ½ **cup coarsely chopped seeded cucumber**
- ½ **cup coarsely chopped yellow and/or red sweet pepper**
- ¼ **cup coarsely chopped red onion**
- ¼ **cup snipped fresh cilantro**
- 3 **tablespoons lime juice or lemon juice**
- 2 **cloves garlic, minced**
- ¼ **to ½ teaspoon bottled hot pepper sauce**

Exchanges: 1 Vegetable, ½ Starch, ½ Other Carbo., ½ Very Lean Meat

1 In a large bowl combine undrained canned tomatoes, fresh tomatoes, garbanzo beans, vegetable juice, broth, cucumber, sweet pepper, onion, cilantro, lime juice, garlic, and hot pepper sauce. Cover and chill for 2 to 24 hours.

2 To serve, ladle soup into bowls or mugs.

Nutrition Facts per serving: 136 cal., 3 g total fat (0 g sat. fat), 0 mg chol., 1,145 mg sodium, 23 g carbo., 6 g fiber, 6 g pro.
Daily Values: 21% vit. A, 89% vit. C, 10% calcium, 9% iron

lunches

ginger-lime CHICKEN SALAD

Yogurt serves as a healthy alternative to mayonnaise in this tangy, quick-to-prepare chicken salad.

Prep: 10 minutes
Chill: 30 minutes
Makes: 4 servings

¼ **cup fat-free plain yogurt**

2 **tablespoons lime juice**

2 **teaspoons grated fresh ginger**

2 **cups chopped, cooked chicken breast**

1 **cup snow pea pods, bias-cut lengthwise**

1 **cup thinly sliced celery**

1 **tablespoon thinly sliced red onion**

Exchanges: 1 Vegetable, 3 Very Lean Meat, ½ Fat

1 In a medium bowl combine yogurt, lime juice, and ginger. Add chicken, stirring to coat. Cover and chill at least 30 minutes. In a medium bowl toss together pea pods, celery, and onion. Place the vegetable mixture in 4 salad bowls. Top with the chicken mixture.

Nutrition Facts per serving: 147 cal., 3 g total fat (1 g sat. fat), 60 mg chol., 86 mg sodium, 5 g carbo., 1 g fiber, 23 g pro.
Daily Values: 2% vit. A, 28% vit. C, 6% calcium, 6% iron

lunches

mango salad WITH TURKEY

To save time prepare the Lime Vinaigrette ahead and cover and chill up to 4 hours. Shake the dressing before drizzling over salad. For an extra burst of citrus flavor, serve the salad with lime wedges.

Start to Finish: 30 minutes
Makes: 4 servings

¼ **cup salad oil**

¼ **teaspoon finely shredded lime peel**

2 **tablespoons lime juice**

¼ **teaspoon grated fresh ginger**

6 **cups torn mixed greens**

4 **mangoes, seeded, peeled, and cut into thin slices**

8 **ounces cooked smoked turkey or chicken, cut into thin bite-size strips**

1 **green onion, thinly sliced**

¼ **cup snipped fresh cilantro**

Lime wedges (optional)

Exchanges: 1½ Vegetable, 2 Fruit, 1½ Very Lean Meat, 2½ Fat

1 In a screw-top jar combine salad oil, lime peel, lime juice, and ginger. Cover and shake well. Divide greens among 4 salad plates. Arrange one-fourth of the mango, smoked turkey, and green onion on each plate of greens. Sprinkle with cilantro. Drizzle vinaigrette over salad. If desired, serve with lime wedges on the side.

Nutrition Facts per serving: 321 cal., 15 g total fat (2 g sat. fat), 25 mg chol., 417 mg sodium, 39 g carbo., 5 g fiber, 12 g pro.
Daily Values: 181% vit. A, 119% vit. C, 7% calcium, 6% iron

lunches

chicken and VEGETABLE SALAD

Remember this salad when it's too hot to cook. All you need are breadsticks, iced tea, and a fresh fruit dessert to complete the meal.

Start to Finish: 25 minutes
Makes: 4 servings

- ½ **cup low-fat cottage cheese or fat-free cottage cheese**
- 1 **tablespoon catsup**
- 1 **hard-cooked egg, chopped (optional)**
- 1 **green onion, thinly sliced**
- 1 **tablespoon sweet pickle relish**
- ⅛ **teaspoon salt**
- 1½ **cups chopped cooked chicken (about 8 ounces)**
- ½ **cup sliced celery**
- ½ **cup chopped red or green sweet pepper**
- **Lettuce leaves**
- 2 **tablespoons sliced almonds, toasted**

Exchanges: ½ Other Carbo., 2½ Lean Meat

1 For dressing, in a food processor bowl combine cottage cheese and catsup. Cover and process until smooth; transfer to a small bowl. Stir in egg (if desired), green onion, pickle relish, and salt. Set aside.

2 In a medium bowl combine chicken, celery, and sweet pepper. Add dressing and gently toss to mix.

3 To serve, divide salad among 4 lettuce-lined dinner plates. Sprinkle with almonds.

Nutrition Facts per serving: 164 cal., 6 g total fat (1 g sat. fat), 49 mg chol., 322 mg sodium, 6 g carbo., 1 g fiber, 20 g pro.
Daily Values: 25% vit. A, 64% vit. C, 5% calcium, 7% iron

lunches

turkey and FRUIT PASTA SALAD

For a slightly smoky flavor, use the turkey ham option. For additional variety and color, use fresh blueberries or raspberries in place of the strawberries.

Prep: 25 minutes
Chill: 4 hours
Makes: 4 servings

- **1 cup dried gemelli pasta or 1⅓ cups dried rotini pasta**
- **1½ cups chopped cooked turkey, chicken, or turkey ham (about 8 ounces)**
- **2 green onions, sliced**
- **⅓ cup lime juice or lemon juice**
- **¼ cup salad oil**
- **1 tablespoon honey**
- **2 teaspoons snipped fresh thyme or ½ teaspoon dried thyme, crushed**
- **2 medium nectarines or large plums, sliced**
- **1 cup halved strawberries**

Exchanges: 1 Fruit, 1½ Starch, 2 Lean Meat, 2 Fat

① Cook pasta according to package directions; drain. Rinse with cold water; drain again.

② In a large bowl combine cooked pasta, turkey, and green onions; toss gently to combine.

③ For dressing, in a screw-top jar combine lime juice, oil, honey, and thyme. Cover and shake well. Pour dressing over pasta mixture; toss gently to coat. Cover and chill for 4 to 24 hours.

④ Just before serving, add the nectarines and strawberries; toss gently to combine.

Nutrition Facts per serving: 382 cal., 17 g total fat (3 g sat. fat), 40 mg chol., 40 mg sodium, 37 g carbo., 3 g fiber, 20 g pro.
Daily Values: 11% vit. A, 54% vit. C, 4% calcium, 12% iron

lunches

ham and CANTALOUPE SALAD

To tote this lush salad for lunch either at your desk or in the park, pack the sliced melon, dressing, and greens mixture in separate containers.

Prep: 25 minutes
Chill: 1 hour
Makes: 4 servings

- **1 small cantaloupe, halved and seeded**
- **4 cups torn romaine lettuce**
- **1 cup torn spinach**
- **8 ounces lean cooked ham, cut into bite-size strips (1½ cups)**
- **2 green onions, thinly sliced**
- **¼ cup unsweetened pineapple juice**
- **1 tablespoon white wine vinegar**
- **1 tablespoon salad oil**
- **1½ teaspoons snipped fresh mint or ½ teaspoon dried mint, crushed**
- **¼ cup sliced almonds, toasted**

Exchanges: 1 Vegetable, 1 Fruit, 2 Lean Meat, 1 Fat

1. Coarsely chop half of the melon; slice remaining melon. In a large bowl combine the chopped melon, lettuce, spinach, ham, and green onions.

2. In a screw-top jar combine pineapple juice, white wine vinegar, salad oil, and mint. Cover and shake well.

3. Arrange melon slices on 4 plates. Pour dressing over greens mixture; toss lightly to coat. Divide salad among plates; sprinkle with almonds.

Nutrition Facts per serving: 230 cal., 11 g total fat (2 g sat. fat), 27 mg chol., 839 mg sodium, 20 g carbo., 4 g fiber, 15 g pro.
Daily Values: 141% vit. A, 144% vit. C, 8% calcium, 14% iron

Nutrition by Color

Cantaloupe is grouped nutritionally with other orange fruits and vegetables like apricots, papayas, butternut squash, and carrots. These orange foods are important to add to your diet for the high amounts of antioxidants they contain, including vitamin C, carotenoids, and bioflavonoids. These nutrients are shown to reduce the risk of heart disease and some cancers. They also help keep the eyes and immune system healthy.

lunches

spinach PASTA SALAD

The basil, prosciutto, and pine nuts—classic Italian favorites—keep this cool pasta salad packed with interesting flavors.

Prep: 25 minutes
Chill: 4 hours
Makes: 6 servings

- **8 ounces dried ziti or other medium pasta**
- **1 cup lightly packed spinach leaves**
- **¼ cup lightly packed basil leaves**
- **2 cloves garlic, quartered**
- **2 tablespoons finely shredded Parmesan cheese**
- **⅛ teaspoon salt**
- **⅛ teaspoon black pepper**
- **1 tablespoon olive oil**
- **1 tablespoon water**
- **½ cup fat-free or light mayonnaise dressing or salad dressing**
- **6 spinach leaves**
- **6 radicchio leaves (optional)**
- **1 ounce chopped prosciutto or ham**
- **2 tablespoons toasted pine nuts**

Exchanges: 2 Starch, ½ Medium-Fat Meat, 2½ Fat

1 Cook pasta according to package directions; drain. Rinse with cold water; drain again. Set aside.

2 Meanwhile, in a blender container or food processor bowl combine the 1 cup spinach, the basil, garlic, cheese, salt, and pepper. Add oil and water; cover and blend or process until nearly smooth and mixture forms a paste, scraping down sides of container frequently. Combine mayonnaise dressing and spinach mixture. Add to pasta and toss until well coated. Cover and chill for 4 to 24 hours.

3 To serve, line a salad bowl with spinach leaves and, if desired, radicchio leaves. Spoon salad into lined bowl. Sprinkle with chopped prosciutto and pine nuts.

Nutrition Facts per serving: 304 cal., 15 g total fat (4 g sat. fat), 18 mg chol., 494 mg sodium, 32 g carbo., 2 g fiber, 12 g pro.
Daily Values: 14% vit. A, 5% vit. C, 17% calcium, 13% iron

lunches

salmon CAESAR SALAD

For a salad that's even lower in carbs, omit the croutons. Or make your own from a low-carb bread.

Start to Finish: 15 minutes
Makes: 3 servings

1 10-ounce package light-version Caesar salad kit (includes lettuce, dressing, and croutons)

½ cup cucumber, quartered lengthwise and sliced

¼ cup sweet pepper, cut into thin strips

6 ounces smoked, poached, or canned salmon, skinned, boned, and broken into chunks (1 cup)

½ of a lemon, cut into 3 wedges (optional)

Exchanges: 1½ Vegetable, 2 Lean Meat, 2 Fat

1 In a large bowl combine lettuce and dressing from the packaged salad, cucumber, and pepper strips; toss gently to coat. Add salmon and the croutons from packaged salad; toss gently to mix. Divide among 3 dinner plates. If desired, squeeze juice from a lemon wedge over each salad.

Nutrition Facts per serving: 238 cal., 17 g total fat (3 g sat. fat), 22 mg chol., 805 mg sodium, 9 g carbo., 3 g fiber, 14 g pro.
Daily Values: 38% vit. A, 67% vit. C, 7% calcium, 9% iron

lunches

mexican FIESTA SALAD

When corn on the cob is in season, use ½ cup fresh corn kernels in this spunky salad and save a few of the cornhusks to line the plates.

Start to Finish: 30 minutes
Makes: 4 servings

- 2 **cups dried penne, mostaccioli, or rotini pasta (about 6 ounces)**
- ½ **cup frozen whole kernel corn**
- ½ **cup light dairy sour cream**
- ⅓ **cup bottled chunky salsa**
- 1 **tablespoon snipped fresh cilantro**
- 1 **tablespoon lime juice**
- 1 **15-ounce can black beans, rinsed and drained**
- 3 **medium roma tomatoes, chopped**
- 1 **medium zucchini, chopped (1¼ cups)**
- ½ **cup shredded sharp cheddar cheese (2 ounces)**
- **Fresh cilantro sprigs (optional)**

Exchanges: ½ Vegetable, 3 Starch, 1 Medium-Fat Meat

❶ Cook pasta according to package directions, adding corn for the last 5 minutes of cooking. Drain pasta and corn. Rinse with cold water; drain again.

❷ Meanwhile, for dressing, in a small bowl stir together sour cream, salsa, snipped cilantro, and lime juice. Set dressing aside.

❸ In a large bowl combine the pasta-corn mixture, black beans, tomatoes, and zucchini. Set aside a little of the cheese for topping; add remaining cheese to pasta mixture. Pour dressing over pasta mixture. Toss lightly to coat. (If desired, cover and chill for up to 24 hours. Before serving, if necessary, stir in enough milk to moisten.) Top with reserved cheese. If desired, garnish with cilantro sprigs.

Nutrition Facts per serving: 330 cal., 8 g total fat (5 g sat. fat), 25 mg chol., 470 mg sodium, 50 g carbo., 7 g fiber, 18 g pro.
Daily Values: 23% vit. A, 37% vit. C, 22% calcium, 16% iron

lunches

grilled DINNERS

Fire up the grill for these mouthwatering entrées. Add some fun to your evening meal with sauce-and-pepper-topped Pizza Burgers. Or host a Mexican-themed party featuring Margarita-Glazed Pork Chops.

jamaican pork WITH MELON

You'll find jerk seasoning in the spice aisle of the supermarket or in food specialty shops. You can also sprinkle it on skinless, boneless chicken breast halves before grilling.

Prep: 15 minutes
Grill: 12 minutes
Makes: 4 servings

- 1 **cup chopped honeydew melon**
- 1 **cup chopped cantaloupe**
- 1 **tablespoon snipped fresh mint**
- 1 **tablespoon honey**
- 4 **teaspoons Jamaican jerk seasoning**
- 4 **boneless pork top loin chops, cut ¾ to 1 inch thick**
- **Star anise (optional)**
- **Fresh mint sprigs (optional)**

Exchanges: ½ Fruit, ½ Other Carbo., 4 Very Lean Meat, 1 Fat

① For salsa, in a medium bowl combine honeydew, cantaloupe, snipped mint, and honey. Cover and chill until ready to serve or for up to 8 hours.

② Sprinkle Jamaican jerk seasoning evenly over both sides of each chop; rub in with your fingers. For a charcoal grill, place chops on the rack of an uncovered grill directly over medium coals. Grill for 12 to 15 minutes or until meat juices run clear (160°F), turning once halfway through grilling. (For a gas grill, preheat grill. Reduce heat to medium. Place chops on grill rack over heat. Cover and grill as above.) Serve salsa with chops. If desired, garnish with star anise and/or mint sprigs.

Nutrition Facts per serving: 240 cal., 7 g total fat (2 g sat. fat), 77 mg chol., 366 mg sodium, 12 g carbo., 1 g fiber, 31 g pro.
Daily Values: 26% vit. A, 48% vit. C, 3% calcium, 7% iron

margarita-glazed PORK CHOPS

You can use tequila or fresh lime juice to make the marinade. Either way the taste is reminiscent of Mexico's most beloved cocktail, the margarita.

Prep: 10 minutes
Grill: 12 minutes
Makes: 8 servings

8 **boneless pork top loin chops, cut 1 inch thick (about 3 pounds total)**

⅔ **cup sugar-free orange marmalade**

2 **fresh jalapeño peppers, seeded and finely chopped***

¼ **cup tequila or lime juice**

2 **teaspoons grated fresh ginger or 1 teaspoon ground ginger**

Snipped fresh cilantro

Lime and orange wedges (optional)

Exchanges: ½ Other Carbo., 5 Very Lean Meat, 2 Fat

1 Trim fat from the pork chops. For glaze, in a small bowl stir together orange marmalade, jalapeño peppers, tequila, and ginger.

2 For a charcoal grill, place chops on the rack of an uncovered grill directly over medium coals. Grill for 12 to 15 minutes or until meat juices run clear (160°F), turning once halfway through grilling and brushing frequently with glaze during the last 5 minutes of grilling. (For a gas grill, preheat grill. Reduce heat to medium. Place chops on grill rack over heat. Cover and grill as above.)

3 To serve, sprinkle with cilantro. If desired, garnish with lime and orange wedges.

***Note:** Because chile peppers, such as jalapeños, contain volatile oils that can burn your skin and eyes, avoid direct contact with them as much as possible. When working with chile peppers, wear plastic or rubber gloves. If your bare hands do touch the chile peppers, wash your hands and nails well with soap and warm water.

Nutrition Facts per serving: 281 cal., 9 g total fat (3 g sat. fat), 93 mg chol., 62 mg sodium, 7 g carbo., 0 g fiber, 38 g pro.
Daily Values: 1% vit. A, 4% vit. C, 3% calcium, 7% iron

grilled dinners

pork WITH PEACHY SALSA

Sliding the pork tenderloin slices onto skewers makes them easier to turn.

Prep: 30 minutes
Grill: 20 minutes
Makes: 6 servings

- ½ cup chopped, peeled peaches or unpeeled nectarines
- ½ cup chopped, seeded cucumber
- ⅓ cup salsa
- 1 tablespoon snipped fresh cilantro or parsley
- 12 slices bacon
- 1½ pounds pork tenderloin (2 tenderloins)

Exchanges: 3 Very Lean Meat, 1 High-Fat Meat, ½ Fat

1. For salsa, in a medium bowl combine peaches, cucumber, salsa, and cilantro. Toss gently. Cover and chill for up to 2 days or until serving time.

2. In a large skillet over medium heat partially cook bacon. Bias-cut pork tenderloin into 1½-inch slices. Wrap a slice of bacon around each piece of pork. If desired, fasten bacon to meat with wooden toothpicks. Thread wrapped meat onto skewers.

3. For a charcoal grill, in a grill with a cover arrange medium-hot coals around a drip pan. Test for medium heat above pan. Place kabobs on grill rack directly over drip pan. Cover and grill for 20 to 22 minutes or until meat juices run clear (160°F), turning once. (For a gas grill, preheat grill. Reduce heat to medium. Place kabobs on grill rack over heat. Cover and grill as above.)

4. Remove meat from skewers. Serve with salsa.

Nutrition Facts per serving: 235 cal., 11 g total fat (4 g sat. fat), 87 mg chol., 338 mg sodium, 2 g carbo., 0 g fiber, 29 g pro.
Daily Values: 4% vit. A, 6% vit. C, 1% calcium, 8% iron

grilled dinners

corn country PORK CHOPS

A little sweet, a little salty, a little garlicky, and altogether perfect for pork chops—this marinade is all of the above.

Prep: 10 minutes
Marinate: 4 hours
Grill: 8 minutes
Makes: 6 servings

6 **boneless pork loin chops, cut ¾ inch thick (about 2¼ pounds total)**

½ **cup chopped onion**

¼ **cup soy sauce**

2 **tablespoons olive oil or cooking oil**

2 **tablespoons catsup**

2 **cloves garlic, minced**

Exchanges: 5½ Very Lean Meat, 1½ Fat

1 Trim fat from meat. Place pork chops in a self-sealing plastic bag set in a deep bowl. For marinade, in a bowl combine onion, soy sauce, oil, catsup, and garlic. Pour marinade over chops; seal bag. Marinate chops in the refrigerator for 4 to 6 hours, turning bag occasionally.

2 Drain chops, discarding marinade. Sprinkle chops with pepper. For a charcoal grill, place chops on the rack of an uncovered grill directly over medium coals. Grill for 8 to 11 minutes or until meat juices run clear (160°F), turning once halfway through grilling. (For a gas grill, preheat grill. Reduce heat to medium. Place chops on grill rack over heat. Cover and grill as above.)

Nutrition Facts per serving: 275 cal., 11 g total fat (4 g sat. fat), 92 mg chol., 406 mg sodium, 1 g carbo., 0 g fiber, 38 g pro.
Daily Values: 1% vit. A, 2% vit. C, 3% calcium, 6% iron

Great Grilling

Grilling is an easy way to make a tasty meal without heating up the kitchen. To ensure even cooking, always grill at medium to medium-low temperatures. Cooking at temperatures that are too high causes the food's outside to burn before the inside is cooked. Be sure to trim excess fat from meats to keep it from dripping into the grill and causing flare-ups. Always use long-handled tongs instead of a fork to turn meat. Doing so keeps your hands away from the heat and prevents the loss of flavorful juices that occurs when meat is pierced with a fork.

grilled dinners

southwest top ROUND STEAK

Marinating the beef all day or overnight in a spicy lime juice–salsa mixture ensures that it will be fork-tender.

Prep: 10 minutes
Marinate: 8 hours
Grill: 16 minutes
Makes: 4 to 6 servings

¼ **cup lime juice**

¼ **cup steak sauce**

¼ **cup salsa**

1 **tablespoon cooking oil**

1 **clove garlic, minced**

½ **teaspoon coarsely ground black pepper**

1 **pound beef top round steak, cut 1 inch thick**

Warm flour tortillas (optional)

Salsa (optional)

Exchanges: 4 Very Lean Meat, ½ Fat

1 For marinade, in a small saucepan combine lime juice, steak sauce, the ¼ cup salsa, oil, garlic, and pepper. Bring to boiling; reduce heat. Simmer, uncovered, for 5 minutes, stirring occasionally. Cool.

2 Place steak in a self-sealing plastic bag set in a shallow dish. Add marinade, turning meat. Close bag securely and marinate in refrigerator 8 hours or overnight, turning occasionally.

3 Remove steak from marinade, discarding marinade. For a charcoal grill, place steak on the rack of an uncovered grill directly over medium coals. Grill for 16 to 18 minutes for medium rare (145°F), turning once. (For a gas grill, preheat grill. Reduce heat to medium. Place steak on grill rack over heat. Cover and grill as above.)

4 Thinly slice meat across the grain. If desired, serve on warm tortillas topped with additional salsa.

Nutrition Facts per serving: 166 cal., 5 g total fat (3 g sat. fat), 64 mg chol., 184 mg sodium, 2 g carbo., 0 g fiber, 26 g pro.
Daily Values: 2% vit. A, 7% vit. C, 1% calcium, 13% iron

grilled dinners

steak RÉMOULADE SANDWICHES

Served in France as an accompaniment to cold meats, fish, and seafood, the classic mayonnaise-based sauce called a rémoulade brings something new to the steak sandwich.

Prep: 15 minutes
Grill: 11 minutes
Makes: 4 servings

¼ cup light mayonnaise
   dressing or salad dressing

1½ teaspoons finely minced
   cornichons or gherkins

1 teaspoon drained capers,
   chopped

¼ teaspoon lemon juice
   Black pepper

2 8-ounce boneless beef top
   loin steaks, cut 1 inch thick

2 teaspoons prepared garlic
   spread or 2 teaspoons
   bottled minced garlic
   (4 cloves)

1 large yellow sweet pepper,
   cut lengthwise into 8 strips

4 kaiser or French-style rolls,
   split and toasted

1 cup arugula or fresh
   spinach leaves

Exchanges: ½ Vegetable, 2½ Starch, 3 Lean Meat, 1 Fat

1 For rémoulade, in a small bowl combine mayonnaise dressing, cornichons, capers, lemon juice, and several dashes black pepper. Cover and refrigerate until ready to serve.

2 Pat steaks dry with a paper towel. Using your fingers, rub garlic spread over steaks. Sprinkle with additional black pepper.

3 For a charcoal grill, place steaks and sweet pepper strips on the rack of an uncovered grill directly over medium coals. Grill until meat is done as desired and sweet pepper strips are crisp-tender, turning once halfway through grilling. Allow 11 to 15 minutes for medium rare (145°F) or 14 to 18 minutes for medium (160°F). (For a gas grill, preheat grill. Reduce heat to medium. Place steaks and sweet pepper strips on grill rack over heat. Cover and grill as above.) Transfer cooked steaks and sweet pepper strips to a cutting board; cut steaks into ¼-inch slices.

4 If desired, grill rolls directly over medium heat about 1 minute or until toasted. Spread rémoulade on cut sides of toasted rolls. Fill rolls with arugula, steak slices, and sweet pepper strips. Add roll tops.

Nutrition Facts per serving: 416 cal., 15 g total fat (4 g sat. fat), 62 mg chol., 517 mg sodium, 37 g carbo., 2 g fiber, 32 g pro.
Daily Values: 6% vit. A, 162% vit. C, 8% calcium, 23% iron

grilled dinners

flank steak WITH CHILI SAUCE

A hint of honey sweetens the spicy tomato sauce. Reduce the chili powder if you don't want so much heat.

Prep: 20 minutes
Grill: 17 minutes
Makes: 6 servings

- ½ **cup water**
- 1 **cup chopped onion**
- 4 **cloves garlic, minced**
- 2 **teaspoons chili powder**
- 1 **8-ounce can low-sodium tomato sauce**
- ⅓ **cup vinegar**
- 2 **tablespoons honey**
- ½ **teaspoon salt**
- ¼ **teaspoon black pepper**
- 1¼ **pounds beef flank steak**

Exchanges: ½ Vegetable, ½ Other Carbo., 3 Very Lean Meat, 1 Fat

1 For sauce, in a medium saucepan bring water to boiling. Add onion, garlic, and chili powder. Reduce heat. Simmer, covered, for 5 minutes or until tender. Stir in tomato sauce, vinegar, honey, salt, and pepper. Return to boiling, stirring constantly. Boil for 5 minutes or until slightly thickened.

2 Meanwhile, trim fat from meat. Score both sides of steak in a diamond pattern by making shallow diagonal cuts at 1-inch intervals. Brush lightly with some of the sauce. For a charcoal grill, place steak on the rack of an uncovered grill directly over medium coals. Grill for 17 to 21 minutes or until medium doneness (160°F), turning once halfway through grilling and brushing with the sauce during the last 5 minutes of grilling. (For a gas grill, preheat grill. Reduce heat to medium. Place steak on grill rack over heat. Cover and grill as above.)

3 In a small saucepan reheat the remaining sauce until bubbly. To serve, thinly slice steak across grain. Pass warmed sauce.

Nutrition Facts per serving: 194 cal., 7 g total fat (3 g sat. fat), 38 mg chol., 262 mg sodium, 12 g carbo., 1 g fiber, 22 g pro.
Daily Values: 10% vit. A, 12% vit. C, 3% calcium, 12% iron

grilled dinners

feta-stuffed BURGERS

Just a little bit of feta cheese adds a rich, tangy flavor to these stuffed burgers. Feta is sometimes referred to as pickled cheese because it is stored in a salty brine similar to pickles.

Prep: 30 minutes
Grill: 12 minutes
Chill: 4 to 24 hours
Makes: 6 servings

¼ cup refrigerated or frozen egg product, thawed
2 tablespoons water
⅓ cup rolled oats
¼ teaspoon black pepper
⅛ teaspoon salt
1 pound lean ground beef
2 teaspoons Dijon-style mustard
⅓ cup crumbled feta cheese
3 English muffins, split and toasted
1 recipe Tomato-Basil Relish
Fresh basil (optional)

Exchanges: 1 Starch, 2½ Lean Meat, ½ Fat

① In a bowl stir together egg product and water. Stir in oats, pepper, and salt. Add beef; mix well. Shape mixture into twelve ¼-inch-thick patties. Spread mustard on one side of 6 patties. Top with crumbled cheese. Place remaining patties on top of cheese, pressing edges to seal.

② For charcoal grill, place patties on the rack of an uncovered grill directly over medium coals. Grill for 12 to 14 minutes or until meat is done (160°F). (For a gas grill, preheat grill. Reduce heat to medium. Place patties on grill rack over heat. Cover and grill as above.)

③ Serve patties on toasted English muffin halves. Top with Tomato-Basil Relish. If desired, garnish with fresh basil.

Tomato-Basil Relish: In a small bowl stir together 2 chopped roma tomatoes; ⅓ cup chopped seeded cucumber; 2 tablespoons thinly sliced green onion; 1 tablespoon red wine vinegar; 1 tablespoon snipped, fresh basil or 1 teaspoon dried basil, crushed; and ⅛ teaspoon black pepper. Cover and chill for at least 4 hours or up to 24 hours.

Nutrition Facts per serving: 239 cal., 10 g total fat (4 g sat. fat), 55 mg chol., 353 mg sodium, 18 g carbo., 2 g fiber, 19 g pro.
Daily Values: 8% vit. A, 10% vit. C, 10% calcium, 15% iron

grilled dinners

pizza BURGERS

Pack all your favorite pizza flavors into a bun: grilled pepper strips, mozzarella cheese, and spaghetti sauce.

Prep: 25 minutes
Grill: 10 minutes
Makes: 8 servings

1 **egg**

1¼ **cups purchased meatless spaghetti sauce**

½ **cup fine dry bread crumbs**

⅓ **cup chopped onion (1 small)**

1 **teaspoon dried basil or oregano, crushed**

2 **cloves garlic, minced**

2 **pounds lean ground beef**

2 **medium green, yellow, and/or red sweet peppers, cut into rings and halved**

1 **tablespoon olive oil or cooking oil**

8 **kaiser rolls, split and toasted**

1 **cup shredded mozzarella cheese (4 ounces)**

Exchanges: ½ Vegetable, 2½ Starch, 3½ Lean Meat, 1 Fat

❶ In a large bowl beat egg and ¼ cup of the spaghetti sauce with a whisk. Stir in bread crumbs, onion, basil, and garlic. Add beef; mix well. Shape meat mixture into eight ½-inch-thick patties.

❷ Tear off an 18×12-inch piece of heavy foil. Place sweet pepper pieces in center of foil; drizzle with oil. Bring up 2 opposite edges of foil and seal with a double fold; fold in remaining edges to enclose the peppers, leaving space for steam to build.

❸ For a charcoal grill, place patties and foil packet on the grill rack directly over medium coals. Grill for 10 to 13 minutes or until meat is done (160°F) and peppers are tender, turning patties and foil packet once halfway through grilling. (For a gas grill, preheat grill. Reduce heat to medium. Place patties and packet on grill rack over heat. Cover and grill as above.)

❹ Meanwhile, heat remaining 1 cup spaghetti sauce. Serve patties on rolls with pepper pieces and cheese. Spoon some of the heated spaghetti sauce over burgers. Pass any remaining spaghetti sauce.

Nutrition Facts per serving: 460 cal., 18 g total fat (6 g sat. fat), 106 mg chol., 742 mg sodium, 42 g carbo., 0 g fiber, 32 g pro.
Daily Values: 6% vit. A, 43% vit. C, 18% calcium, 27% iron

roasted GARLIC STEAK

Roasting the garlic with fresh or dried basil and rosemary boosts the flavor to a great new level.

Prep: 15 minutes
Grill: 30 minutes
Makes: 6 servings

- 1 or 2 whole garlic bulb(s)
- 3 to 4 teaspoons snipped fresh basil or 1 teaspoon dried basil, crushed
- 1 tablespoon snipped fresh rosemary or 1 teaspoon dried rosemary, crushed
- 2 tablespoons olive oil or cooking oil
- 1½ pounds boneless beef ribeye steaks or sirloin steak, cut 1 inch thick
- 1 to 2 teaspoons cracked black pepper
- ½ teaspoon salt

Exchanges: 3 Lean Meat, ½ Fat

1. Using a sharp knife, cut off the top ½ inch from each garlic bulb to expose the ends of the individual cloves. Leaving garlic bulb(s) whole, remove any loose, papery outer layers.

2. Fold a 20×18-inch piece of heavy foil in half crosswise. Trim into a 10-inch square. Place garlic bulb(s) cut side up in center of foil square. Sprinkle garlic with basil and rosemary and drizzle with oil. Bring up 2 opposite edges of foil and seal with a double fold. Fold remaining edges together to enclose garlic, leaving space for steam to build.

3. For a charcoal grill, place garlic packet on the rack of an uncovered grill directly over medium coals. Grill about 30 minutes or until garlic feels soft when packet is squeezed, turning garlic occasionally.

4. Meanwhile, trim fat from steaks. Sprinkle pepper and salt evenly over both sides of steaks; rub in with your fingers. While garlic is grilling, add steaks to grill. Grill until done as desired, turning once halfway through grilling. For ribeye steaks, allow 11 to 15 minutes for medium rare (145°F) and 14 to 18 minutes for medium (160°F). For sirloin steak, allow 14 to 18 minutes for medium rare (145°F) and 18 to 22 minutes for medium (160°F). (For a gas grill, preheat grill. Reduce heat to medium. Place garlic, then steaks on grill rack over heat. Cover and grill as above.)

5. To serve, cut steaks into 6 serving-size pieces. Remove garlic from foil, reserving the oil mixture. Squeeze garlic pulp from each clove onto steaks. Mash pulp slightly with a fork; spread over steaks. Drizzle with the reserved oil mixture.

Nutrition Facts per serving: 189 cal., 9 g total fat (2 g sat. fat), 52 mg chol., 139 mg sodium, 4 g carbo., 0 g fiber, 22 g pro.
Daily Values: 1% vit. A, 6% vit. C, 3% calcium, 14% iron

grilled dinners

fennel-cumin LAMB CHOPS

You can make the spice rub in advance and store it in an airtight jar for up to 1 week. You'll like it with pork chops or a pork roast too.

Prep: 15 minutes
Marinate: 30 minutes
Grill: 10 minutes
Makes: 2 servings

- 1 **large clove garlic, minced**
- ¾ **teaspoon fennel seed, crushed**
- ¾ **teaspoon ground cumin**
- ¼ **teaspoon ground coriander**
- ¼ **teaspoon salt**
- ⅛ **teaspoon black pepper**
- 4 **lamb rib chops, cut about 1 inch thick**

Exchanges: 4 Lean Meat, ½ Fat

1 For rub, combine garlic, fennel, cumin, coriander, salt, and pepper. Sprinkle mixture over both sides of chops; rub in with your fingers. Place chops on a plate; cover with plastic wrap and chill for 30 minutes to 24 hours.

2 For a charcoal grill, place chops on the rack of an uncovered grill directly over medium coals. Grill until done as desired. Allow 10 to 14 minutes for medium rare (145°F) and 14 to 16 minutes for medium (160°F). (For a gas grill, preheat grill. Reduce heat to medium. Place chops on grill rack over heat. Cover and grill as above.)

Nutrition Facts per serving: 208 cal., 11 g total fat (4 g sat. fat), 80 mg chol., 368 mg sodium, 1 g carbo., 0 g fiber, 25 g pro.
Daily Values: 1% vit. C, 4% calcium, 14% iron

What's Fennel?

Fennel, a vegetable that originated in the Mediterranean area, has a big white bulb with green leaves and stalks growing out of it. Its mildly sweet taste is similar to that of anise or licorice. When buying fennel be sure to choose bulbs that are firm and fragrant, and use it within a week for the best flavor and quality. Nutritionally speaking, fennel is a good source of potassium and also contains vitamin C and folic acid.

grilled dinners

plum chicken KABOBS

Lean chicken breasts, fresh pineapple, sugar snap peas, and sweet pepper form the lineup for these meal-in-one kabobs. Serve with a simply seasoned rice pilaf.

Prep: 20 minutes
Grill: 8 minutes
Makes: 4 servings

1 **pound skinless, boneless chicken breast halves, cut into 1-inch pieces**

1½ **teaspoons Jamaican jerk seasoning**

1 **cup sugar snap peas or pea pods, strings and tips removed**

1 **cup pineapple cubes**

1 **medium red sweet pepper, cut into 1-inch pieces**

¼ **cup plum preserves or jam**

Exchanges: ½ Vegetable, ½ Fruit, 1 Other Carbo., 3½ Lean Meat

1 Sprinkle chicken with about half of the jerk seasoning; toss gently to coat. Cut any large snap peas in half crosswise.

2 On 4 long or 8 short skewers, alternately thread chicken, sugar snap peas, pineapple, and sweet pepper, leaving a ¼-inch space between pieces. For sauce, in a small saucepan stir remaining jerk seasoning into plum preserves. Cook and stir just until preserves are melted; set aside.

3 For a charcoal grill, place kabobs on the rack of an uncovered grill directly over medium coals. Grill for 8 to 12 minutes or until chicken is no longer pink and vegetables are tender, turning once and brushing occasionally with sauce during the last 5 minutes of grilling. (For a gas grill, preheat grill. Reduce heat to medium. Place kabobs on grill rack directly over heat. Cover and grill as above.)

Nutrition Facts per serving: 221 cal., 2 g total fat (1 g sat. fat), 66 mg chol., 185 mg sodium, 23 g carbo., 2 g fiber, 27 g pro.
Daily Values: 43% vit. A, 111% vit. C, 4% calcium, 8% iron

grilled dinners

117

rosemary CHICKEN

You may have to fend off the neighbors once they get a whiff of this aromatic grilled chicken. Better yet, invite them to join your family for a backyard picnic.

Prep: 15 minutes
Grill: 35 minutes
Marinate: 6 hours
Makes: 6 servings

- 2 to 2½ **pounds meaty chicken pieces (breasts, thighs, and drumsticks)**
- ½ **cup dry white wine or chicken broth**
- 2 **tablespoons olive oil**
- 4 **cloves garlic, minced**
- 4 **teaspoons snipped fresh rosemary**
- 1 **tablespoon finely shredded lemon peel**
- ¼ **teaspoon salt (optional)**
- ¼ **teaspoon black pepper (optional)**

Exchanges: 3 Lean Meat, 1 Fat

1 If desired, skin chicken. Place chicken in a self-sealing plastic bag set in a shallow dish.

2 For marinade, in a blender container or food processor bowl combine wine, oil, garlic, snipped rosemary, lemon peel, and, if desired, salt and pepper. Cover and blend or process about 15 seconds or until well combined. Pour over chicken. Close bag. Marinate in the refrigerator for 6 hours or overnight, turning bag occasionally.

3 Drain chicken, reserving marinade. For a charcoal grill, place chicken bone side up on the rack of an uncovered grill directly over medium coals. Grill for 35 to 45 minutes or until no longer pink (170°F for breasts, 180°F for thighs and drumsticks), turning and brushing once with marinade halfway through grilling. (For a gas grill, preheat grill. Reduce heat to medium. Place chicken on grill rack; cover and grill as above.) Discard any remaining marinade.

Nutrition Facts per serving: 227 cal., 13 g total fat (3 g sat. fat), 69 mg chol., 62 mg sodium, 1 g carbo., 0 g fiber, 22 g pro.
Daily Values: 3% vit. C, 2% calcium, 6% iron

grilled dinners

chicken WITH ROQUEFORT

French Roquefort cheese lends a touch of old-world elegance to this creamy chicken dish.

Prep: 15 minutes
Grill: 12 minutes
Makes: 4 servings

½ cup fat-free plain yogurt

¼ cup chopped red onion

2 tablespoons crumbled Roquefort or other blue cheese

1 tablespoon snipped fresh chives

⅛ teaspoon white pepper

2 small pears, halved lengthwise, cored, and stemmed

Lemon juice

4 medium skinless, boneless chicken breast halves (1 pound)

Salt

Black pepper

Exchanges: 1 Fruit, 3½ Very Lean Meat, ½ Fat

1 For sauce, in a small bowl combine yogurt, onion, Roquefort cheese, chives, and white pepper. Cover and chill until ready to serve. Brush cut sides of pears with lemon juice. Set aside.

2 Sprinkle chicken with salt and pepper. For a charcoal grill, place chicken on the rack of an uncovered grill directly over medium coals. Grill for 5 minutes. Turn chicken. Place pears on grill, cut side down. Grill chicken and pears for 7 to 10 minutes or until chicken is no longer pink (170°F). (For a gas grill, preheat grill. Reduce heat to medium. Place chicken, then pears on grill rack over heat. Cover and grill as above.) Serve chicken and pears with sauce.

Nutrition Facts per serving: 199 cal., 5 g total fat (2 g sat. fat), 63 mg chol., 168 mg sodium, 14 g carbo., 2 g fiber, 25 g pro.
Daily Values: 2% vit. A, 9% vit. C, 8% calcium, 6% iron

grilled dinners

119

apple and chicken SALAD

The same sweet-savory mixture of apple jelly and horseradish mustard that's brushed on the grilled chicken serves as the dressing for the mixed greens, apples, and walnuts.

Prep: 20 minutes
Grill: 12 minutes
Makes: 4 servings

⅓ **cup apple jelly**

3 **tablespoons horseradish mustard**

4 **skinless, boneless chicken breast halves (1 pound)**

4 **cups mesclun or torn mixed salad greens**

2 **tart medium apples, cored and sliced**

⅓ **cup coarsely chopped walnuts, toasted**

1 **tablespoon cider vinegar**

1 **tablespoon salad oil**

Exchanges: 1 Vegetable, ½ Fruit, 1½ Other Carbo., 4 Very Lean Meat, 2 Fat

❶ In a small saucepan melt apple jelly over low heat. Remove from heat; stir in mustard. Set aside 2 tablespoons of the jelly mixture to brush on chicken. Reserve remaining jelly mixture for dressing.

❷ For a charcoal grill, place chicken on the rack of an uncovered grill directly over medium coals. Grill for 12 to 15 minutes or until no longer pink (170°F), turning once. (For a gas grill, preheat grill. Reduce heat to medium. Place chicken on grill rack over heat. Cover and grill as above.) Brush chicken with the 2 tablespoons jelly mixture. Transfer chicken to a cutting board; cool slightly and bias-slice.

❸ Meanwhile, in a large bowl toss together mesclun, apples, and walnuts. For dressing, stir together the reserved jelly mixture, vinegar, and oil. Divide greens mixture among 4 dinner plates. Arrange chicken on the greens; drizzle with some of the reserved jelly mixture.

Nutrition Facts per serving: 352 cal., 13 g total fat (2 g sat. fat), 66 mg chol., 175 mg sodium, 32 g carbo., 4 g fiber, 29 g pro.
Daily Values: 5% vit. A, 13% vit. C, 4% calcium, 8% iron

grilled dinners

easy marinated CHICKEN

LESS THAN 10 GRAMS OF CARBS

Widely used in Chinese cooking, hoisin sauce is thick, dark, and spicy-sweet. Stir it into marinades or pass as a table condiment.

Prep: 10 minutes
Grill: 12 minutes
Marinate: 2 hours
Makes: 8 servings

- 8 skinless, boneless chicken breast halves (2 pounds)
- ½ cup bottled oil and vinegar salad dressing
- 3 tablespoons soy sauce
- 2 tablespoons bottled hoisin sauce
- ½ teaspoon ground ginger

  Bottled hoisin sauce

Exchanges: 5 Very Lean Meat

1 Place chicken breasts in a self-sealing plastic bag set in a deep bowl. For marinade, in a small bowl combine salad dressing, soy sauce, the 2 tablespoons hoisin sauce, and ginger. Pour marinade over chicken; seal bag. Marinate in the refrigerator for 2 to 24 hours, turning bag occasionally. Drain chicken, discarding marinade.

2 For a charcoal grill, place chicken on the rack of an uncovered grill directly over medium coals. Grill for 12 to 15 minutes or until no longer pink (170°F). (For a gas grill, preheat grill. Reduce heat to medium. Place chicken on grill rack over heat. Cover and grill as above.) Pass additional hoisin sauce for dipping.

Nutrition Facts per serving: 189 cal., 5 g total fat (1 g sat. fat), 82 mg chol., 286 mg sodium, 1 g carbo., 0 g fiber, 33 g pro.
Daily Values: 1% vit. A, 2% vit. C, 2% calcium, 5% iron

Marinating Dos and Don'ts

Marinating meats adds both flavor and tenderness. For the best results follow these guidelines: Always marinate in the refrigerator to keep the food at the proper temperature. Never save and reuse a marinade. If you plan to baste or make a sauce with the marinade, set some aside before adding the meat. Or, if the marinade has been in contact with the meat, bring it to a rolling boil for 1 to 2 minutes before using as a sauce. To make cleanup easy, marinate in a self-sealing plastic bag instead of a dish.

grilled dinners

turkey with cilantro PESTO

Cilantro pesto is the southwestern answer to Italy's basil pesto. Savor it with chicken, fish, or shrimp.

Prep: 15 minutes
Grill: 12 minutes
Makes: 8 servings

2 **pounds turkey breast tenderloins**

 Salt

 Black pepper

1½ **cups lightly packed fresh cilantro sprigs and/or fresh basil leaves**

⅓ **cup walnuts**

3 **tablespoons olive oil**

2 **tablespoons lime juice**

2 **cloves garlic, minced**

¼ **teaspoon salt**

 Lime wedges or lemon wedges (optional)

Exchanges: 4 Very Lean Meat, 1½ Fat

❶ Split each turkey breast tenderloin in half horizontally. Sprinkle turkey with salt and pepper; set aside.

❷ For cilantro pesto, in a blender container or food processor bowl combine cilantro, walnuts, oil, lime juice, garlic, and the ¼ teaspoon salt. Cover and blend or process until nearly smooth. Divide pesto in half. Chill half of the pesto to serve with turkey.

❸ For a charcoal grill, place turkey on the rack of an uncovered grill directly over medium coals. Grill for 7 minutes; turn. Brush lightly with the unchilled half of the cilantro pesto. Grill for 5 to 8 minutes more or until turkey is no longer pink (170°F). (For a gas grill, preheat grill. Reduce heat to medium. Place turkey on grill rack over heat. Cover and grill as above.) Discard remainder of cilantro pesto used as a brush-on.

❹ Serve turkey with remaining chilled pesto. If desired, serve with lime wedges to squeeze over turkey.

Nutrition Facts per serving: 209 cal., 9 g total fat (1 g sat. fat), 70 mg chol., 195 mg sodium, 2 g carbo., 1 g fiber, 29 g pro.
Daily Values: 18% vit. A, 11% vit. C, 3% calcium, 9% iron

grilled dinners

123

salmon WITH MANGO SALSA

The mango is more than just another pretty fruit. It's a nutrition powerhouse that contains generous amounts of vitamins A, C, and E plus lots of fiber.

Prep: 15 minutes
Grill: 20 minutes
Marinate: 4 hours
Makes: 4 servings

- 4 **6- to 8-ounce fresh or frozen salmon fillets (with skin), 1 inch thick**
- 2 **tablespoons sugar**
- 1½ **teaspoons finely shredded lime peel**
- ¾ **teaspoon salt**
- ¼ **teaspoon cayenne pepper**
- 1 **large ripe mango, peeled, seeded, and cut into thin bite-size strips**
- ½ **of a medium cucumber, seeded and cut into thin bite-size strips**
- 2 **green onions, sliced**
- 3 **tablespoons lime juice**
- 1 **tablespoon snipped fresh cilantro or 2 teaspoons snipped fresh mint**
- 1 **small jalapeño pepper, seeded and chopped***
- 1 **clove garlic, minced**

1 Thaw fish, if frozen. Rinse fish; pat dry. Place fish skin side down in a shallow dish.

2 For rub, in a small bowl stir together sugar, lime peel, ½ teaspoon of the salt, and the cayenne pepper. Sprinkle rub evenly over fish; rub in with your fingers. Cover and marinate in the refrigerator for 4 to 24 hours.

3 Meanwhile, for salsa, in a medium bowl combine mango, cucumber, green onions, lime juice, cilantro, jalapeño pepper, garlic, and remaining ¼ teaspoon salt. Cover and chill until ready to serve.

4 In a grill with a cover arrange medium-hot coals around a drip pan. Test for medium heat above the pan. Place fish skin side down on the greased grill rack directly over drip pan, tucking under any thin edges. Cover and grill for 20 to 25 minutes or until fish flakes easily when tested with a fork. If desired, remove skin from fish. Serve fish with salsa.

***Note:** Because chile peppers, such as jalapeños, contain volatile oils that can burn your skin and eyes, avoid direct contact with them as much as possible. When working with chile peppers, wear plastic or rubber gloves. If your bare hands do touch the chile peppers, wash your hands and nails well with soap and warm water.

Nutrition Facts per serving: 352 cal., 15 g total fat (3 g sat. fat), 105 mg chol., 520 mg sodium, 18 g carbo., 2 g fiber, 37 g pro.
Daily Values: 50% vit. A, 38% vit. C, 3% calcium, 6% iron

grilled dinners

orange SHRIMP KABOBS

With shrimp, turkey bacon, and a special orange-flavored sauce and sweet pepper combo, this dish is definitely company fare.

Prep: 30 minutes
Grill: 8 minutes
Makes: 4 servings

- 16 fresh or frozen jumbo shrimp in shells (about 1 pound total)
- 8 slices turkey bacon, halved crosswise
- 2 red and/or yellow sweet peppers, cut into 1-inch pieces
- 2 teaspoons finely shredded orange peel
- 2 tablespoons orange juice
- 2 teaspoons snipped fresh rosemary
- 2 cups hot cooked rice
- 1 cup cooked or canned black beans, rinsed and drained

Exchanges: ½ Vegetable, 2½ Starch, 3 Very Lean Meat, ½ Fat

1 Thaw shrimp, if frozen. Peel and devein shrimp, leaving tails intact. Rinse shrimp; pat dry with paper towels.

2 Wrap each shrimp in a half slice of the bacon. On long metal skewers, alternately thread bacon-wrapped shrimp and sweet pepper pieces, leaving a ¼-inch space between pieces. In a small bowl combine 1 teaspoon of the orange peel, the orange juice, and rosemary. Brush over kabobs.

3 For a charcoal grill, place kabobs on the greased rack of an uncovered grill directly over medium coals. Grill for 8 to 10 minutes or until shrimp are opaque and bacon is crisp, turning once halfway through grilling. (For a gas grill, preheat grill. Reduce heat to medium. Place kabobs on greased grill rack over heat. Cover and grill as above.)

4 Meanwhile, in a medium saucepan stir together remaining orange peel, cooked rice, and black beans; heat through. Serve with shrimp and peppers.

Nutrition Facts per serving: 340 cal., 7 g total fat (1 g sat. fat), 149 mg chol., 509 mg sodium, 40 g carbo., 5 g fiber, 28 g pro.
Daily Values: 8% vit. A, 253% vit. C, 8% calcium, 23% iron

grilled dinners

herb-pecan CRUSTED SNAPPER

Butter, chopped pecans, fresh herbs, and a touch of lemon and garlic make a toasty crust for meaty red snapper. This combination is terrific on fresh walleye too.

Prep: 15 minutes
Grill: 4 to 6 minutes per ½-inch thickness
Makes: 4 servings

- 4 **5- or 6-ounce fresh or frozen red snapper fillets with skin, ½ to 1 inch thick**
- ⅓ **cup finely chopped pecans**
- 2 **tablespoons fine dry bread crumbs**
- 2 **tablespoons butter or margarine, softened**
- 1 **teaspoon finely shredded lemon peel**
- 1 **teaspoon bottled minced garlic (2 cloves)**
- 1 **tablespoon snipped fresh flat-leaf parsley**
- ¼ **teaspoon salt**
- ⅛ **teaspoon black pepper**
  Dash cayenne pepper
  Snipped fresh flat-leaf parsley (optional)
  Lemon wedges (optional)

Exchanges: 4½ Very Lean Meat, 2½ Fat

❶ Thaw fish, if frozen; rinse and pat dry with paper towels. Measure thickness of fish. In a small bowl combine pecans, bread crumbs, butter, lemon peel, garlic, the 1 tablespoon parsley, salt, black pepper, and cayenne pepper.

❷ For a charcoal grill, place fish skin side down on the greased rack of an uncovered grill directly over medium coals. Spoon pecan mixture on top of fillets; spread slightly. Grill until fish flakes easily when tested with a fork. Allow 4 to 6 minutes per ½-inch thickness of fish. (For a gas grill, preheat grill. Reduce heat to medium. Place fish on greased grill rack over heat. Spoon pecan mixture on top of fillets; spread slightly. Cover and grill as above.) If desired, sprinkle fish with additional snipped parsley and serve with lemon wedges.

Nutrition Facts per serving: 276 cal., 16 g total fat (5 g sat. fat), 68 mg chol., 395 mg sodium, 4 g carbo., 1 g fiber, 31 g pro.
Daily Values: 9% vit. A, 4% vit. C, 5% calcium, 7% iron

grilled dinners

127

spicy black BEAN PATTIES

These vegetarian burgers infused with cilantro, chipotle pepper, and cumin are a great source of protein with little fat.

Prep: 20 minutes
Grill: 8 minutes
Makes: 4 servings

½ **of a medium avocado, seeded and peeled**

1 **tablespoon lime juice**

Salt

Black pepper

2 **slices whole wheat bread, torn**

3 **tablespoons fresh cilantro leaves**

2 **cloves garlic**

1 **15-ounce can black beans, rinsed and drained**

1 **canned chipotle pepper in adobo sauce**

1 **to 2 teaspoons adobo sauce**

1 **teaspoon ground cumin**

1 **beaten egg**

1 **small roma tomato, chopped**

Exchanges: ½ Vegetable, ½ Starch, ½ Lean Meat

1 For guacamole, in a small bowl mash the avocado. Stir in lime juice; season to taste with salt and black pepper. Cover surface with plastic wrap and chill until ready to serve.

2 Place the torn bread in a food processor bowl. Cover and process or blend until bread resembles coarse crumbs. Transfer to a large bowl; set aside.

3 Place cilantro and garlic in the food processor bowl. Cover and process until finely chopped. Add beans, chipotle pepper, adobo sauce, and cumin. Cover and process until beans are coarsely chopped and mixture begins to pull away from the side of the bowl or container. Add mixture to bread crumbs. Add egg; mix well. Shape into four ½-inch-thick patties.

4 For a charcoal grill, place patties on the lightly greased rack of an uncovered grill directly over medium coals. Grill for 8 to 10 minutes or until patties are heated through, turning once halfway through grilling. (For a gas grill, lightly grease grill rack; preheat grill. Reduce heat to medium. Place patties on grill rack over heat. Cover and grill as above.)

5 To serve, top with guacamole and chopped tomato.

Nutrition Facts per serving: 178 cal., 7 g total fat (1 g sat. fat), 53 mg chol., 487 mg sodium, 25 g carbo., 9 g fiber, 11 g pro.
Daily Values: 9% vit. A, 12% vit. C, 7% calcium, 16% iron

Spicing It Up

Adding extra zip to low-fat cooking makes healthy eating a lot more enjoyable. This is even more true for such meatless dishes as vegetables, pastas, and beans, which tend to have milder flavors than meat, poultry, and fish. Spices are the perfect addition. They come from plants native to tropical areas and are known for their strong flavors and aromas. In addition to traditional combinations, more unique mixtures, such as cinnamon and chili powder or cumin and curry, will get you good results.

veggie-filled BURGERS

To keep these turkey burgers juicy, be careful not to overcook them. Use an instant-read thermometer to check the temperature at the center of the patties.

Prep: 25 minutes
Grill: 12 minutes
Makes: 4 servings

2 tablespoons milk

½ cup finely shredded carrot

¼ cup thinly sliced green onion

¼ cup soft whole wheat bread crumbs

¼ teaspoon dried Italian seasoning, crushed

¼ teaspoon garlic salt

⅛ teaspoon black pepper

¾ pound lean ground turkey or chicken

¼ cup Dijon-style mustard

½ teaspoon curry powder

4 whole wheat hamburger buns, toasted

4 lettuce leaves (optional)

½ cup shredded zucchini (optional)

1 medium sliced tomato (optional)

Exchanges: 1½ Starch, 2 Lean Meat, ½ Fat

1 In a medium bowl stir together milk, carrot, green onion, bread crumbs, Italian seasoning, garlic salt, and pepper. Add ground turkey; mix well. Shape the mixture into four ½-inch-thick patties.

2 For a charcoal grill, place patties on the greased rack of an uncovered grill directly over medium-hot coals. Grill, uncovered, about 12 minutes or until an instant-read thermometer inserted into the side of a patty registers 165°F, turning once. (For a gas grill, grease rack; preheat grill. Reduce heat to medium-hot. Place patties on grill rack; cover and grill patties as directed above.)

3 Meanwhile, stir together mustard and curry powder. Serve patties on buns. If desired, top with lettuce leaves, shredded zucchini, sliced tomato, and mustard mixture.

Nutrition Facts per serving: 257 cal., 9 g total fat (4 g sat. fat), 54 mg chol., 409 mg sodium, 24 g carbo., 3 g fiber, 20 g pro.
Daily Values: 71% vit. A, 4% vit. C, 17% iron

grilled dinners

slow cooker
SUPPERS

It's such a good feeling to come home and have dinner ready when you walk in the door. That's the appeal of the slow cooker. But don't limit yourself to soups and roasts when there are so many fantastic slow cooker recipes, like Easy Beef Burgundy and Hot Pepper Pork Sandwiches.

Spicy Steak and Beans, *recipe page 132*

spicy steak AND BEANS

Queso fresco (KAY-so FRESK-o) means "fresh cheese" in Spanish, and you can find it in large supermarkets and Mexican food stores.

Prep: 25 minutes
Cook: 7 to 9 hours (low) or
3½ to 4½ hours (high);
plus 30 minutes (high)
Makes: 6 servings

1½ pounds beef flank steak

1 10-ounce can chopped tomatoes with green chile peppers, undrained

½ cup chopped onion

2 cloves garlic, minced

1 tablespoon snipped fresh oregano or 1 teaspoon dried oregano, crushed

1 teaspoon chili powder

1 teaspoon ground cumin

¼ teaspoon salt

¼ teaspoon black pepper

2 small green, red, and/or yellow sweet peppers, cut into strips

1 15-ounce can pinto beans, rinsed and drained

Hot cooked brown rice (optional)

Crumbled queso fresco or feta cheese (optional)

Exchanges: 1 Vegetable, 1 Starch, 3½ Very Lean Meat, 1 Fat

1 Trim fat from meat. Place meat in a 3½- or 4-quart slow cooker. In a bowl stir together undrained tomatoes, onion, garlic, dried oregano (if using), chili powder, cumin, salt, and black pepper. Pour over meat.

2 Cover and cook on low-heat setting for 7 to 9 hours or on high-heat setting for 3½ to 4½ hours.

3 If using low-heat setting, turn to high-heat setting. Stir in sweet pepper strips and pinto beans. Cover and cook for 30 minutes more. Remove meat; cool slightly. Shred or thinly slice meat across the grain. Stir fresh oregano (if using) into bean mixture.

4 If desired, spoon rice into soup bowls. Arrange meat on top of rice. Spoon bean mixture over meat. If desired, sprinkle with cheese.

Nutrition Facts per serving: 262 cal., 8 g total fat (3 g sat. fat), 45 mg chol., 452 mg sodium, 17 g carbo., 4 g fiber, 29 g pro.
Daily Values: 9% vit. A, 37% vit. C, 8% calcium, 18% iron

jerk beef ROAST

Jamaican jerk seasoning is the must-have ingredient for this roast. You'll enjoy its spicy-sweet combination of chiles, thyme, cinnamon, ginger, allspice, and cloves.

Prep: 30 minutes
Cook: 8 to 10 hours (low) or
4 to 5 hours (high)
Makes: 6 servings

1 2- to 2½-pound boneless
beef chuck pot roast

¾ cup water

¼ cup raisins

¼ cup steak sauce

3 tablespoons balsamic vinegar

2 tablespoons sugar (optional)

2 tablespoons quick-cooking
tapioca

1 teaspoon cracked black
pepper

1 teaspoon Jamaican jerk
seasoning

2 cloves garlic, minced
Hot cooked brown rice
(optional)

Exchanges: 1 Other Carbo., 5 Very Lean Meat, ½ Fat

1 Trim fat from meat. If necessary, cut roast to fit into a 3½- or 4-quart slow cooker. Place meat in the cooker. In a bowl combine the water, raisins, steak sauce, balsamic vinegar, sugar (if desired), tapioca, pepper, Jamaican jerk seasoning, and garlic. Pour mixture over roast.

2 Cover and cook on low-heat setting for 8 to 10 hours or on high-heat setting for 4 to 5 hours. Skim fat from the cooking liquid. Serve beef with the cooking liquid and, if desired, hot cooked rice.

Nutrition Facts per serving: 237 cal., 6 g total fat (2 g sat. fat), 89 mg chol., 310 mg sodium, 12 g carbo., 1 g fiber, 33 g pro.
Daily Values: 2% vit. A, 4% vit. C, 2% calcium, 23% iron

slow cooker

Picking the Right Roast

Selecting a roast may be more difficult than it seems. At the meat counter you're faced with many types of roasts from rib to chuck arm pot to round tip. In addition to looking for a lean roast, you must consider how you're going to cook it. The leanest roasts are round roasts, a category that includes eye round, top round, bottom round, and tenderloin roast. All of these—except the bottom round—are excellent for roasting or cooking at a high heat. For bottom round, you're better off with moist cooking, such as in a covered pot with liquid.

133

sloppy joes WITH A KICK

There's nothing ho-hum about this familiar favorite! Sassy ingredients give it a lively twist.

Prep: 20 minutes
Cook: 6 to 8 hours (low) or
3 to 4 hours (high)
Makes: 8 servings

1½ pounds lean ground beef

1 cup chopped onion

1 clove garlic, minced

1 6-ounce can vegetable juice

½ cup catsup

½ cup water

2 tablespoons no-calorie, heat-stable granular sugar substitute

2 tablespoons chopped, canned jalapeño peppers (optional)

1 tablespoon prepared mustard

2 teaspoons chili powder

1 teaspoon Worcestershire sauce

8 whole wheat hamburger buns, split and toasted

Shredded reduced-fat cheddar cheese (optional)

Sweet pepper strips (optional)

Exchanges: 2 Starch, 2 Lean Meat, 2 Fat

1 In a large skillet cook ground beef, onion, and garlic until meat is brown and onion is tender. Drain off fat.

2 Meanwhile, in a 3½- or 4-quart slow cooker combine vegetable juice, catsup, water, sugar substitute, jalapeño peppers (if desired), mustard, chili powder, and Worcestershire sauce. Stir in meat mixture.

3 Cover and cook on low-heat setting for 6 to 8 hours or on high-heat setting for 3 to 4 hours. Spoon meat mixture onto bun halves. If desired, sprinkle with cheese and serve with sweet pepper strips.

Nutrition Facts per serving: 310 cal., 13 g total fat (5 g sat. fat), 53 mg chol., 522 mg sodium, 27 g carbo., 3 g fiber, 21 g pro.
Daily Values: 12% vit. A, 13% vit. C, 7% calcium, 21% iron

slow cooker

135

round steak WITH HERBS

Cream of celery soup is the flavor base in this beef recipe. If you like, try other soup varieties such as cream of mushroom or onion.

Prep: 10 minutes
Cook: 10 to 12 hours (low) or
5 to 6 hours (high)
Makes: 6 servings

2 pounds beef round steak, cut ¾ inch thick

1 medium onion, sliced

1 10¾-ounce can condensed cream of celery soup

½ teaspoon dried oregano, crushed

¼ teaspoon dried thyme, crushed

¼ teaspoon black pepper

Hot cooked whole wheat pasta (optional)

Exchanges: 5 Very Lean Meat, 1½ Fat

❶ Trim fat from meat. Cut steak into serving-size portions. Place onion in a 3½- or 4-quart slow cooker; place meat on top of onion. In a small bowl combine soup, oregano, thyme, and pepper; pour over meat.

❷ Cover and cook on low-heat setting for 10 to 12 hours or on high-heat setting for 5 to 6 hours. If desired, serve steak with hot cooked pasta.

Nutrition Facts per serving: 249 cal., 9 g total fat (3 g sat. fat), 78 mg chol., 475 mg sodium, 5 g carbo., 1 g fiber, 34 g pro.
Daily Values: 3% vit. A, 1% vit. C, 3% calcium, 17% iron

easy BEEF BURGUNDY

The canned soups and onion soup mix do most of the work—all you have to do is cut up the meat and mushrooms.

Prep: 20 minutes
Cook: 8 to 10 hours (low) or
4 to 5 hours (high)
Makes: 6 servings

1½ **pounds beef stew meat, trimmed and cut into 1-inch pieces**

2 **tablespoons cooking oil**

1 **10¾-ounce can reduced-fat and reduced-sodium condensed cream of celery soup**

1 **10¾-ounce can reduced-fat and reduced-sodium condensed cream of mushroom soup**

¾ **cup Burgundy**

1 **envelope (½ of a 2-ounce package) onion soup mix**

3 **cups sliced fresh mushrooms (8 ounces)**

Hot cooked whole wheat pasta or brown rice (optional)

Exchanges: ½ Vegetable, ½ Other Carbo., 3½ Lean Meat, ½ Fat

1 In a large skillet brown meat, half at a time, in hot oil. Drain off fat. In a 3½- to 5-quart slow cooker combine celery soup, mushroom soup, Burgundy, and onion soup mix. Stir in meat and mushrooms.

2 Cover and cook on low-heat setting for 8 to 10 hours or on high-heat setting for 4 to 5 hours. If desired, serve over hot cooked pasta.

Nutrition Facts per serving: 301 cal., 13 g total fat (3 g sat. fat), 58 mg chol., 628 mg sodium, 12 g carbo., 0 g fiber, 27 g pro.
Daily Values: 1% calcium, 16% iron

Wine for Flavor

Cooking with wine is a great way to boost flavor without adding fat and with few extra calories. Common knowledge dictates the use of cheap, not necessarily great tasting, wine in cooking, but you might want to rethink this advice. When you cook with wine, the liquid evaporates, leaving a more concentrated flavor. Of course you don't need to break the bank, but you should at least use wine that you like to be sure you'll enjoy the stronger flavor brought out by the cooking.

so-easy PEPPER STEAK

In the mood for Mexican, Cajun, or Italian? Choose the appropriately seasoned tomatoes for robust flavor that usually comes only from a long list of seasonings.

Prep: 15 minutes
Cook: 10 to 12 hours (low) or
5 to 6 hours (high)
Makes: 8 servings

2 pounds boneless beef round steak, cut ¾ to 1 inch thick

Salt and black pepper

1 14½-ounce can Cajun-, Mexican-, or Italian-style stewed tomatoes, undrained

⅓ cup Italian-style tomato paste

½ teaspoon bottled hot pepper sauce

1 16-ounce package frozen sweet pepper stir-fry vegetables (yellow, green, and red peppers and onion)

Hot cooked noodles or hot mashed potatoes

❶ Trim fat from meat. Cut meat into 8 serving-size pieces. Lightly sprinkle with salt and black pepper. Place meat in a 3½- or 4-quart slow cooker. In a medium bowl combine tomatoes, tomato paste, and hot pepper sauce. Pour over meat in cooker. Add frozen vegetables.

❷ Cover and cook on low-heat setting for 10 to 12 hours or on high-heat setting for 5 to 6 hours. Serve over hot cooked noodles.

Nutrition Facts per serving: 303 cal., 6 g total fat (2 g sat. fat), 80 mg chol., 416 mg sodium, 29 g carbo., 2 g fiber, 30 g pro.
Daily Values: 7% vit. A, 47% vit. C, 2% calcium, 22% iron

slow cooker

beef WITH MUSHROOMS

Cook a package of frozen mashed potatoes to serve with this saucy round steak. If you like, stir snipped fresh basil or grated Parmesan cheese into the cooked potatoes.

slow cooker

Prep: 10 minutes
Cook: 8 to 10 hours (low) or
4 to 5 hours (high)
Makes: 4 servings

1 pound boneless beef round steak, cut 1 inch thick

1 medium onion, sliced

1 4-ounce jar whole mushrooms, drained

1 12-ounce jar beef gravy

¼ cup water

Exchanges: 2 Vegetable, 3½ Very Lean Meat, ½ Fat

1 Trim fat from meat. Cut meat into 4 serving-size pieces. Place onion slices in a 3½- or 4-quart slow cooker. Arrange mushrooms over onions; add beef. In a small bowl stir together gravy and water. Pour over beef.

2 Cover and cook on low-heat setting for 8 to 10 hours or on high-heat setting for 4 to 5 hours.

Nutrition Facts per serving: 193 cal., 4 g total fat (2 g sat. fat), 47 mg chol., 744 mg sodium, 9 g carbo., 2 g fiber, 29 g pro.
Daily Values: 3% vit. A, 2% calcium, 16% iron

brisket IN ALE

The flavorful gravy—made from the beer-spiked cooking liquid—is the finishing touch to this tender meat dish.

Prep: 25 minutes
Cook: 10 to 12 hours (low) or
5 to 6 hours (high); plus
10 minutes
Makes: 10 servings

1 **3- to 4-pound fresh beef
brisket**

2 **medium onions, thinly sliced
and separated into rings**

1 **bay leaf**

1 **12-ounce can beer**

¼ **cup chili sauce**

2 **tablespoons no-calorie, heat-
stable granular sugar
substitute**

½ **teaspoon dried thyme,
crushed**

¼ **teaspoon salt**

¼ **teaspoon black pepper**

1 **clove garlic, minced**

2 **tablespoons cornstarch**

2 **tablespoons cold water**

Exchanges: ½ Other Carbo., 2½ Lean Meat

❶ Trim fat from meat. If necessary, cut brisket to fit into a 3½- to 6-quart slow cooker. Place the onions, bay leaf, and brisket in the cooker. In a medium bowl combine beer, chili sauce, sugar substitute, thyme, salt, pepper, and garlic; pour over meat.

❷ Cover and cook on low-heat setting for 10 to 12 hours or on high-heat setting for 5 to 6 hours.

❸ Using a slotted spoon, transfer brisket and onions to a serving platter; cover with foil to keep warm. Discard bay leaf.

❹ For gravy, pour juices into a large measuring cup; skim fat. Measure 2½ cups liquid; discard remaining liquid. In a medium saucepan stir together cornstarch and water; stir in the cooking liquid. Cook and stir until thickened and bubbly; cook and stir for 2 minutes more. Pass gravy with meat.

Nutrition Facts per serving: 170 cal., 6 g total fat (2 g sat. fat), 46 mg chol., 216 mg sodium, 6 g carbo., 1 g fiber, 20 g pro.
Daily Values: 2% vit. A, 4% vit. C, 2% calcium, 12% iron

slow cooker

super-simple BEEF STEW

Super-simple is right. It's hard to believe so few ingredients add up to such a satisfying one-dish winner.

Prep: 15 minutes
Cook: 8 to 9 hours (low) or
4 to 4½ hours (high);
plus 10 minutes (high)
Makes: 4 servings

12 **ounces small red potatoes, quartered (about 2 cups)**

4 **medium carrots, cut into ½-inch pieces**

1 **small red onion, cut into wedges**

1 **pound beef stew meat**

1 **10¾-ounce can condensed cream of mushroom or cream of celery soup**

1 **cup beef broth**

½ **teaspoon dried marjoram or dried thyme, crushed**

1 **9-ounce package frozen cut green beans, thawed**

1 In a 3½- or 4-quart slow cooker place potatoes, carrots, onion, stew meat, soup, beef broth, and marjoram. Stir to combine.

2 Cover and cook on low-heat setting for 8 to 9 hours or on high-heat setting for 4 to 4½ hours.

3 If using low-heat setting, turn to high-heat setting. Stir in thawed green beans. Cover and cook for 10 to 15 minutes more or just until green beans are tender.

Nutrition Facts per serving: 365 cal., 13 g total fat (4 g sat. fat), 54 mg chol., 830 mg sodium, 32 g carbo., 6 g fiber, 31 g pro.
Daily Values: 315% vit. A, 44% vit. C, 9% calcium, 27% iron

slow cooker

143

seeded PORK ROAST

A savory blend of anise, fennel, caraway, dill, and celery seeds creates a crustlike coating for this ultratender pork roast. The cooking liquid contains apple juice, which lends a subtle sweetness.

Prep: 25 minutes
Cook: 9 to 11 hours (low) or
4½ to 5½ hours (high);
plus 10 minutes (high)
Makes: 8 servings

- 1   2½- to 3-pound boneless pork shoulder roast
- 1   tablespoon soy sauce
- 2   teaspoons anise seeds, crushed
- 2   teaspoons fennel seeds, crushed
- 2   teaspoons caraway seeds, crushed
- 2   teaspoons dillseeds, crushed
- 2   teaspoons celery seeds, crushed
- ½   cup beef broth
- ⅔   cup apple juice
- 1   tablespoon cornstarch

Exchanges: 4 Lean Meat

1 Remove netting from roast, if present. If necessary, cut roast to fit into a 3½- to 5-quart slow cooker. Trim fat from meat. Brush soy sauce over surface of roast. On a large piece of foil combine the anise seeds, fennel seeds, caraway seeds, dillseeds, and celery seeds. Roll roast in seeds to coat evenly.

2 Place roast in cooker. Pour broth and ⅓ cup of the apple juice around roast.

3 Cover and cook on low-heat setting for 9 to 11 hours or on high-heat setting for 4½ to 5½ hours.

4 Transfer roast to a serving platter. For gravy, strain cooking juices and skim fat; transfer juices to small saucepan. Combine remaining apple juice and cornstarch; add to juices in saucepan. Cook and stir until thickened and bubbly. Cook and stir 2 minutes more. Pass gravy with roast.

Nutrition Facts per serving: 220 cal., 9 g total fat (3 g sat. fat), 92 mg chol., 285 mg sodium, 5 g carbo., 0 g fiber, 29 g pro.
Daily Values: 3% vit. C, 4% calcium, 14% iron

brunswick STEW

Early Virginia settlers made this hearty stew with squirrel meat. Our updated version simmers all day in your slow cooker and features chicken and ham.

Prep: 20 minutes
Cook: 8 to 10 hours (low) or
4 to 5 hours (high); plus
45 minutes (high)
Makes: 6 servings

- **3 medium onions, cut into thin wedges**
- **2 pounds meaty chicken pieces (breasts, thighs, drumsticks), skinned**
- **1½ cups diced cooked ham (8 ounces)**
- **1 14½-ounce can diced tomatoes, undrained**
- **1 14-ounce can chicken broth**
- **4 cloves garlic, minced**
- **1 tablespoon Worcestershire sauce**
- **1 teaspoon dry mustard**
- **1 teaspoon dried thyme, crushed**
- **¼ teaspoon black pepper**
- **¼ teaspoon bottled hot pepper sauce**
- **1 10-ounce package frozen sliced okra**
- **1 cup frozen baby lima beans**
- **1 cup frozen whole kernel corn**

Exchanges: 1 Vegetable, 1 Starch, 1 Other Carbo., 5 Very Lean Meat, 1½ Fat

1 Place onion in a 3½- to 4-quart slow cooker. Top with chicken and ham. In a small bowl combine undrained tomatoes, broth, garlic, Worcestershire sauce, mustard, thyme, pepper, and hot pepper sauce; pour over chicken and ham.

2 Cover and cook on low-heat setting for 8 to 10 hours or on high-heat setting for 4 to 5 hours.

3 If desired, remove chicken; cool slightly. (Keep lid on the slow cooker.) Remove meat from chicken bones; cut meat into bite-size pieces. Return chicken to cooker; discard bones.

4 Add okra, lima beans, and corn to slow cooker. If using low-heat setting turn to high-heat setting. Cover and cook 45 minutes more or until vegetables are tender.

Nutrition Facts per serving: 417 cal., 11 g total fat (3 g sat. fat), 124 mg chol., 1,252 mg sodium, 36 g carbo., 7 g fiber, 43 g pro.
Daily Values: 17% vit. A, 65% vit. C, 15% calcium, 26% iron

hot pepper pork SANDWICHES

You can adjust the heat level by varying the number of jalapeños you use. Want to turn up the heat even more?
Leave the pepper seeds intact.

Prep: 20 minutes
Cook: 11 to 12 hours (low) or
      5½ to 6 hours (high)
Makes: 8 servings

1 **2½- to 3-pound boneless pork shoulder roast**

2 **teaspoons fajita seasoning**

1 **or 2 fresh jalapeño peppers, seeded, if desired, and finely chopped,* or 1 large green or red sweet pepper, seeded and cut into bite-size strips**

2 **10-ounce cans enchilada sauce**

8 **whole grain hamburger buns or kaiser rolls, split and, if desired, toasted**

Exchanges: 1½ Starch, 2½ Lean Meat

1 Trim fat from meat. If necessary, cut roast to fit into a 3½- or 4-quart slow cooker. Place meat in the cooker. Sprinkle meat with fajita seasoning. Add peppers and enchilada sauce.

2 Cover and cook on low-heat setting for 11 to 12 hours or on high-heat setting for 5½ to 6 hours. Transfer roast to a cutting board. Using 2 forks, shred meat. Stir shredded meat into juices in slow cooker. Using a slotted spoon, spoon shredded meat mixture into toasted buns.

*Note: Because chile peppers, such as jalapeños, contain volatile oils that can burn your skin and eyes, avoid direct contact with them as much as possible. When working with chile peppers, wear plastic or rubber gloves. If your bare hands do touch the chile peppers, wash your hands and nails well with soap and warm water.

Nutrition Facts per serving: 262 cal., 9 g total fat (3 g sat. fat), 58 mg chol., 778 mg sodium, 23 g carbo., 3 g fiber, 22 g pro.
Daily Values: 4% vit. A, 6% vit. C, 7% calcium, 18% iron

slow cooker

thyme and garlic CHICKEN

Thyme, garlic, a little orange juice, and a splash of balsamic vinegar flavor these moist, fork-tender chicken breasts.

slow cooker

Prep: 15 minutes
Cook: 5 to 6 hours (low) or
2½ to 3 hours (high);
plus 10 minutes
Makes: 6 to 8 servings

6 cloves garlic, minced

1½ teaspoons dried thyme, crushed

3 to 4 pounds whole chicken breasts (with bone), halved and skinned

¼ cup orange juice

1 tablespoon balsamic vinegar

Exchanges: 5 Very Lean Meat

❶ Sprinkle garlic and thyme over chicken pieces. Place chicken in a 3½- or 4-quart slow cooker. Pour orange juice and vinegar over chicken.

❷ Cover and cook on low-heat setting for 5 to 6 hours or on high-heat setting for 2½ to 3 hours.

❸ Remove chicken from cooker; cover with foil to keep warm. Skim fat from cooking juices. Strain juices into a saucepan. Bring to boiling; reduce heat. Boil gently, uncovered, about 10 minutes or until reduced to 1 cup. Pass juices with chicken.

Nutrition Facts per serving: 178 cal., 2 g total fat (0 g sat. fat), 85 mg chol., 78 mg sodium, 3 g carbo., 0 g fiber, 34 g pro.
Daily Values: 2% vit. A, 13% vit. C, 3% calcium, 7% iron

mediterranean CHICKEN

If you think you've served chicken in every way imaginable, you'll love this dish. The flavors of artichokes, olives, and thyme lend a Mediterranean accent.

Prep: 20 minutes
Cook: 7 to 8 hours (low) or
3½ to 4 hours (high)
Makes: 6 servings

2 cups sliced fresh mushrooms

1 14½-ounce can diced
tomatoes, undrained

1 8- or 9-ounce package frozen
artichoke hearts

1 cup chicken broth

½ cup chopped onion

½ cup sliced, pitted ripe olives
or ¼ cup capers, drained

¼ cup dry white wine or
chicken broth

3 tablespoons quick-cooking
tapioca

2 to 3 teaspoons curry powder

¾ teaspoon dried thyme,
crushed

¼ teaspoon salt

¼ teaspoon black pepper

1½ pounds skinless, boneless
chicken breast halves and/or
thighs

Hot cooked brown rice
(optional)

Exchanges: 1 Vegetable, ½ Other Carbo., 4 Very Lean Meat, ½ Fat

1 In a 3½- or 4-quart slow cooker place mushrooms, undrained tomatoes, frozen artichoke hearts, broth, onion, olives, and wine. Stir in tapioca, curry powder, thyme, salt, and pepper. Add chicken; spoon some of the tomato mixture over the chicken.

2 Cover and cook on low-heat setting for 7 to 8 hours or on high-heat setting for 3½ to 4 hours. If desired, serve with hot cooked rice.

Nutrition Facts per serving: 227 cal., 4 g total fat (1 g sat. fat), 66 mg chol., 578 mg sodium, 15 g carbo., 4 g fiber, 29 g pro.
Daily Values: 3% vit. A, 22% vit. C, 8% calcium, 13% iron

Oh, Tomato!

Canned tomatoes are a terrific pantry staple. They're available whole, pureed, diced, and seasoned. With few calories, tomatoes boost both the flavor and the nutritional impact of a recipe. They're loaded with the antioxidant lycopene, which may prevent prostate cancer as well as other cancers and heart disease. Canned tomatoes, because they are cooked, have a much higher level of lycopene.

chicken IN WINE SAUCE

Chicken and hearty vegetables are simmered in a delicate wine-flavored sauce. Choose dark meat chicken—thighs or drumsticks—for this dish.

Prep: 20 minutes
Cook: 8 to 9 hours (low) or
4 to 4½ hours (high);
plus 10 minutes
Makes: 6 servings

4 medium red-skin potatoes, quartered

4 medium carrots, cut into ½-inch pieces

2 stalks celery, cut into 1-inch pieces

1 small onion, sliced

3 pounds chicken thighs or drumsticks, skinned

1 tablespoon snipped fresh parsley

½ teaspoon salt

½ teaspoon dried rosemary, crushed

½ teaspoon dried thyme, crushed

¼ teaspoon black pepper

1 clove garlic, minced

1 cup chicken broth

½ cup dry white wine

3 tablespoons butter or margarine

3 tablespoons all-purpose flour

Snipped fresh thyme (optional)

Exchanges: ½ Vegetable, 1½ Starch, 3½ Lean Meat

1 In a 5- or 6-quart slow cooker place potatoes, carrots, celery, and onion. Place chicken pieces on top of vegetables. Sprinkle with parsley, salt, rosemary, dried thyme, pepper, and garlic; add broth and wine.

2 Cover and cook on low-heat setting for 8 to 9 hours or on high-heat setting for 4 to 4½ hours. Using a slotted spoon, transfer chicken and vegetables to a serving platter; cover with foil to keep warm.

3 For gravy, skim fat from cooking juices; strain juices. In a large saucepan melt butter. Stir in flour and cook for 1 minute. Add cooking juices. Cook and stir until thickened and bubbly. Cook and stir 2 minutes more. If desired, sprinkle chicken and vegetables with snipped fresh thyme. Pass gravy with the chicken and vegetables.

Nutrition Facts per serving: 328 cal., 11 g total fat (5 g sat. fat), 124 mg chol., 544 mg sodium, 24 g carbo., 3 g fiber, 29 g pro.
Daily Values: 213% vit. A, 33% vit. C, 5% calcium, 14% iron

ginger-tomato CHICKEN

Chicken drumsticks and thighs are great for the slow cooker. They stay moist and tender during the long cooking time.

Prep: 20 minutes
Cook: 6 to 7 hours (low) or
3 to 3½ hours (high)
Makes: 6 servings

12 chicken drumsticks and/or thighs, skinned (2½ to 3 pounds)

2 14½-ounce cans tomatoes

2 tablespoons quick-cooking tapioca

1 tablespoon grated fresh ginger

1 tablespoon snipped fresh cilantro or parsley

4 cloves garlic, minced

2 teaspoons brown sugar (optional)

½ teaspoon crushed red pepper

½ teaspoon salt

Hot cooked brown rice (optional)

Exchanges: 1 Vegetable, ½ Other Carbo., 3 Very Lean Meat

1 Place chicken pieces in a 3½- or 4-quart slow cooker.

2 Drain 1 can of tomatoes; chop tomatoes from both cans. For sauce, in a medium bowl combine chopped tomatoes and the juice from 1 can, the tapioca, ginger, cilantro, garlic, brown sugar (if using), crushed red pepper, and salt. Pour sauce over chicken.

3 Cover and cook on low-heat setting for 6 to 7 hours or on high-heat setting for 3 to 3½ hours. Skim fat from sauce. Serve chicken with sauce in shallow bowls. If desired, serve with rice.

Nutrition Facts per serving: 168 cal., 4 g total fat (1 g sat. fat), 81 mg chol., 472 mg sodium, 10 g carbo., 1 g fiber, 23 g pro.
Daily Values: 18% vit. A, 40% vit. C, 6% calcium, 10% iron

italian chicken AND PASTA

For a colorful variation, try spinach or red pepper fettuccine.

Prep: 15 minutes
Cook: 5 to 6 hours (low) or
2½ to 3 hours (high)
Makes: 4 servings

12 ounces skinless, boneless
chicken thighs

1 9-ounce package frozen
Italian-style green beans

1 cup fresh mushrooms,
quartered

1 small onion, sliced ¼ inch
thick

1 14½-ounce can Italian-style
stewed tomatoes, undrained

1 6-ounce can Italian-style
tomato paste

1 teaspoon dried Italian
seasoning, crushed

2 cloves garlic, minced

6 ounces fettuccine, cooked
and drained

3 tablespoons finely shredded
Parmesan cheese

Exchanges: 1 Vegetable, 3½ Starch, 2 Lean Meat

1 Cut chicken into 1-inch pieces; set aside. In a 3½- or 4-quart slow cooker place green beans, mushrooms, and onion. Place chicken on vegetables.

2 In a small bowl combine undrained tomatoes, tomato paste, Italian seasoning, and garlic. Pour over chicken.

3 Cover and cook on low-heat setting for 5 to 6 hours or on high-heat setting for 2½ to 3 hours. Serve over hot cooked fettuccine. Sprinkle with Parmesan cheese.

Nutrition Facts per serving: 405 cal., 7 g total fat (2 g sat. fat), 75 mg chol., 728 mg sodium, 55 g carbo., 4 g fiber, 28 g pro.
Daily Values: 7% vit. A, 46% vit. C, 15% calcium, 26% iron

slow cooker

teriyaki and orange CHICKEN

Here's a sauce that's sweet and full of flavor. Use orange sections or slices to garnish the meal.

Prep: 15 minutes
Cook: 4 to 5 hours (low) or
2 to 2½ hours (high)
Makes: 4 servings

1 **16-ounce package frozen loose-pack broccoli, carrots, and water chestnuts**

2 **tablespoons quick-cooking tapioca**

1 **pound skinless, boneless chicken breast halves or thighs, cut into 1-inch pieces**

¾ **cup chicken broth**

3 **tablespoons orange marmalade**

2 **tablespoons bottled teriyaki sauce**

1 **teaspoon dry mustard**

½ **teaspoon ground ginger**

2 **cups hot cooked brown rice**

Exchanges: 1 Vegetable, 2 Starch, 1 Other Carbo., 3 Very Lean Meat

1 In a 3½- or 4-quart slow cooker combine frozen vegetables and tapioca. Add chicken.

2 In a small bowl combine chicken broth, orange marmalade, teriyaki sauce, dry mustard, and ginger. Pour over mixture in cooker.

3 Cover and cook on low-heat setting for 4 to 5 hours or on high-heat setting for 2 to 2½ hours. Serve with hot cooked rice.

Nutrition Facts per serving: 375 cal., 4 g total fat (1 g sat. fat), 79 mg chol., 790 mg sodium, 52 g carbo., 4 g fiber, 30 g pro.
Daily Values: 40% vit. A, 16% vit. C, 3% calcium, 17% iron

slow cooker

155

barbecued TURKEY THIGHS

Who needs a grill for barbecue? These shapely, saucy thighs keep their form nicely during slow heat cooking and can hold their own among other grilled turkey dishes.

Prep: 15 minutes
Cook: 10 to 12 hours (low) or
5 to 6 hours (high)
Makes: 4 to 6 servings

½ cup catsup

2 tablespoons no-calorie, heat-stable granular sugar substitute

1 tablespoon quick-cooking tapioca

1 tablespoon vinegar

1 teaspoon Worcestershire sauce

¼ teaspoon ground cinnamon

¼ teaspoon crushed red pepper

2 to 2½ pounds turkey thighs (about 2 thighs) or meaty chicken pieces (breasts, thighs, and drumsticks), skinned

Hot cooked brown rice or whole wheat pasta (optional)

Exchanges: 1 Other Carbo., 4 Very Lean Meat, 1 Fat

1 In a 3½- or 4-quart slow cooker combine catsup, sugar substitute, tapioca, vinegar, Worcestershire sauce, cinnamon, and red pepper. Place turkey thighs meaty side down on catsup mixture.

2 Cover and cook on low-heat setting for 10 to 12 hours or high-heat setting for 5 to 6 hours. Transfer turkey to a serving dish. Pour cooking juices into a small bowl; skim off fat. Serve turkey with cooking juices and, if desired, hot cooked rice.

Nutrition Facts per serving: 225 cal., 6 g total fat (2 g sat. fat), 100 mg chol., 444 mg sodium, 12 g carbo., 1 g fiber, 30 g pro.
Daily Values: 8% vit. A, 9% vit. C, 5% calcium, 17% iron

Slow Cooker Tips

After a long day there's nothing like coming home to the aroma of a hot meal cooking in a slow cooker. While the time saved at night is terrific, putting the meal together in the morning is a bit more challenging. To eliminate this problem, simply prepare the meal the night before. Brown meats, if necessary, cut and chop veggies, and measure liquids. If your slow cooker has a removable cook well, place all the ingredients in it and refrigerate overnight. If not, place everything in a plastic bag to refrigerate overnight and put into the slow cooker in the morning.

turkey CHABLIS

Only wines grown in the village of Chablis, France, are truly Chablis wines. But did you know that the grape used in these wines is Chardonnay? You can use a Chardonnay in this recipe or your favorite dry white wine.

Prep: 15 minutes
Cook: 9 to 10 hours (low) or
4½ to 5 hours (high)
Makes: 6 to 8 servings

¾ **cup dry white wine**

½ **cup chopped onion**

1 **bay leaf**

1 **clove garlic, minced**

1 **3½- to 4-pound frozen boneless turkey, thawed**

1 **teaspoon dried rosemary, crushed**

¼ **teaspoon black pepper**

⅓ **cup half-and-half, light cream, or milk**

2 **tablespoons cornstarch**

Exchanges: ½ Other Carbo., 8 Very Lean Meat, 1½ Fat

1 In a 3½- to 6-quart slow cooker combine wine, onion, bay leaf, and garlic. Remove netting from turkey, if present. Remove gravy packet, if present, and chill for another use. In a small bowl combine rosemary and pepper. Sprinkle rosemary mixture evenly over turkey; rub in with your fingers. Place turkey in cooker.

2 Cover and cook on low-heat setting for 9 to 10 hours or on high-heat setting for 4½ to 5 hours. Remove turkey from cooker, reserving juices. Cover turkey and keep warm.

3 For gravy, strain juices into a glass measuring cup; skim off fat. Measure 1⅓ cups juices. Pour juices into a small saucepan. Combine half-and-half and cornstarch; stir into juices in saucepan. Cook and stir over medium heat until thickened and bubbly. Cook and stir for 2 minutes more.

4 Slice turkey; arrange on a serving platter. Spoon some of the gravy over turkey. Pass remaining gravy.

Nutrition Facts per serving: 365 cal., 9 g total fat (3 g sat. fat), 176 mg chol., 193 mg sodium, 5 g carbo., 0 g fiber, 58 g pro.
Daily Values: 1% vit. A, 2% vit. C, 6% calcium, 23% iron

slow cooker

bean-and-rice-stuffed PEPPERS

Five easy ingredients make a delicious, healthy meatless meal.

Prep: 15 minutes
Cook: 6 to 6½ hours (low) or
3 to 3½ hours (high)
Makes: 4 servings

4 medium green, red, or yellow sweet peppers

1 cup cooked converted rice

1 15-ounce can chili beans with chili gravy

4 ounces Monterey Jack cheese, shredded (1 cup)

1 15-ounce can chunky tomato sauce with onion, celery, and green pepper

Exchanges: 1½ Vegetable, 1½ Starch, ½ Other Carbo., 1 Medium-Fat Meat, 1 Fat

❶ Halve the sweet peppers lengthwise, removing tops, membranes, and seeds. Stir together rice, beans, and ½ cup of the cheese; spoon into peppers. Pour tomato sauce into the bottom of a 5- or 6-quart slow cooker. Place peppers filled side up in cooker.

❷ Cover and cook on low-heat setting for 6 to 6½ hours or on high heat setting for 3 to 3½ hours. Transfer peppers to a serving plate. Spoon tomato sauce over peppers; sprinkle with remaining cheese.

Nutrition Facts per serving: 323 cal., 11 g total fat (5 g sat. fat), 25 mg chol., 918 mg sodium, 41 g carbo., 9 g fiber, 16 g pro.
Daily Values: 86% vit. A, 206% vit. C, 34% calcium, 16% iron

slow cooker

pasta WITH EGGPLANT SAUCE

Chunks of eggplant cook in a traditional spaghetti sauce, making a tasty low-calorie alternative to ground beef or sausage.

Prep: 20 minutes
Cook: 7 to 8 hours (low) or
3½ to 4 hours (high)
Makes: 6 servings

- 1 **medium eggplant**
- ½ **cup chopped onion**
- 1 **28-ounce can Italian-style tomatoes, undrained and cut up**
- 1 **6-ounce can Italian-style tomato paste**
- 1 **4-ounce can sliced mushrooms, drained**
- 2 **cloves garlic, minced**
- ¼ **cup dry red wine**
- ¼ **cup water**
- 1½ **teaspoons dried oregano, crushed**
- ½ **cup pitted kalamata olives or pitted ripe olives, sliced**
- 2 **tablespoons snipped fresh parsley**
  Salt
  Black pepper
- 4 **cups hot cooked penne pasta**
- ⅓ **cup grated or shredded Parmesan cheese**
- 2 **tablespoons toasted pine nuts (optional)**

Exchanges: 2½ Vegetable, 2 Starch, 1 Fat

1 Peel eggplant, if desired; cut eggplant into 1-inch cubes. In a 3½- to 5-quart slow cooker combine eggplant, onion, undrained tomatoes, tomato paste, mushrooms, garlic, wine, water, and oregano.

2 Cover and cook on low-heat setting for 7 to 8 hours or on high-heat setting for 3½ to 4 hours. Stir in olives and parsley. Season to taste with salt and pepper. Serve over pasta. Top with Parmesan cheese and, if desired, toasted pine nuts.

Nutrition Facts per serving: 259 cal., 6 g total fat (1 g sat. fat), 4 mg chol., 804 mg sodium, 42 g carbo., 7 g fiber, 10 g pro.
Daily Values: 18% vit. A, 37% vit. C, 13% calcium, 20% iron

meatless BURRITOS

Everyone likes burritos, and this recipe makes enough to serve a crowd. For easy accompaniments pick up a fruit salad from the deli and a package or two of Mexican-style rice mix.

Prep: 20 minutes
Cook: 6 to 8 hours (low) or
3 to 4 hours (high)
Makes: 16 servings

- **3 15-ounce cans red kidney and/or black beans, rinsed and drained**
- **1 14½-ounce can diced tomatoes, undrained**
- **1½ cups bottled salsa or picante sauce**
- **1 11-ounce can whole kernel corn with sweet peppers, drained**
- **1 fresh jalapeño chile pepper, seeded and finely chopped (optional)**
- **2 teaspoons chili powder**
- **2 cloves garlic, minced**
- **16 8- to 10-inch flour tortillas, warmed**
- **2 cups shredded lettuce**
- **1 cup shredded taco cheese or cheddar cheese (4 ounces)**
- **Sliced green onions and/or dairy sour cream (optional)**

Exchanges: ½ Vegetable, 2 Starch, ½ Very Lean Meat

1 In a 3½- or 4-quart slow cooker combine beans, undrained tomatoes, salsa, corn, jalapeño pepper (if desired), chili powder, and garlic.

2 Cover and cook on low-heat setting for 6 to 8 hours or on high-heat setting for 3 to 4 hours.

3 To serve, spoon some bean mixture just below center of each tortilla. Top with lettuce and cheese. If desired, top with green onions and/or sour cream. Fold bottom edge of each tortilla up and over filling. Fold in opposite sides; roll up from bottom.

Nutrition Facts per serving: 205 cal., 3 g total fat (2 g sat. fat), 7 mg chol., 471 mg sodium, 34 g carbo., 6 g fiber, 8 g pro.
Daily Values: 10% vit. A, 14% vit. C, 12% calcium, 13% iron

slow cooker

161

vegetable chili WITH PASTA

Finely chop the onion to ensure that it's fully cooked. When you're ready to serve this family-style supper, sprinkle each serving with cheese.

Prep: 20 minutes
Cook: 4 to 5 hours (low) or
 2 to 2½ hours (high)
Makes: 5 servings

- 1 15-ounce can garbanzo beans, rinsed and drained
- 1 15-ounce can red kidney beans, rinsed and drained
- 2 14½-ounce cans diced tomatoes, undrained
- 1 8-ounce can tomato sauce
- 1 cup finely chopped onion
- ½ cup chopped green or yellow sweet pepper
- 2 cloves garlic, minced
- 2 to 3 teaspoons chili powder
- ½ teaspoon dried oregano, crushed
- ⅛ teaspoon ground red pepper (optional)
- 1 cup wagon wheel pasta or elbow macaroni
  Shredded cheddar cheese (optional)

Exchanges: 3 Starch, 1½ Vegetable

1 In a 3½- or 4-quart slow cooker combine beans, undrained tomatoes, tomato sauce, onion, sweet pepper, garlic, chili powder, oregano, and, if desired, red pepper.

2 Cover; cook on low-heat setting for 4 to 5 hours or on high-heat setting for 2 to 2½ hours.

3 Cook pasta according to package directions; drain. Stir cooked pasta into bean mixture. Serve in bowls and, if desired, sprinkle with cheddar cheese.

Nutrition Facts per serving: 273 cal., 2 g total fat (0 g sat. fat), 0 mg chol., 868 mg sodium, 53 g carbo., 10 g fiber, 14 g pro.
Daily Values: 13% vit. A, 57% vit. C, 13% calcium, 22% iron

Being Vegetarian

People become vegetarian for different reasons, whether they're personal, religious, or health related. If you have diabetes, a vegetarian diet can be both safe and healthy as long as you choose your foods wisely. Plant-based foods such as nuts, peanut butter, tofu, and other soy foods can provide the protein in your diet.

Also, low-fat dairy foods such as skim (fat-free) milk and yogurt, along with eggs, are good sources of protein. In addition, include a variety of fruits, vegetables, and whole grains and limit foods high in fats, added sugars, and sodium.

sloppy veggie SANDWICHES

Instead of making sandwiches, try serving the vegetable mixture on tostada shells with shredded lettuce, chopped tomato, and shredded cheese for a taco-style salad.

Prep: 20 minutes
Cook: 3 to 3½ hours (high), plus 30 minutes (high)
Makes: 8 sandwiches

1 cup chopped carrots

1 cup chopped celery

⅔ cup brown lentils, rinsed and drained

⅔ cup uncooked regular brown rice

½ cup chopped onion

2 tablespoons brown sugar

2 tablespoons prepared mustard

½ teaspoon salt

⅛ to ¼ teaspoon cayenne pepper

1 clove garlic, minced

2 14-ounce cans vegetable or chicken broth

1 15-ounce can tomato sauce

2 tablespoons cider vinegar

8 whole wheat hamburger buns or French-style rolls, split and toasted

Exchanges: 3 Starch, ½ Vegetable

1 In a 3½- or 4-quart slow cooker combine carrots, celery, lentils, brown rice, onion, brown sugar, mustard, salt, cayenne pepper, and garlic. Stir in vegetable broth.

2 Cover and cook on high-heat setting for 3 to 3½ hours. Stir in tomato sauce and vinegar. Cover and cook for 30 minutes more. Serve mixture on toasted buns.

Nutrition Facts per sandwich: 261 cal., 4 g total fat (1 g sat. fat), 0 mg chol., 1,036 mg sodium, 50 g carbo., 8 g fiber, 11 g pro.
Daily Values: 78% vit. A, 5% vit. C, 7% calcium, 21% iron

slow cooker

squash AND LENTIL SOUP

The magic of this soup is garam masala, found in the spice aisle of most supermarkets. This blend of ground spices can include cinnamon, nutmeg, cloves, coriander, cumin, cardamom, pepper, chiles, fennel, and mace.

Prep: 25 minutes
Cook: 8 to 9 hours (low) or
      4 to 4½ hours (high)
Makes: 5 to 6 servings

1 **cup dry lentils**

2½ **cups peeled butternut squash, cut into ¾-inch pieces**

½ **cup chopped onion**

½ **cup chopped carrot**

½ **cup chopped celery**

2 **cloves garlic, minced**

1 **teaspoon garam masala**

4 **cups chicken broth or vegetable broth**

Exchanges: 2 Starch, 1½ Very Lean Meat

① Rinse and drain lentils. In a 3½- or 4-quart slow cooker combine lentils, squash, onion, carrot, and celery. Sprinkle garlic and garam masala over vegetables. Pour broth over all.

② Cover and cook on low-heat setting for 8 to 9 hours or on high-heat setting for 4 to 4½ hours. Ladle into bowls.

Nutrition Facts per serving: 199 cal., 2 g total fat (0 g sat. fat), 0 mg chol., 639 mg sodium, 31 g carbo., 13 g fiber, 16 g pro.
Daily Values: 107% vit. A, 17% vit. C, 6% calcium, 22% iron

indian VEGETABLE SOUP

Chock-full of nutty garbanzo beans, red-skin potatoes, and chunks of eggplant, this curried soup makes a hearty meal.

Prep: 30 minutes
Cook: 8 to 10 hours (low) or
      4 to 5 hours (high)
Makes: 6 to 8 servings

1 medium eggplant, cut into ½-inch cubes (5 to 6 cups)

1 pound red-skin potatoes, cut into 1-inch pieces (3 cups)

2 cups chopped tomatoes or one 14½-ounce can low-sodium tomatoes, undrained and cut up

1 15-ounce can garbanzo beans (chickpeas), rinsed and drained

1 tablespoon grated fresh ginger

1½ teaspoons mustard seeds

1½ teaspoons ground coriander

1 teaspoon curry powder

¼ teaspoon black pepper

4 cups vegetable broth or chicken broth

2 tablespoons snipped fresh cilantro

Exchanges: 1½ Vegetable, 1½ Starch

❶ In a 4- to 6-quart slow cooker combine eggplant, potatoes, undrained tomatoes, and garbanzo beans. Sprinkle vegetables with ginger, mustard seeds, coriander, curry powder, and pepper. Pour broth over all.

❷ Cover and cook on low-heat setting for 8 to 10 hours or on high-heat setting for 4 to 5 hours. Ladle into bowls and sprinkle with cilantro.

Nutrition Facts per serving: 162 cal., 2 g total fat (0 g sat. fat), 0 mg chol., 889 mg sodium, 30 g carbo., 7 g fiber, 8 g pro.
Daily Values: 7% vit. A, 33% vit. C, 4% calcium, 10% iron

slow cooker

skillet
MEALS

For a fast dinner that doesn't heat up the kitchen, grab your skillet! It's great for stir-fries, sauces, hot sandwiches, and more. With these recipes, you can choose from a variety of soon-to-be favorites such as Cilantro Chicken with Nuts, Crunchy Parmesan Turkey, and Grilled Brie Sandwiches.

Chicken-Broccoli Stir-Fry, *recipe page 162*

chicken-broccoli STIR-FRY

Thirty minutes to a fresh, hot, homemade stir-fry—that beats takeout any day. Seasoned with hoisin sauce and sesame oil, this stir-fry isn't missing a thing.

Start to Finish: 30 minutes
Makes: 4 servings

- ½ **cup water**
- 2 **tablespoons soy sauce**
- 2 **tablespoons hoisin sauce**
- 2 **teaspoons cornstarch**
- 1 **teaspoon grated fresh ginger**
- 1 **teaspoon toasted sesame oil**
- 1 **pound broccoli**
- 1 **yellow sweet pepper**
- 2 **tablespoons cooking oil**
- 12 **ounces skinless, boneless chicken breasts or thighs, cut into bite-size pieces**
- 2 **cups chow mein noodles or hot cooked rice**

Exchanges: 2 Vegetable, 1½ Starch, 2 Lean Meat, 1½ Fat

1 For sauce, in a small bowl stir together the water, soy sauce, hoisin sauce, cornstarch, ginger, and sesame oil. Set aside.

2 Cut florets from broccoli stems and separate florets into small pieces. Cut broccoli stems crosswise into ¼-inch slices. Cut pepper into short, thin strips.

3 In a wok or large skillet heat 1 tablespoon of the cooking oil over medium-high heat. Cook and stir broccoli stems in hot oil for 1 minute. Add broccoli florets and sweet pepper; cook and stir for 3 to 4 minutes or until crisp-tender. Remove from wok; set aside.

4 Add remaining oil to wok or skillet. Add chicken; cook and stir for 2 to 3 minutes or until no longer pink. Push chicken from center of wok. Stir sauce; pour into center of wok. Cook and stir until thickened and bubbly. Return cooked vegetables to wok; stir to coat with sauce. Cook and stir 1 minute more or until heated through. Serve with chow mein noodles.

Nutrition Facts per serving: 378 cal., 16 g total fat (3 g sat. fat), 49 mg chol., 877 mg sodium, 31 g carbo., 6 g fiber, 29 g pro.
Daily Values: 18% vit. A, 272% vit. C, 8% calcium, 13% iron

keys-style citrus CHICKEN

The sunshine-inspired cooking of the Florida Keys draws on the best of both island and mainland. Here it combines fresh Florida citrus with the Caribbean penchant for fiery peppers.

Start to Finish: 20 minutes
Makes: 4 servings

- 4 **medium skinless, boneless chicken breast halves (1 pound)**
- 2 **or 3 cloves garlic, peeled and thinly sliced**
- 1 **tablespoon butter or margarine**
- 1 **teaspoon finely shredded lime peel**
- 2 **tablespoons lime juice**
- ¼ **teaspoon ground ginger**
- ⅛ **teaspoon crushed red pepper**
- 1 **orange**

Exchanges: 5 Very Lean Meat, ½ Fat

1 In a large skillet cook chicken and garlic in butter over medium heat for 8 to 10 minutes or until chicken is no longer pink (170°F), turning chicken once and stirring garlic occasionally.

2 Meanwhile, in a small bowl combine lime peel, lime juice, ginger, and red pepper; set aside. Peel orange. Reserving juice, cut orange in half lengthwise, then cut crosswise into slices. Add reserved orange juice and the lime juice mixture to skillet. Place orange slices on top of chicken. Cover and cook for 1 to 2 minutes more or until heated through.

3 To serve, spoon any reserved drippings over chicken.

Nutrition Facts per serving: 202 cal., 5 g total fat (2 g sat. fat), 90 mg chol., 105 mg sodium, 5 g carbo., 1 g fiber, 33 g pro.
Daily Values: 4% vit. A, 37% vit. C, 3% calcium, 6% iron

skillet meals

Maximize Your Iron

The mineral iron carries oxygen throughout the body. It's primarily found in beef and other meats, as well as fortified breads and cereals. Vitamin C enhances iron absorption. So be sure to eat foods high in iron with foods high in vitamin C. In addition to oranges and orange juice, vitamin C is found in red peppers, strawberries, kiwifruits, and potatoes.

chicken WITH WHITE BEANS

White kidney beans, also called cannellini beans, are popular in the Tuscany region of Italy. As American chefs become increasingly interested in Tuscan cooking, the beans are becoming much loved stateside too.

Start to Finish: 35 minutes
Makes: 6 servings

- 6 skinless, boneless chicken thighs (1 pound)
- 1 tablespoon olive oil or cooking oil
- ½ cup dry white wine or water
- 1 teaspoon instant chicken bouillon granules
- 2 cloves garlic, minced
- 1 teaspoon dried oregano, crushed
- ¾ teaspoon dried thyme, crushed
- ½ teaspoon dried savory, crushed
- ⅛ teaspoon black pepper
- 1 pound banana, buttercup, or butternut squash, peeled, seeded, and cut into ½-inch pieces (about 2½ cups)
- 1 15-ounce can white kidney (cannellini) beans, rinsed and drained
- 1 14½-ounce can diced tomatoes, undrained
- 2 tablespoons snipped fresh parsley
  Fresh parsley sprig (optional)

Exchanges: 1 Starch, ½ Other Carbo., 2½ Very Lean Meat, ½ Fat

1 In a large skillet cook chicken in hot oil over medium-high heat until light brown, turning to brown evenly. Remove chicken from skillet. Drain off fat.

2 Add wine, bouillon granules, and garlic to skillet. Bring to boiling; reduce heat. Boil gently, uncovered, 3 minutes or until liquid is reduced by about half, scraping up any crusty browned bits from bottom of skillet.

3 Stir in oregano, thyme, savory, and pepper. Return chicken to skillet. Add squash. Bring to boiling; reduce heat. Cover and simmer for 15 to 20 minutes or until chicken is no longer pink (180°F) and squash is nearly tender. Stir in beans and undrained tomatoes. Simmer, uncovered, about 5 minutes more or until bean mixture is slightly thickened.

4 To serve, spoon the bean mixture into shallow bowls. Place chicken on top of bean mixture. Sprinkle with parsley. If desired, garnish with fresh parsley sprig.

Nutrition Facts per serving: 219 cal., 6 g total fat (1 g sat. fat), 60 mg chol., 462 mg sodium, 21 g carbo., 5 g fiber, 21 g pro.
Daily Values: 62% vit. A, 34% vit. C, 19% calcium, 16% iron

skillet meals

171

pesto chicken AND SQUASH

Purchased pesto simplifies the preparation here. Look for jars of pesto near the spaghetti sauce in your grocery store.

Start to Finish: 20 minutes
Makes: 4 servings

- **4 skinless, boneless chicken breast halves (1 pound)**
- **1 tablespoon olive oil**
- **2 cups finely chopped yellow summer squash or zucchini**
- **2 tablespoons purchased basil pesto**
- **2 tablespoons finely shredded Asiago or Parmesan cheese**

Exchanges: 1 Vegetable, 3 Very Lean Meat, 1½ Fat

1 In a large nonstick skillet cook chicken in hot oil over medium heat for 6 minutes.

2 Turn chicken; add squash. Cook for 6 to 9 minutes more or until the chicken is no longer pink (170°F) and squash is crisp-tender, stirring squash gently once or twice. Transfer chicken and squash to 4 dinner plates. Spread pesto over chicken; sprinkle with cheese.

Nutrition Facts per serving: 186 cal., 10 g total fat (2 g sat. fat), 55 mg chol., 129 mg sodium, 2 g carbo., 1 g fiber, 23 g pro.
Daily Values: 4% vit. A, 10% vit. C, 7% calcium, 5% iron

skillet meals

fettuccine and SWEET PEPPERS

To make Romano cheese shavings, firmly pull a vegetable peeler or a cheese shaver over the edge of a block of Romano.

Start to Finish: 25 minutes
Makes: 4 servings

- ½ **cup chicken broth**
- 1 **teaspoon cornstarch**
- 1 **16-ounce package frozen sweet pepper stir-fry vegetables (yellow, green, and red sweet peppers and onion)**
- 1 **9-ounce package refrigerated fettuccine or linguine**
- 1 **tablespoon olive oil**
- 12 **ounces skinless, boneless chicken breasts, cut into bite-size pieces**
- 4 **cloves garlic, minced**
- ¼ **to ½ teaspoon crushed red pepper**
- ½ **cup chopped tomatoes**
- ¼ **cup snipped fresh basil**
  Shaved Romano cheese

Exchanges: 1 Vegetable, 2½ Starch, 3½ Very Lean Meat, 1 Fat

1 In a small bowl stir together chicken broth and cornstarch; set aside.

2 Bring a Dutch oven of salted water to boiling. Add frozen pepper mixture and pasta. Return to boiling and cook for 2 minutes or just until pasta is tender. Drain and return to Dutch oven. Toss with 1 teaspoon of the oil. Keep pasta warm.

3 Meanwhile, in a large skillet cook chicken, garlic, and crushed red pepper in remaining oil over medium-high heat for 2 to 3 minutes or until chicken is no longer pink, stirring often. Push chicken to side of skillet. Stir cornstarch mixture; add to center of skillet. Cook and stir until thickened and bubbly. Cook and stir for 2 minutes more. Stir in chicken to coat with sauce.

4 Remove chicken and sauce from heat; toss with cooked pasta mixture, tomatoes, and basil. Serve topped with shaved Romano cheese.

Nutrition Facts per serving: 397 cal., 9 g total fat (2 g sat. fat), 118 mg chol., 309 mg sodium, 44 g carbo., 5 g fiber, 33 g pro.
Daily Values: 25% vit. A, 38% vit. C, 11% calcium, 19% iron

skillet meals

Sweet Nutrition

As with most vegetables, sweet peppers are very low in calories and contain virtually no fat or salt. Available in a rainbow of colors including red, green, yellow, orange, and purple, they are loaded with nutrition. Each color represents a different set of phytochemicals such as anthocyanins, lutein, and lycopene. Put them all together and you have a mixture that can help lower the risk of some cancers, improve heart health, and help maintain eye health, memory, and urinary tract health.

cilantro chicken WITH NUTS

Served over shredded cabbage, this fabulous chicken dish is like a main-dish salad. Substitute rice if you want a more traditional Asian flavor.

Start to Finish: 25 minutes
Makes: 4 servings

1 **pound skinless, boneless chicken breasts, cut into 1-inch strips**

2 **teaspoons roasted peanut oil**

1 **ounce honey-roasted peanuts**

1 **tablespoon soy sauce**

2 **teaspoons rice vinegar**

1 **teaspoon toasted sesame oil**

1 **cup fresh cilantro leaves**

4 **cups finely shredded napa cabbage or 2 cups hot cooked rice**

Fresh cilantro sprigs (optional)

Lime wedges (optional)

Exchanges: 1 Vegetable, 1 Other Carbo., 3 Very Lean Meat, 1 Fat

1 In a heavy 10-inch skillet cook and stir chicken in hot peanut oil over high heat for 2 minutes. Add peanuts. Cook and stir for 3 minutes more or until chicken is no longer pink.

2 Add soy sauce, vinegar, and sesame oil. Cook and stir for 2 minutes more. Remove from heat. Stir in cilantro leaves.

3 To serve, spoon chicken mixture over cabbage or rice. If desired, garnish with cilantro sprigs and lime wedges.

Nutrition Facts per serving: 254 cal., 8 g total fat (1 g sat. fat), 49 mg chol., 322 mg sodium, 20 g carbo., 4 g fiber, 25 g pro.
Daily Values: 78% vit. A, 98% vit. C, 9% calcium, 13% iron

skillet meals

turkey and wild rice PILAF

Another time chill the cooked mixture—it's delicious served as a main-dish salad.

Prep: 20 minutes
Cook: 43 minutes
Makes: 4 servings

- 1 **cup sliced celery**
- ¼ **cup chopped onion**
- 1 **tablespoon butter or margarine**
- ⅓ **cup wild rice, rinsed and drained**
- 1 **14-ounce can reduced-sodium chicken broth**
- ⅓ **cup long grain rice**
- 12 **ounces cooked smoked turkey, cubed**
- 2 **medium red apples, coarsely chopped**
- 1 **large carrot, peeled and cut into thin, bite-size strips**
- 2 **tablespoons snipped fresh parsley**

Exchanges: 1 Vegetable, ½ Fruit, 1½ Starch, 2½ Lean Meat, ½ Fat

1 In a large skillet cook celery and onion in hot butter over medium heat about 10 minutes or until tender. Add uncooked wild rice; cook and stir for 3 minutes. Add broth. Bring to boiling; reduce heat. Cover and simmer for 20 minutes. Stir in uncooked long grain rice. Return to boiling; reduce heat. Cover and simmer about 20 minutes more or until wild rice and long grain rice are tender and most of the liquid is absorbed.

2 Stir in turkey, apples, and carrot. Cook, uncovered, for 3 to 4 minutes more or until heated through and liquid is absorbed. Stir in parsley.

Nutrition Facts per serving: 289 cal., 7 g total fat (2 g sat. fat), 44 mg chol., 1,231 mg sodium, 37 g carbo., 3 g fiber, 21 g pro.
Daily Values: 65% vit. A, 14% vit. C, 3% calcium, 12% iron

crunchy parmesan TURKEY

Wheat germ adds crunch to the cheesy coating on these turkey steaks.

Start to Finish: 25 minutes
Makes: 4 servings

- ¼ **cup seasoned fine dry bread crumbs**
- ¼ **cup toasted wheat germ**
- ¼ **cup grated Parmesan cheese**
- 2 **teaspoons sesame seeds or ¼ teaspoon dried Italian seasoning, crushed**
- 1 **egg**
- ¼ **teaspoon seasoned salt or ¼ teaspoon each salt and black pepper**
- 4 **turkey breast slices, cut ½ inch thick (about 1 pound)**
- 1 **tablespoon olive oil or cooking oil**

Exchanges: ½ Starch, 5 Very Lean Meat, 1 Fat

1 For coating, in a plastic bag combine bread crumbs, wheat germ, Parmesan cheese, and sesame seeds. Seal bag; shake to combine. In a small shallow bowl beat egg with a fork. Stir in the seasoned salt.

2 Dip turkey breast slices into the egg mixture, allowing excess to drain off. Coat with bread crumb mixture.

3 In a large nonstick skillet cook turkey in hot oil over medium heat for 6 to 8 minutes or until no longer pink (170°F), turning once. Transfer turkey to serving platter.

Nutrition Facts per serving: 258 cal., 9 g total fat (2 g sat. fat), 127 mg chol., 432 mg sodium, 9 g carbo., 1 g fiber, 35 g pro.
Daily Values: 2% vit. A, 1% vit. C, 10% calcium, 13% iron

skillet meals

beef-vegetable RAGOÛT

This recipe fits the bill for a casual get-together and it's ready in only 30 minutes.

Start to Finish: 30 minutes
Makes: 4 servings

  8 ounces dried wide noodles
 12 ounces beef tenderloin, cut into ¾-inch cubes
  2 tablespoons olive oil or cooking oil
 1½ cups packaged sliced fresh crimini or button mushrooms
  ½ cup chopped onion
  2 cloves garlic, minced
  3 tablespoons all-purpose flour
  ½ teaspoon salt
  ¼ teaspoon black pepper
  1 14-ounce can beef broth
  ¼ cup port wine or dry sherry
  2 cups sugar snap peas
  1 cup cherry tomatoes, halved

Exchanges: 1 Vegetable, 3½ Starch, 2½ Medium-Fat Meat, ½ Fat

1 In a large saucepan, cook the noodles according to the package directions.

2 Meanwhile, in a large skillet cook and stir the beef in hot oil over medium heat for 2 to 3 minutes or until meat is done as desired. Remove meat, reserving drippings in skillet. Set meat aside.

3 Cook mushrooms, onion, and garlic in reserved drippings for 4 to 5 minutes or until tender. Sprinkle flour, salt, and pepper over mushroom mixture; stir in. Carefully add broth and wine. Cook and stir until thickened and bubbly.

4 Stir sugar snap peas into the mushroom mixture. Cook for 2 to 3 minutes more or until peas are tender. Stir in meat and tomatoes; heat through.

5 Drain noodles; transfer to a serving platter. Spoon the meat and vegetable mixture over noodles.

Nutrition Facts per serving: 535 cal., 16 g total fat (4 g sat. fat), 97 mg chol., 694 mg sodium, 61 g carbo., 5 g fiber, 31 g pro.
Daily Values: 6% vit. A, 48% vit. C, 7% calcium, 36% iron

skillet meals

italian BEEF SKILLET

The preparation for this beef and vegetable dish takes about 35 minutes. Then sit back and you can relax while it simmers.

skillet meals

Prep: 35 minutes
Cook: 1¼ hours
Makes: 4 servings

1 **pound boneless beef round steak**

Nonstick cooking spray

2 **cups sliced fresh mushrooms**

1 **cup chopped onion**

1 **cup coarsely chopped green sweet pepper**

½ **cup chopped celery**

2 **cloves garlic, minced**

1 **14½-ounce can diced tomatoes, undrained**

½ **teaspoon dried basil, crushed**

¼ **teaspoon dried oregano, crushed**

⅛ **to ¼ teaspoon crushed red pepper**

2 **tablespoons grated Parmesan cheese**

Hot cooked pasta (optional)

Exchanges: 2½ Vegetable, 3½ Very Lean Meat, ½ Fat

❶ Trim fat from meat. Cut meat into 4 serving-size pieces. Lightly coat a large skillet with cooking spray. Heat over medium heat. Add meat and cook until brown, turning to brown evenly. Remove meat from skillet; set aside.

❷ Add mushrooms, onion, sweet pepper, celery, and garlic to skillet. Cook until vegetables are nearly tender. Stir in undrained tomatoes, basil, oregano, and crushed red pepper. Return meat to skillet, spooning vegetable mixture over meat. Cover and simmer about 1¼ hours or until meat is tender, stirring occasionally.

❸ Transfer meat to a serving platter. Spoon vegetable mixture over meat and sprinkle with Parmesan cheese. If desired, serve with hot cooked pasta.

Nutrition Facts per serving: 212 cal., 4 g total fat (1 g sat. fat), 51 mg chol., 296 mg sodium, 14 g carbo., 3 g fiber, 30 g pro.
Daily Values: 6% vit. A, 74% vit. C, 11% calcium, 20% iron

Cooking with Herbs

Using herbs is a great way to add flavor to foods, especially when you're trying to control salt and fat. Some recipes call for fresh herbs; others call for dried. What's the difference? Fresh herbs add more flavor, but they have a less concentrated taste that fades quickly. When substituting one for the other, you can replace 1 tablespoon of fresh herbs with 1 teaspoon of dried herbs. Crush dried herbs in your hands before using to bring out the essential oils. If using fresh herbs wait until near the end of the cooking time to add them to avoid losing the flavor.

saucy beef AND ONIONS

With the variety of fat-free and reduced-fat products available in grocery stores, low-fat cooking is easier than ever. Here light sour cream and a jar of fat-free gravy create a saucy hamburger stroganoff.

Start to Finish: 35 minutes
Makes: 4 servings

12 ounces lean ground beef
 2 cups sliced fresh mushrooms
 2 medium onions, cut into
    thin wedges
 1 clove garlic, minced
 1 12-ounce jar fat-free
    beef gravy
⅔ cup light dairy sour cream
 1 tablespoon Worcestershire
    sauce
¾ teaspoon snipped fresh
    thyme or sage or
    ¼ teaspoon dried thyme
    or sage, crushed
⅛ teaspoon black pepper
 2 cups hot cooked rice
    or noodles
 2 tablespoons snipped
    fresh parsley

Exchanges: 1 Vegetable, 2 Starch, 3 Medium-Fat Meat

1 In a large skillet cook ground beef, mushrooms, onions, and garlic until meat is brown and onions are tender. Drain off fat.

2 In a medium bowl stir together beef gravy, sour cream, Worcestershire sauce, thyme, and pepper. Stir into meat mixture. Cook and stir until heated through.

3 Serve meat mixture over hot cooked rice. Sprinkle with fresh parsley.

Nutrition Facts per serving: 396 cal., 15 g total fat (6 g sat. fat), 83 mg chol., 972 mg sodium, 35 g carbo., 1 g fiber, 32 g pro.
Daily Values: 7% vit. A, 9% vit. C, 10% calcium, 22% iron

skillet meals

ginger BEEF STIR-FRY

When you crave steak but not the high fat and calories that go with it, try this stir-fry. Lean beef and crispy spring vegetables make up a full-flavored dinner you can toss together in minutes.

Start to Finish: 30 minutes
Makes: 4 servings

8 ounces beef top round steak

½ cup reduced-sodium beef broth

3 tablespoons reduced-sodium soy sauce

2½ teaspoons cornstarch

1 teaspoon sugar

1 teaspoon grated fresh ginger

Nonstick cooking spray

1¼ pounds fresh asparagus spears, trimmed and cut into 2-inch pieces (3 cups), or 3 cups small broccoli florets

1½ cups sliced fresh mushrooms

4 green onions, bias-sliced into 2-inch pieces

1 tablespoon cooking oil

2 cups hot cooked rice

Exchanges: 1½ Vegetable, 1½ Starch, 1½ Lean Meat, ½ Fat

1 If desired, partially freeze beef for easier slicing. Trim fat from beef. Thinly slice beef across the grain into bite-size strips. Set aside. For sauce, in a small bowl stir together beef broth, soy sauce, cornstarch, sugar, and ginger; set aside.

2 Lightly coat an unheated wok or large skillet with nonstick cooking spray. Heat over medium-high heat. Add asparagus, mushrooms, and green onions. Stir-fry for 3 to 4 minutes or until vegetables are crisp-tender. Remove from wok or skillet.

3 Carefully add the oil to wok or skillet. Add beef; stir-fry for 2 to 3 minutes or until brown. Push the beef from center of the wok or skillet. Stir sauce. Add sauce to center of wok or skillet. Cook and stir until thickened and bubbly.

4 Return vegetables to wok or skillet. Stir all ingredients together to coat with sauce; heat through. Serve immediately over hot cooked rice.

Nutrition Facts per serving: 258 cal., 7 g total fat (2 g sat. fat), 25 mg chol., 523 mg sodium, 31 g carbo., 3 g fiber, 19 g pro.
Daily Values: 10% vit. A, 20% vit. C, 5% calcium, 18% iron

skillet meals

183

veal SCALOPPINE

Serve this fat- and calorie-trimmed classic with hot cooked broccoli and whole wheat dinner rolls.

Start to Finish: 30 minutes
Makes: 4 servings

- **12 ounces boneless veal leg round steak, veal leg sirloin steak, or beef top round steak, cut ¼ inch thick and trimmed of separable fat**
- **Salt**
- **Black pepper**
- **½ cup chopped onion**
- **¼ cup water**
- **2 cloves garlic, minced**
- **1 14½-ounce can diced tomatoes, undrained**
- **3 tablespoons dry white wine**
- **1 tablespoon snipped fresh oregano or 1 teaspoon dried oregano, crushed**
- **1 tablespoon capers, drained (optional)**
- **⅛ teaspoon black pepper**
- **Nonstick cooking spray**
- **2 cups hot cooked noodles**

Exchanges: 1 Vegetable, 1½ Starch, 2½ Very Lean Meat

1 Cut meat into 8 pieces. Place each piece of meat between 2 pieces of plastic wrap. Working from center to edges, pound with flat side of a meat mallet to about ⅛-inch thickness. Remove plastic wrap. Sprinkle meat lightly with salt and pepper to taste. Set aside.

2 For sauce, in a medium covered saucepan combine onion, water, and garlic. Cook until onion is tender. Stir in undrained tomatoes, wine, oregano, capers (if desired), and ⅛ teaspoon pepper. Bring to boiling; reduce heat. Simmer, uncovered, about 15 minutes or until desired consistency. Keep warm.

3 Meanwhile, lightly coat a large skillet with nonstick cooking spray. Heat over medium-high heat. Cook meat, half at a time, for 2 to 4 minutes or until done as desired, turning once. Transfer meat to a serving platter. Keep warm.

4 To serve, spoon the sauce over meat. Serve with hot cooked noodles.

Nutrition Facts per serving: 235 cal., 3 g total fat (1 g sat. fat), 93 mg chol., 279 mg sodium, 27 g carbo., 2 g fiber, 23 g pro.
Daily Values: 13% vit. A, 27% vit. C, 5% calcium, 14% iron

skillet meals

veal with APPLE-MARSALA

Veal may be labeled "scaloppine" in your supermarket meat section. Scaloppine technically describes a thin scallop of meat that is quickly sautéed. It's generally cut ⅛ inch thick, and you don't have to pound it.

Start to Finish: 25 minutes
Makes: 4 servings

Nonstick cooking spray

12 **ounces veal scaloppine or boneless veal leg round steak or beef top round steak,* cut ¼ inch thick and trimmed of separable fat**

1 **apple, thinly sliced**

1 **clove garlic, minced**

½ **cup dry Marsala**

⅓ **cup reduced-sodium chicken broth**

1 **tablespoon snipped fresh parsley**

Exchanges: 1 Starch, 2 Very Lean Meat, 1½ Fruit, 2 Fat

① Lightly coat an unheated large skillet with nonstick cooking spray. Heat over medium-high heat. Cook meat, half at a time, for 4 to 5 minutes or until no pink remains, turning once. Transfer to a serving platter. Keep warm.

② Add sliced apple and garlic to skillet. Stir in Marsala and chicken broth. Bring to boiling; reduce heat. Boil gently, uncovered, for 4 to 5 minutes or until mixture is reduced by half. Spoon over meat. Sprinkle with parsley.

*Note: If using round or beef steak, cut steak into 8 pieces. Place 1 piece of the cut steak between 2 pieces of plastic wrap. Working from center to edges, pound with flat side of meat mallet to ⅛-inch thickness. Remove plastic wrap. Repeat with remaining meat.

Nutrition Facts per serving: 133 cal., 2 g total fat (0 g sat. fat), 66 mg chol., 97 mg sodium, 6 g carbo., 1 g fiber, 19 g pro.
Daily Values: 1% vit. A, 6% vit. C, 1% calcium, 4% iron

skillet meals

Picking the Best Apple for the Job

There are more than 7,500 known varieties of apples. Certainly personal preference is important when choosing apples, but you must also consider what you'll be doing with them. Are they for baking, for applesauce, or for eating out of hand? For baking, the best apples are those that keep their shape and don't get too mushy, such as Rome Beauty and Idared. When making applesauce choose apples that don't turn brown easily such as Cortland and McIntosh. For eating as is, firm, juicy, tasty apples are the ones to pick, such as Empire and Gala.

pork DIANE

Worcestershire sauce, Dijon mustard, and a double dose of lemon—fresh lemon juice and lemon-pepper seasoning—add zest to tender pork loin chops.

Start to Finish: 30 minutes
Makes: 4 servings

1 tablespoon white wine Worcestershire sauce

1 tablespoon water

1 teaspoon lemon juice

1 teaspoon Dijon-style mustard

4 boneless pork top loin chops, cut ¾ to 1 inch thick

½ to 1 teaspoon lemon-pepper seasoning

2 tablespoons butter or margarine

1 tablespoon snipped fresh chives or parsley

Exchanges: 2½ Lean Meat, 1 Fat

1 For sauce, in a small bowl stir together Worcestershire sauce, water, lemon juice, and mustard. Set sauce aside.

2 Sprinkle both sides of chops with lemon-pepper seasoning. In a large skillet cook chops in hot butter over medium heat for 8 to 12 minutes or until meat is done (160°F) and juices run clear, turning once. Remove skillet from heat. Transfer chops to a serving platter; keep warm.

3 Pour sauce into skillet. Cook and stir to loosen any browned bits in bottom of skillet. Spoon sauce over chops. Sprinkle with chives.

Nutrition Facts per serving: 178 cal., 11 g total fat (5 g sat. fat), 66 mg chol., 302 mg sodium, 1 g carbo., 0 g fiber, 18 g pro.
Daily Values: 6% vit. A, 2% vit. C, 2% calcium, 4% iron

skillet meals

snapper VERACRUZ

Snapper Veracruz, one of Mexico's best-known fish recipes, is a melding of flavors. The recipe includes Spanish green olives and capers with jalapeño peppers from Jalapa, the capital of the state of Veracruz.

Start to Finish: 30 minutes
Makes: 6 servings

- 1½ **pounds fresh or frozen skinless red snapper or other fish fillets, ½ to ¾ inch thick**
- ⅛ **teaspoon salt**
- ⅛ **teaspoon black pepper**
- 1 **large onion, sliced and separated into rings**
- 2 **cloves garlic, minced**
- 1 **tablespoon cooking oil**
- 2 **large tomatoes, chopped (2 cups)**
- ¼ **cup sliced pimiento-stuffed green olives**
- ¼ **cup dry white wine**
- 2 **tablespoons capers, drained**
- 1 **to 2 fresh jalapeño or serrano chile peppers, seeded and chopped,* or 1 to 2 canned jalapeño chile peppers, rinsed, drained, seeded, and chopped**
- ½ **teaspoon sugar**
- 1 **bay leaf**

Exchanges: ½ Vegetable, 3½ Very Lean Meat, 1 Fat

❶ Thaw fish, if frozen. Rinse fish; pat dry with paper towels. Cut fish into 6 serving-size pieces. Sprinkle fish with salt and black pepper.

❷ For sauce, in a large skillet cook onion and garlic in hot oil until onion is tender. Stir in tomatoes, olives, wine, capers, jalapeño peppers, sugar, and bay leaf. Bring to boiling. Add fish to skillet. Return to boiling; reduce heat. Cover and simmer for 6 to 10 minutes or until fish flakes easily when tested with a fork. Use a slotted spatula to carefully transfer fish from skillet to a serving platter. Cover and keep warm.

❸ Gently boil sauce in skillet for 5 to 6 minutes or until reduced to about 2 cups, stirring occasionally. Discard bay leaf. Spoon sauce over fish.

*Note: Because chile peppers, such as jalapeños, contain volatile oils that can burn your skin and eyes, avoid direct contact with them as much as possible. When working with chile peppers, wear plastic or rubber gloves. If your bare hands do touch the chile peppers, wash your hands and nails well with soap and warm water.

Nutrition Facts per serving: 178 cal., 6 g total fat (1 g sat. fat), 41 mg chol., 384 mg sodium, 6 g carbo., 1 g fiber, 25 g pro.
Daily Values: 12% vit. A, 26% vit. C, 4% calcium, 7% iron

skillet meals

sesame-teriyaki SEA BASS

Golden teriyaki glaze and toasty sesame seeds make a tantalizing coat for these lightly panfried sea bass fillets. Complete the meal with braised mixed cabbage and couscous pilaf.

Start to Finish: 30 minutes
Makes: 4 servings

- 4 **4-ounce fresh or frozen sea bass fillets, 1 inch thick**
- ¼ **teaspoon black pepper**
- 3 **tablespoons soy sauce**
- 3 **tablespoons sweet rice wine (mirin)**
- 2 **tablespoons dry white wine**
- 1½ **teaspoons sugar**
- 1½ **teaspoons honey**
- 2 **teaspoons cooking oil**
- 1 **tablespoon white or black sesame seeds, toasted***

Exchanges: 1½ Lean Meat

① Thaw fish, if frozen. Rinse fish; pat dry with paper towels. Sprinkle the fish with pepper; set aside.

② For glaze, in a small saucepan combine soy sauce, rice wine, dry white wine, sugar, and honey. Bring to boiling; reduce heat. Simmer, uncovered, about 10 minutes or until glaze is reduced to about ¼ cup.

③ Meanwhile, in a large nonstick skillet cook the fish in hot oil over medium heat for 8 to 12 minutes or until fish flakes easily when tested with a fork, gently turning once.

④ To serve, arrange the fish on a serving platter. Drizzle the glaze over the fish; sprinkle with sesame seeds.

*Note: To toast sesame seeds, in a nonstick skillet cook and stir sesame seeds over medium heat about 1 minute or just until golden brown. Watch closely so the seeds don't burn. Remove from heat and transfer to a bowl to cool completely.

Nutrition Facts per serving: 185 cal., 6 g total fat (1 g sat. fat), 47 mg chol., 851 mg sodium, 6 g carbo., 0 g fiber, 22 g pro.
Daily Values: 5% vit. A, 4% vit. C, 1% calcium, 5% iron

Something's Fishy

Sea bass is a saltwater fish sometimes referred to as sea perch. A 3-ounce serving contains about 100 calories and only 2 grams of fat. Incorporating more fish into one's diet is often recommended to people trying to eat healthier, but buying fresh fish can be intimidating. Follow these simple tips to ensure you're buying fresh, healthy fish: Choose fish with firm, shiny flesh and a mild salty scent. Avoid fish with a very strong fishy odor. Select fish that's moist, not dry.

skillet meals

couscous cakes WITH SALSA

Couscous is made with ground semolina, as are some pastas, but it acts like a grain in this recipe and often substitutes for barley or bulgur.

Start to Finish: 20 minutes
Makes: 4 servings

- ½ **of a 15-ounce can (about ¾ cup) black beans, rinsed and drained**
- ⅔ **cup purchased corn relish**
- 2 **small roma tomatoes, chopped**
- 1½ **teaspoons lime juice**
- ¼ **teaspoon ground cumin**
- ½ **cup quick-cooking couscous**
- 2 **tablespoons whole wheat flour**
- ½ **teaspoon sugar**
- ¼ **teaspoon baking soda**
- ⅛ **teaspoon salt**
- ¾ **cup buttermilk or sour milk***
- 1 **slightly beaten egg**
- 1 **tablespoon cooking oil**

Exchanges: 2 Starch, 1 Other Carbo., ½ Very Lean Meat, ½ Fat

1 For salsa, in a medium bowl combine beans, corn relish, tomatoes, lime juice, and cumin. Set aside.

2 In another medium bowl combine uncooked couscous, whole wheat flour, sugar, baking soda, and salt. In a small bowl combine buttermilk, egg, and oil. Stir buttermilk mixture into flour mixture. Lightly grease a griddle or skillet; heat over medium heat. For each cake, spoon about 2 tablespoons of batter onto the hot griddle or skillet. Cook for 4 to 6 minutes or until browned, turning to other sides when bottoms are lightly browned and edges are slightly dry.

3 To serve, spoon salsa mixture over cakes.

*Note: To make ¾ cup sour milk, place 2 teaspoons lemon juice or vinegar in a glass measuring cup. Add enough fat-free milk to make ¾ cup total liquid; stir. Let stand for 5 minutes before using.

Nutrition Facts per serving: 262 cal., 6 g total fat (1 g sat. fat), 55 mg chol., 453 mg sodium, 46 g carbo., 5 g fiber, 10 g pro.
Daily Values: 7% vit. A, 15% vit. C, 8% calcium, 7% iron

skillet meals

ravioli with SWEET PEPPERS

This pretty vegetable and pasta main dish scores high in flavor and nutrients. Each serving provides more than 100 percent of your daily vitamin A and C needs.

skillet meals

Start to Finish: 20 minutes
Makes: 4 servings

- **1 9-ounce package refrigerated light cheese ravioli**
- **⅔ cup chopped red sweet pepper**
- **⅔ cup chopped green sweet pepper**
- **1 medium carrot, cut into thin bite-size strips**
- **⅓ cup chopped onion**
- **2 cloves garlic, minced**
- **1 tablespoon olive oil**
- **1 cup chopped tomato**
- **¼ cup reduced-sodium chicken broth or vegetable broth**
- **3 tablespoons snipped fresh basil or 2 teaspoons dried basil, crushed**

Exchanges: 2 Vegetable, 2 Starch, ½ Lean Meat

1 Cook pasta according to package directions, except omit any oil or salt. Drain. Return pasta to saucepan; cover and keep warm.

2 Meanwhile, in a large nonstick skillet cook sweet pepper, carrot, onion, and garlic in hot oil over medium-high heat about 5 minutes or until vegetables are tender. Stir in tomato, broth, and basil. Cook and stir about 2 minutes more or until heated through.

3 Add vegetable mixture to the cooked pasta; toss gently to combine.

Nutrition Facts per serving: 280 cal., 9 g total fat (4 g sat. fat), 26 mg chol., 381 mg sodium, 39 g carbo., 2 g fiber, 14 g pro.
Daily Values: 137% vit. A, 115% vit. C, 32% calcium, 13% iron

grilled brie SANDWICHES

Another time try this sophisticated grilled cheese with watercress in place of half of the spinach.

2 cloves garlic, minced

1 tablespoon olive oil or cooking oil

8 ounces torn fresh spinach (6 cups)

8 ounces cold Brie, cut into ⅛-inch slices

8 slices firm-texture whole grain bread

Butter or margarine

Exchanges: 1 Vegetable, 1½ Starch, 1½ Medium-Fat Meat, 4 Fat

1 In a large skillet cook garlic in hot oil for 30 seconds. Add spinach. Cook over medium heat, tossing until spinach begins to wilt; remove from heat. Set aside.

2 Divide cheese among 4 slices of the bread. Top with spinach-garlic mixture. Cover with remaining bread slices. Lightly spread the outside of each sandwich with butter.

3 In a large skillet cook 2 sandwiches over medium-low heat for 5 to 7 minutes or until golden. Turn sandwiches and cook for 2 minutes more or until sandwiches are golden and cheese melts. Transfer to a warm oven. Repeat with remaining sandwiches.

Nutrition Facts per serving: 427 cal., 29 g total fat (16 g sat. fat), 79 mg chol., 762 mg sodium, 24 g carbo., 6 g fiber, 18 g pro.
Daily Values: 64% vit. A, 20% vit. C, 20% calcium, 29% iron

skillet meals

oven
ENTRÉES

Like slow cooker meals, foods made in the oven are pretty much fix-it-and forget-it recipes. You do the prep work, then let the oven finish the job while you do something else. Just add a tossed salad or rolls and dinner is done. In some cases, an oven meal is complete all by itself.

Herbed Beef Tenderloin, *recipe page 198*

herbed BEEF TENDERLOIN

Stir fresh parsley, rosemary, and thyme into Dijon mustard to create a flavorful herb rub for roast beef. Mustard-spiked sour cream makes a refreshing condiment.

Prep: 5 minutes
Roast: 30 minutes
Stand: 15 minutes
Oven: 325°F
Makes: 8 servings

- 1 **2-pound beef tenderloin roast**
- ¼ **cup snipped fresh parsley**
- 2 **tablespoons Dijon-style mustard**
- 1 **tablespoon snipped fresh rosemary**
- 2 **teaspoons snipped fresh thyme**
- 1 **teaspoon olive oil or cooking oil**
- ½ **teaspoon coarsely ground black pepper**
- 2 **cloves garlic, minced**
- ½ **cup light dairy sour cream**
- 2 **teaspoons Dijon-style mustard**
  Coarsely ground black pepper

Exchanges: 3½ Very Lean Meat, 2 Fat

1 Trim fat from meat. In small bowl stir together parsley, the 2 tablespoons mustard, the rosemary, thyme, oil, pepper, and garlic. Rub over top and sides of meat.

2 Place meat on a rack in a shallow roasting pan. Insert an oven-going meat thermometer into center of meat. Roast in a 325° oven for 30 to 45 minutes or until meat thermometer registers 135°F. Cover with foil and let stand 15 minutes. (The meat's temperature will rise 10°F while it stands.)

3 Meanwhile, for sauce, stir together sour cream and the 2 teaspoons mustard. Thinly slice meat. Serve with sauce. If desired, sprinkle with additional pepper.

Nutrition Facts per serving: 215 cal., 11 g total fat (4 g sat. fat), 75 mg chol., 178 mg sodium, 2 g carbo., 0 g fiber, 25 g pro.
Daily Values: 4% vit. A, 5% vit. C, 4% calcium, 18% iron

oven entrées

mustard STEAK SANDWICHES

Save calories by serving this sandwich with just the bottom half of the roll. Use a knife and fork for easier eating.

Prep: 10 minutes
Broil: 15 minutes
Makes: 6 servings

2 tablespoons Dijon-style
  mustard
1 teaspoon brown sugar
½ teaspoon cracked black
  pepper
1 clove garlic, minced
1 pound beef flank steak,
  trimmed of separable fat
3 hoagie rolls, split and toasted
1 cup shredded lettuce
  Thinly sliced tomato
  Dijon-style mustard (optional)

Exchanges: 2½ Starch, 2 Lean Meat, ½ Fat

1 In a small bowl stir together mustard, brown sugar, pepper, and garlic. Set aside.

2 Place meat on the unheated rack of a broiler pan. Score steak on both sides by making shallow cuts at 1-inch intervals in a diamond pattern. Brush steak with some of the mustard mixture. Broil steak 4 to 5 inches from the heat for 7 minutes. Turn and brush steak with remaining mustard mixture. Broil until done as desired, allowing 8 to 11 minutes more for medium (160°F).

3 To serve, thinly slice meat diagonally across the grain. Top each hoagie half with some of the lettuce and sliced tomato. Layer meat slices on each sandwich. If desired, serve with additional mustard.

Nutrition Facts per serving: 333 cal., 9 g total fat (3 g sat. fat), 30 mg chol., 500 mg sodium, 38 g carbo., 2 g fiber, 22 g pro.
Daily Values: 7% vit. A, 11% vit. C, 6% calcium, 19% iron

oven entrées

Fatless Flavor

It's no secret that fat, salt, and sugar give food flavor, so when it comes to eating healthfully, replacing these things with other ingredients is important. Certainly ingredients like mustard, pepper, vinegar, and salsa are great low-cal, fat-free flavorings. And there are so many varieties of each of these that the possibilities are endless. Consider hot or honey mustard, balsamic or raspberry vinegar, and tomato or black bean salsa. The list goes on. As long as you're willing to experiment, you'll never run out of variations.

beef WITH MUSHROOM SAUCE

For a more elegant dinner, broil beef tenderloin instead of eye round steaks and make the sauce using ⅓ cup dry red wine and ⅓ cup water in place of the vegetable juice.

Prep: 20 minutes
Broil: 10 minutes
Makes: 4 servings

⅛ teaspoon black pepper

4 3-ounce beef eye round steaks, trimmed of separable fat

1 cup sliced fresh mushrooms

½ cup sliced green onions

2 cloves garlic, minced

2 teaspoons butter or margarine

2 teaspoons cornstarch

⅔ cup low-sodium vegetable juice

½ teaspoon instant beef bouillon granules

Exchanges: 3 Lean Meat, 1½ Fat

1 Rub pepper over meat. Place meat on the unheated rack of a broiler pan. Broil 4 to 5 inches from the heat until done as desired, turning once. Allow 10 to 12 minutes for medium rare (145°F) or 12 to 15 minutes for medium (160°F).

2 Meanwhile, in a saucepan cook mushrooms, onions, and garlic in hot butter until vegetables are tender. Stir in cornstarch. Add vegetable juice and beef bouillon granules. Cook and stir until thickened and bubbly. Cook and stir 2 minutes more. Keep warm while cooking meat. Serve the sauce over meat.

Nutrition Facts per serving: 170 cal., 7 g total fat (3 g sat. fat), 51 mg chol., 181 mg sodium, 5 g carbo., 1 g fiber, 20 g pro.
Daily Values: 11% vit. A, 21% vit. C, 2% calcium, 10% iron

oven entrées

roast with SPICY POTATOES

Tri-tip roast is a boneless cut of beef from the bottom sirloin. Because of its shape, it's also sometimes called triangular roast. This versatile cut tastes wonderful roasted, grilled, or broiled, and it's low in calories.

Prep: 25 minutes
Roast: 30 minutes
Stand: 15 minutes
Oven: 425°F
Makes: 6 to 8 servings

1½ **pounds tiny new potatoes (15 to 18), halved**
1½ **teaspoons chili powder**
½ **teaspoon ground cumin**
¼ **teaspoon garlic powder**
¼ **teaspoon salt**
¼ **teaspoon dried oregano, crushed**
⅛ **teaspoon cayenne pepper**
3 **tablespoons lemon juice**
1 **tablespoon cooking oil**
1 **1½- to 2-pound boneless tri-tip roast**

Exchanges: 1½ Starch, 3 Medium-Fat Meat

1 In a covered medium saucepan cook potatoes in a small amount of boiling salted water about 10 minutes or until nearly tender. Drain well.

2 Meanwhile, in a small bowl combine chili powder, cumin, garlic powder, salt, oregano, and cayenne pepper. Gently toss potatoes with 2 tablespoons of the lemon juice and the oil. Sprinkle with 1½ teaspoons of the chili powder mixture. Toss again to coat potatoes evenly. Arrange potatoes in a single layer in a lightly greased 15×10×1-inch baking pan; set aside.

3 Brush both sides of roast with remaining 1 tablespoon lemon juice. Sprinkle with remaining chili powder mixture. Place roast on a rack set in a shallow roasting pan. Insert a meat thermometer into center of roast. Roast, uncovered, in a 425° oven until done as desired. Allow 30 to 35 minutes for medium rare (140°F) or 40 to 45 minutes for medium (155°F). Remove roast from oven. Cover with foil and let stand for 15 minutes. (The meat's temperature will rise 5°F while it stands.)

4 Meanwhile, while roast is standing, place the potatoes in the 425° oven. Bake, uncovered, 15 minutes or until potatoes are tender and brown, carefully turning potatoes once.

5 To serve, thinly slice roast across the grain. Serve potatoes with roast.

Nutrition Facts per serving: 265 cal., 8 g total fat (2 g sat. fat), 54 mg chol., 175 mg sodium, 20 g carbo., 2 g fiber, 28 g pro.
Daily Values: 5% vit. A, 34% vit. C, 2% calcium, 22% iron

oven entrées

spinach-stuffed FLANK STEAK

Dried tomatoes have a sweet, tart flavor. To save on calories and fat, choose those that are not packed in oil. Soften the tomatoes in hot water for 10 minutes before using.

Prep: 20 minutes
Broil: 10 minutes
Makes: 4 servings

¼ cup dried tomatoes (not oil packed)
1 1-pound beef flank steak or top round steak, trimmed of separable fat
⅛ teaspoon salt
⅛ teaspoon black pepper
1 10-ounce package frozen chopped spinach, thawed and well drained
2 tablespoons grated Parmesan cheese
2 tablespoons snipped fresh basil

Exchanges: 1 Vegetable, 4 Very Lean Meat, 1 Fat

1 In a small bowl soak the dried tomatoes in enough hot water to cover for 10 minutes. Drain. Snip into small pieces.

2 Meanwhile, score both sides of steak in a diamond pattern by making shallow diagonal cuts at 1-inch intervals. Place meat between 2 pieces of plastic wrap. Working from center to edges, pound with the flat side of a meat mallet into a 12×8-inch rectangle. Remove plastic wrap. Sprinkle with the salt and pepper.

3 Spread the spinach over the steak. Sprinkle with the softened tomatoes, Parmesan cheese, and basil. Roll the steak up from a short side. Secure with wooden toothpicks at 1-inch intervals, starting ½ inch from an end. Cut between the toothpicks into eight 1-inch slices.

4 Place slices cut side down on the unheated rack of a broiler pan. Broil 3 to 4 inches from the heat until done as desired, turning once. Allow 10 to 12 minutes for medium rare (145°F) or 12 to 16 minutes for medium (160°F). Before serving, remove the toothpicks.

Nutrition Facts per serving: 214 cal., 9 g total fat (4 g sat. fat), 47 mg chol., 348 mg sodium, 4 g carbo., 2 g fiber, 28 g pro.
Daily Values: 207% vit. A, 11% vit. C, 10% calcium, 14% iron

oven entrées

mustard-maple PORK ROAST

Dijon mustard and maple syrup make a wonderful glaze for pork. Let the roast stand for 15 minutes before carving—this allows the temperature to rise to 160°F and makes the roast easier to slice.

Prep: 20 minutes
Roast: 1½ hours
Stand: 15 minutes
Oven: 325°F
Makes: 8 to 10 servings

1 2- to 2½-pound boneless pork loin roast (single loin)

2 tablespoons Dijon-style mustard

1 tablespoon maple-flavor syrup

2 teaspoons dried sage, crushed

1 teaspoon finely shredded orange peel

¼ teaspoon salt

¼ teaspoon black pepper

20 to 24 tiny new potatoes (about 1¾ pounds)

16 ounces packaged, peeled baby carrots

1 tablespoon olive oil

¼ teaspoon salt

Exchanges: 1 Vegetable, 1½ Starch, 2½ Lean Meat, ½ Fat

1 Trim fat from meat. Stir together mustard, syrup, sage, orange peel, the ¼ teaspoon salt, and the pepper. Spoon mixture onto meat. Place roast fat side up on a rack in a shallow roasting pan. Insert a meat thermometer. Roast, uncovered, in a 325° oven for 45 minutes.

2 Meanwhile, peel a strip of skin from the center of each potato. Cook potatoes in boiling salted water for 5 minutes. Add carrots; cook 5 minutes more. Drain.

3 Toss together potatoes, carrots, olive oil, and ¼ teaspoon salt. Place in roasting pan around pork roast. Roast, uncovered, for 45 minutes to 1 hour more or until meat thermometer registers 155°F. Cover with foil and let stand for 15 minutes. (The meat's temperature will rise 5°F while it stands.)

Nutrition Facts per serving: 281 cal., 10 g total fat (3 g sat. fat), 51 mg chol., 309 mg sodium, 29 g carbo., 3 g fiber, 19 g pro.
Daily Values: 128% vit. A, 24% vit. C, 3% calcium, 17% iron

oven entrées

205

pork with pear STUFFING

This dish is both elegant and easy to prepare. The stuffing makes a swirl of color in each slice and provides a sweet, nutty counterpoint to the tender pork.

Prep: 20 minutes
Roast: 35 minutes
Oven: 425°F
Makes: 4 servings

½ **cup chopped pear**

¼ **cup chopped hazelnuts (filberts) or almonds, toasted**

¼ **cup finely shredded carrot**

¼ **cup soft bread crumbs**

2 **tablespoons chopped onion**

1 **teaspoon grated fresh ginger**

¼ **teaspoon salt**

¼ **teaspoon black pepper**

1 **12-ounce pork tenderloin**

1 **teaspoon cooking oil**

2 **tablespoons sugar-free orange marmalade**

Exchanges: ½ Starch, 2½ Lean Meat

1 For stuffing, in a small bowl combine pear, nuts, carrot, bread crumbs, onion, ginger, salt, and black pepper; set aside.

2 Trim any fat from meat. Butterfly meat by making a lengthwise slit down the center to within ½ inch of the underside. Open flat; pound with the flat side of a meat mallet to about ¼-inch thickness.

3 Spread stuffing over meat. Fold in ends. Starting from a long side, roll up meat. Secure with 100-percent-cotton string or wooden toothpicks. Place meat roll on a rack in a shallow roasting pan. Brush lightly with oil. Insert a meat thermometer into center of meat.

4 Roast in a 425° oven for 30 to 40 minutes or until meat thermometer registers 155°F. Brush orange marmalade over top of meat. Roast about 5 minutes more or until meat thermometer registers 160°F.

Nutrition Facts per serving: 191 cal., 9 g total fat (1 g sat. fat), 55 mg chol., 193 mg sodium, 9 g carbo., 2 g fiber, 20 g pro.
Daily Values: 43% vit. A, 5% vit. C, 2% calcium, 9% iron

oven entrées

Using Ginger

Often used in Asian cooking, fresh ginger adds a slightly peppery flavor to any kind of food. When buying ginger, look for pieces that are firm and mold-free. Once home simply pop it in the fridge where it will last two to three weeks, or freeze it to keep indefinitely. To use ginger, peel it first (no need to thaw if frozen), then slice, grate, mince, or julienne it. If you like a strong ginger flavor, add it near the end of cooking. For milder flavor add it near the beginning.

german-style CHICKEN

Germany's most famous mustard took its name from one of Germany's most famous cities—Düsseldorf. It's a dark, mild ingredient that harmonizes with the other flavors in this dish.

Prep: 5 minutes
Bake: 45 minutes
Oven: 375°F
Makes: 4 servings

- **4 medium chicken breast halves (2 pounds)**
- **¼ cup Düsseldorf or horseradish mustard**
- **2 tablespoons dry sherry**
- **½ teaspoon sweet Hungarian paprika or ¼ teaspoon hot Hungarian paprika**
- **½ cup soft rye bread crumbs**

Exchanges: ½ Starch, 4 Very Lean Meat, 1 Fat

① Skin chicken breasts. In a small bowl combine mustard, sherry, and paprika. Brush 2 tablespoons of the mustard mixture evenly over top of chicken. Place chicken mustard side up in a 3-quart rectangular baking dish. Sprinkle with bread crumbs, patting lightly.

② Bake, uncovered, in a 375° oven for 45 to 50 minutes or until chicken is no longer pink (170°F). Serve with remaining mustard mixture.

Nutrition Facts per serving: 232 cal., 9 g total fat (2 g sat. fat), 83 mg chol., 306 mg sodium, 4 g carbo., 0 g fiber, 31 g pro.
Daily Values: 4% vit. A, 3% calcium, 10% iron

oven entrées

asian CHICKEN AND VEGGIES

Five-spice powder, a blend available on the grocery shelf, and a bottled cooking sauce give budget chicken pieces an Asian flair.

Prep: 10 minutes
Bake: 40 minutes
Oven: 400°F
Makes: 4 servings

8 **chicken drumsticks and/or thighs, skinned (2 pounds)**

1 **tablespoon cooking oil**

1½ **teaspoons five-spice powder**

⅓ **cup bottled plum sauce or sweet-and-sour sauce**

1 **14-ounce package frozen loose-pack baby whole potatoes, broccoli, carrots, baby corn, and red pepper mix or one 16-ounce package frozen stir-fry vegetables (any combination)**

Exchanges: 1 Vegetable, 1 Starch, 4 Very Lean Meat, 1 Fat

1 Arrange chicken pieces in a 13×9×2-inch baking pan, making sure pieces don't touch. Brush chicken pieces with cooking oil; sprinkle with 1 teaspoon of the five-spice powder. Bake, uncovered, in a 400° oven for 25 minutes.

2 Meanwhile, in a large bowl combine remaining ½ teaspoon five-spice powder and plum sauce. Add frozen vegetables; toss to coat.

3 Move chicken pieces to one side of the baking pan. Add vegetable mixture to the other side of the pan. Bake for 15 to 20 minutes more or until chicken is no longer pink (180°F), stirring vegetables once during baking. Using a slotted spoon, transfer chicken and vegetables to a serving platter.

Nutrition Facts per serving: 277 cal., 9 g total fat (2 g sat. fat), 98 mg chol., 124 mg sodium, 21 g carbo., 2 g fiber, 30 g pro.
Daily Values: 21% vit. A, 19% vit. C, 5% calcium, 11% iron

oven entrées

garlic-clove CHICKEN

Cooking garlic within the clove's casing imparts only a mild garlic flavor to foods cooked with it. That's why you'll never believe 25 cloves are used here.

Prep: 20 minutes
Bake: 45 minutes
Oven: 325°F
Makes: 4 servings

Nonstick cooking spray

2 **to 2½ pounds meaty chicken pieces (breasts, thighs, and drumsticks), skinned**

25 **cloves garlic (about ½ cup or 2 to 3 bulbs)**

¼ **cup dry white wine**

Salt

Cayenne pepper

Exchanges: ½ Other Carbo., 4½ Very Lean Meat, ½ Fat

1 Lightly coat a large skillet with nonstick cooking spray. Heat skillet over medium heat. Add chicken and cook for 10 minutes, turning to brown evenly. Place chicken in a 2-quart square baking dish. Add unpeeled garlic cloves. Pour wine over chicken. Lightly sprinkle chicken with salt and cayenne pepper.

2 Bake, covered, in a 325° oven for 45 to 50 minutes or until chicken is no longer pink (170°F for breasts, 180°F for thighs and drumsticks).

Nutrition Facts per serving: 194 cal., 3 g total fat (1 g sat. fat), 96 mg chol., 232 mg sodium, 6 g carbo., 0 g fiber, 31 g pro.
Daily Values: 1% vit. A, 14% vit. C, 5% calcium, 8% iron

oven entrées

LESS THAN
10 GRAMS
OF **CARBS**

roast tarragon CHICKEN

Tarragon's bold, aniselike flavor complements the sweetness of the roasted tomatoes and onions. You can also use rosemary or thyme.

Prep: 15 minutes
Roast: 45 minutes
Oven: 375°F
Makes: 6 servings

- **3 tablespoons olive oil**
- **2½ teaspoons dried tarragon, crushed**
- **2 cloves garlic, minced**
- **½ teaspoon coarsely ground black pepper**
- **¼ teaspoon salt**
- **1 pound cherry tomatoes**
- **8 small shallots**
- **2½ to 3 pounds meaty chicken pieces (breasts, thighs, and drumsticks)**

Exchanges: 1 Vegetable, 3 Medium-Fat Meat

1 In a medium bowl stir together olive oil, tarragon, garlic, pepper, and salt. Add tomatoes and shallots; toss gently to coat. Use a slotted spoon to remove tomatoes and shallots from bowl, reserving the olive oil mixture.

2 If desired, skin chicken. Place chicken in a shallow roasting pan. Brush chicken with the reserved olive oil mixture.

3 Roast chicken in a 375° oven for 20 minutes. Add shallots; roast for 15 minutes. Add tomatoes; roast for 10 to 12 minutes more or until chicken is no longer pink (170°F for breasts; 180°F for thighs and drumsticks) and vegetables are tender.

Nutrition Facts per serving: 266 cal., 17 g total fat (4 g sat. fat), 66 mg chol., 166 mg sodium, 6 g carbo., 1 g fiber, 21 g pro.
Daily Values: 12% vit. A, 24% vit. C, 2% calcium, 8% iron

oven entrées

Roasting Vegetables

Finding ways to enhance foods' natural flavor in lieu of adding fat, salt, and sugar makes healthy eating easy. Roasting vegetables is only one of the ways to do this. Roasting (cooking with a high, dry heat) brings out the natural sugars in vegetables and concentrates their flavors. The natural flavor of the vegetables is good, but you can add any combination of dried herbs for variety.

211

pizza WITH RED PEPPER SAUCE

Queso fresco's mild, salty flavor fares well as a topper for this chicken-and-roasted-pepper pizza.

Prep: 30 minutes
Bake: 10 minutes
Oven: 425°F
Makes: 6 servings

Nonstick cooking spray

2 **medium red sweet peppers**

1 **Anaheim pepper**

1 **tablespoon olive oil**

1 **clove garlic, cut up**

½ **teaspoon salt**

½ **teaspoon crushed cumin
   seeds**

1 **12-inch Italian bread shell**

6 **ounces coarsely shredded
   deli-roasted or rotisserie
   chicken (about 2 cups)**

2 **green onions, sliced**

2 **ounces crumbled or shredded
   queso fresco and/or
   Monterey Jack cheese
   (about ½ cup)**

3 **tablespoons dairy sour cream**

¼ **cup fresh cilantro leaves**

1 **small avocado, halved,
   seeded, peeled, and thinly
   sliced (optional)**

1 **serrano pepper or jalapeño
   pepper, thinly sliced
   (optional)**

Exchanges: 1½ Vegetable, 2 Starch, 1½ Lean Meat, ½ Fat

1 Line a baking sheet with foil; lightly coat foil with nonstick cooking spray. Set baking sheet aside. Cut sweet peppers and Anaheim pepper in half lengthwise. Remove seeds and membranes. Place pepper halves cut side down on prepared baking sheet. Roast in a 425° oven for 20 minutes or until skins are blistered. Wrap pepper halves in the foil; let stand for 10 minutes to steam. Peel and discard pepper skins. Coarsely chop peppers.

2 In a blender container or food processor bowl combine peppers, oil, garlic, salt, and cumin seeds. Cover and blend or process until smooth. (Store sauce in a covered container in the refrigerator for up to 10 days.)

3 Place bread shell on a preheated baking stone or 12-inch pizza pan. Spread with the red pepper sauce. Bake in the 425° oven for 5 minutes. Top with chicken, green onions, and cheese. Bake 5 minutes more. Top with sour cream, cilantro, and, if desired, avocado and sliced pepper.

Nutrition Facts per serving: 299 cal., 9 g total fat (2 g sat. fat), 28 mg chol., 642 mg sodium, 38 g carbo., 1 g fiber, 18 g pro.
Daily Values: 60% vit. A, 190% vit. C, 16% calcium, 6% iron

oven entrées

213

tortilla-crusted CHICKEN

Crushed tortillas make an irresistible coating for oven-fried chicken. Although chips have a reputation for being high in fat and calories, they lend lots of flavor and crunch, so you need to use only a few.

Prep: 10 minutes
Bake: 25 minutes
Oven: 375°F
Makes: 4 servings

Nonstick cooking spray

1 **cup finely crushed tortilla chips**

½ **teaspoon dried oregano, crushed**

¼ **teaspoon ground cumin**

¼ **teaspoon black pepper**

1 **egg**

4 **skinless, boneless chicken breast halves (1 pound)**

Salsa (optional)

Exchanges: 1 Starch, 4½ Very Lean Meat, 1½ Fat

1 Coat a 15×10×1-inch baking pan with nonstick cooking spray; set aside. In a shallow dish combine tortilla chips, oregano, cumin, and pepper. Place the egg in another shallow dish; beat slightly. Dip chicken in beaten egg and coat with tortilla chip mixture.

2 Arrange chicken in the prepared baking pan. Bake in a 375° oven about 25 minutes or until chicken is no longer pink (170°F). If desired, serve the chicken with salsa.

Nutrition Facts per serving: 305 cal., 10 g total fat (2 g sat. fat), 135 mg chol., 225 mg sodium, 16 g carbo., 2 g fiber, 36 g pro.
Daily Values: 3% vit. A, 2% vit. C, 7% calcium, 9% iron

Turn Up the Heat with Salsa

Salsa is a lot more than a low-fat dip for chips or vegetables. There are countless varieties of salsa, each with its own unique flavor. In addition to the classic tomato–hot pepper salsa, you can try roasted corn, fruit, tomatillo, and many, many others. Adjust the heat level by carefully selecting the kind and amount of hot peppers you use. Consider using salsas as spreads on sandwiches, as garnishes for chicken or pork, or to add flavor to soups.

oven entrées

chicken with MOZZARELLA

This recipe requires that you pound the chicken breasts to flatten them, but take care not to pound them so hard that you tear the flesh, making holes through which the delicious filling can escape.

Prep: 40 minutes
Bake: 25 minutes
Oven: 400°F
Makes: 6 servings

6   skinless, boneless chicken breast halves (1½ pounds)

Salt

Black pepper

¼   cup finely chopped shallots or onion

1   clove garlic, minced

2   teaspoons olive oil

½   of a 10-ounce package frozen chopped spinach, thawed and well drained

3   tablespoons pine nuts or walnuts, toasted

¾   cup shredded smoked mozzarella cheese (3 ounces)

¼   cup seasoned fine dry bread crumbs

¼   cup grated Parmesan cheese

1   tablespoon olive oil

Exchanges: ½ Other Carbo., 4½ Very Lean Meat, ½ Medium-Fat Meat, 1 Fat

1 Place 1 chicken breast half between 2 pieces of plastic wrap. Pound lightly with the flat side of a meat mallet into a rectangle about ⅛ inch thick. Remove plastic wrap. Season with salt and pepper. Repeat with remaining chicken breasts.

2 For filling, in a medium skillet cook shallots and garlic in the 2 teaspoons hot oil until tender. Remove from heat; stir in spinach, nuts, and smoked mozzarella. In a shallow bowl combine bread crumbs and Parmesan cheese.

3 Place 2 to 3 tablespoons of filling on each chicken breast. Fold in the bottom and sides; then roll up. Secure with wooden toothpicks.

4 Lightly brush each roll with the 1 tablespoon olive oil; coat with bread crumb mixture. Place rolls seam side down in a shallow baking pan. Bake, uncovered, in a 400° oven about 25 minutes or until chicken is no longer pink (170°F). Remove toothpicks before serving.

Nutrition Facts per serving: 274 cal., 11 g total fat (3 g sat. fat), 77 mg chol., 368 mg sodium, 6 g carbo., 1 g fiber, 35 g pro.
Daily Values: 39% vit. A, 6% vit. C, 18% calcium, 8% iron

oven entrées

balsamic chicken OVER GREENS

A bed of greens serves as a low-carb alternative to a bed of rice for marinated chicken breasts.

Prep: 15 minutes
Broil: 12 minutes
Marinate: 1 hour
Makes: 4 servings

4 skinless, boneless chicken breast halves (1 pound)

1 cup bottled balsamic vinaigrette salad dressing

3 cloves garlic, minced

¼ teaspoon crushed red pepper

8 cups torn mixed greens

Exchanges: 2 Vegetable, 4 Very Lean Meat, 2 Fat

1 Place chicken breast halves in a self-sealing plastic bag set in a shallow dish. For marinade, stir together ½ cup of the vinaigrette, the garlic, and crushed red pepper. Pour marinade over the chicken; close bag. Marinate in the refrigerator for 1 to 4 hours, turning bag occasionally.

2 Drain chicken, reserving marinade. Place chicken on the unheated rack of a broiler pan. Broil 4 to 5 inches from heat for 12 to 15 minutes or until chicken is no longer pink (170°F), turning once and brushing with marinade halfway through broiling. Discard any remaining marinade.

3 Arrange greens on serving plates. Cut chicken into strips. Place chicken on top of greens. Serve with remaining vinaigrette.

Nutrition Facts per serving: 284 cal., 13 g total fat (2 g sat. fat), 82 mg chol., 525 mg sodium, 7 g carbo., 1 g fiber, 34 g pro.
Daily Values: 21% vit. A, 14% vit. C, 6% calcium, 8% iron

oven entrées

nut-crusted TURKEY BREAST

Diners won't miss turkey drumsticks when they have slices of this aromatic roast on their plates. Many cooks find roasting a breast portion more manageable than cooking a whole bird.

Prep: 20 minutes
Roast: 1 hour
Stand: 15 minutes
Oven: 375°F
Makes: 8 to 10 servings

- 1   3- to 3½-pound turkey breast half with bone
- 1   tablespoon olive oil or cooking oil
- 1   clove garlic, minced
- ¼   teaspoon salt
- ⅓   cup slivered almonds
- ⅓   cup pine nuts or slivered almonds
- 1   teaspoon ground coriander
- ¼   teaspoon ground cinnamon
- ¼   teaspoon coarsely ground black pepper
- ¼   cup sugar-free orange marmalade

oven entrées

Exchanges: ½ Other Carbo., 5½ Very Lean Meat, 1 Fat

1 Remove skin from turkey breast. Place turkey breast on a lightly greased rack in a shallow roasting pan. Combine oil, garlic, and salt. Brush over turkey breast. Insert a meat thermometer into the thickest part of the breast; thermometer should not touch bone. Roast, uncovered, in a 375° oven for 30 minutes.

2 Meanwhile, in a blender container or food processor bowl blend or process almonds and pine nuts until finely chopped. In a small bowl stir together the nuts, coriander, cinnamon, and black pepper. Set aside.

3 Remove turkey breast from oven. Brush surface with orange marmalade; sprinkle nut mixture over the turkey, pressing gently so nuts adhere. Continue roasting, uncovered, for 30 to 45 minutes longer or until meat thermometer registers 170°F. Remove from oven.

4 Let the turkey stand about 15 minutes before slicing.

Make-ahead directions: Prepare nut mixture up to 1 day before using. Place in a small bowl; cover and store at room temperature.

Nutrition Facts per serving: 321 cal., 18 g total fat (4 g sat. fat), 99 mg chol., 141 mg sodium, 5 g carbo., 1 g fiber, 36 g pro.
Daily Values: 5% calcium, 15% iron

turkey breast WITH ASPARAGUS

Remember this recipe when spring's first tender shoots of asparagus begin to appear. You'll love the perfect pairing of tarragon and Dijon mustard and the bright, vibrant colors of the asparagus, parsley, and red peppers.

Prep: 30 minutes
Roast: 1½ hours
Stand: 10 minutes
Oven: 325°F
Makes: 10 to 12 servings

¼ **cup butter or margarine, softened**

2 **teaspoons Dijon-style mustard**

¾ **teaspoon dried tarragon, crushed**

¼ **teaspoon salt**

⅛ **teaspoon black pepper**

2 **1¼- to 1½-pound boneless turkey breast halves (with skin on)**

1 **7-ounce jar roasted red sweet peppers, drained and coarsely chopped**

½ **cup snipped fresh parsley**

1½ **pounds asparagus spears, trimmed**

1 **tablespoon olive oil**

¼ **teaspoon salt**

Exchanges: 4 Lean Meat

1 In a small bowl combine softened butter, mustard, tarragon, ¼ teaspoon salt, and black pepper; set aside.

2 Remove skin from turkey; set skin aside. Lay one turkey breast half boned side up on work surface. Make 4 or 5 shallow cuts in thickest part of the breast (do not cut through). Place turkey breast between 2 pieces of plastic wrap. Using the flat side of a meat mallet, lightly pound turkey breast to a uniform ¾-inch thickness. Remove plastic wrap. Repeat with the remaining turkey breast half. Dot turkey with half of the butter mixture; set the remaining mixture aside. Top turkey evenly with roasted peppers and parsley. Starting from a short side, roll up each turkey breast into a spiral. Wrap the reserved skin around each roll; tie with 100-percent-cotton string. Place on a rack in a shallow roasting pan.

3 Melt the remaining butter mixture; brush over surface of turkey. Insert a meat thermometer into center of one of the turkey rolls. Roast in a 325° oven for 1½ to 1¾ hours or until turkey is no longer pink (170°F).

4 Meanwhile, in a large bowl toss together asparagus, oil, and ¼ teaspoon salt. Place asparagus in the roasting pan next to turkey the last 15 to 20 minutes of roasting.

5 Cover turkey and asparagus with foil and let stand for 10 to 15 minutes before slicing. Serve turkey with roasted asparagus.

Nutrition Facts per serving: 245 cal., 14 g total fat (5 g sat. fat), 86 mg chol., 247 mg sodium, 2 g carbo., 1 g fiber, 27 g pro.
Daily Values: 8% vit. A, 91% vit. C, 3% calcium, 11% iron

oven entrées

salmon-vegetable PACKETS

The packets go straight from the oven to the dinner plate. It's easy enough for any day of the week.

Prep: 25 minutes
Bake: 30 minutes
Oven: 350°F
Makes: 4 servings

4 **4-ounce fresh or frozen skinless salmon fillets, ¾ inch thick**

2 **cups thinly bias-sliced carrots**

2 **cups sliced fresh mushrooms**

4 **green onions, sliced**

2 **teaspoons finely shredded orange peel**

2 **teaspoons snipped fresh oregano or ½ teaspoon dried oregano, crushed**

4 **cloves garlic, halved**

¼ **teaspoon salt**

¼ **teaspoon black pepper**

4 **teaspoons olive oil**

2 **medium oranges, thinly sliced**

4 **sprigs fresh oregano (optional)**

Exchanges: 1 Vegetable, ½ Fruit, 1½ Lean Meat

1 Thaw fish, if frozen. Rinse fish; pat dry with paper towels. Set aside. In a small saucepan cook carrots, covered, in a small amount of boiling water for 2 minutes. Drain and set aside. Tear off four 24-inch pieces of heavy foil. Fold each in half to make an 18×12-inch rectangle.

2 In a large bowl combine carrots, mushrooms, green onions, orange peel, oregano, garlic, salt, and pepper. Divide vegetable mixture among foil rectangles.

3 Place fish on top of the vegetable mixture. Drizzle fish with oil; sprinkle lightly with additional salt and pepper. Top with orange slices and, if desired, oregano sprigs. For each packet, bring up 2 opposite edges of foil and seal with a double fold. Fold remaining ends to completely enclose the food, allowing space for steam to build. Place the foil packets in a single layer in a large baking pan.

4 Bake in a 350° oven about 30 minutes or until fish flakes easily when tested with a fork and carrots are tender. Transfer the packets to dinner plates. Open slowly to allow steam to escape.

Nutrition Facts per serving: 226 cal., 9 g total fat (1 g sat. fat), 20 mg chol., 288 mg sodium, 19 g carbo., 5 g fiber, 19 g pro.
Daily Values: 198% vit. A, 71% vit. C, 6% calcium, 14% iron

salmon with TROPICAL RICE

The key here is the complex flavor of coriander seeds—a cross between caraway and sage, with a lemon bite. Because it takes so little time to snip, shred, and crush the ingredients in this recipe, put the rice on to cook first.

Start to Finish: 30 minutes
Oven: 450°F
Makes: 4 servings

- 1 **1½-pound fresh or frozen salmon fillet**
- 2 **tablespoons coriander seeds, coarsely crushed**
- 1 **tablespoon packed brown sugar**
- 1 **teaspoon lemon-pepper seasoning**
- 1 **tablespoon butter or margarine, melted**
- 2 **cups cooked rice**
- 1 **medium mango, seeded, peeled, and chopped**
- 1 **tablespoon snipped fresh cilantro**
- 1 **teaspoon finely shredded lemon peel**

Exchanges: ½ Fruit, 1½ Starch, 3½ Lean Meat, ½ Fat

1 Thaw salmon, if frozen. Rinse fish; pat dry with paper towels. Measure thickness of fish. Place fish skin side down in a greased shallow baking pan.

2 In a small bowl stir together coriander seeds, brown sugar, and lemon-pepper seasoning. Brush top and sides of fish with melted butter. Sprinkle fish with coriander mixture, pressing in slightly.

3 Stir together rice, mango, cilantro, and lemon peel. Spoon rice mixture around fish. Bake, uncovered, in a 450° oven for 4 to 6 minutes per ½-inch thickness of fish or until fish flakes easily when tested with a fork.

4 To serve, cut fish into 4 serving-size pieces. Serve fish on top of rice mixture.

Nutrition Facts per serving: 384 cal., 10 g total fat (3 g sat. fat), 96 mg chol., 421 mg sodium, 36 g carbo., 3 g fiber, 37 g pro.
Daily Values: 47% vit. A, 28% vit. C, 6% calcium, 17% iron

oven entrées

vegetable-topped FISH

Salsa and summer squash make a tasty but amazingly easy sauce for baked fillets.

Start to Finish: 15 minutes
Oven: 450°F
Makes: 4 servings

1 **pound fresh or frozen fish fillets**

2 **teaspoons butter or margarine, melted**

⅛ **teaspoon salt**

⅛ **teaspoon black pepper**

1 **8-ounce jar (about 1 cup) salsa**

1 **small yellow summer squash or zucchini, halved lengthwise and cut into ¼-inch slices**

Exchanges: ½ Vegetable, 3 Very Lean Meat

① Thaw fish, if frozen. Rinse fish and pat dry. Measure thickness of fish. Place fish in a greased shallow baking pan, tucking under any thin edges. Brush fish with melted butter. Sprinkle with salt and pepper. Bake, uncovered, in a 450° oven until fish flakes easily when tested with a fork (allow 4 to 6 minutes per ½-inch thickness).

② Meanwhile, in a small saucepan stir together salsa and summer squash. Bring to boiling; reduce heat. Cover and simmer for 5 to 6 minutes or until squash is crisp-tender. Serve squash mixture over fish.

Nutrition Facts per serving: 131 cal., 3 g total fat (0 g sat. fat), 48 mg chol., 403 mg sodium, 5 g carbo., 1 g fiber, 22 g pro.
Daily Values: 10% vit. A, 21% vit. C, 4% calcium, 6% iron

oven entrées

223

GREAT FOR KIDS

corn and tomato PUDDING

The classic bread pudding dessert is reinvented as a luscious meatless main course. If using the French bread option, choose only firm, dry bread—fresh bread is too soft to soak up the milk and eggs and hold its shape.

Prep: 20 minutes
Bake: 30 minutes
Oven: 375°F
Makes: 6 servings

- **3 tablespoons snipped dried tomatoes (not oil-packed)**
- **4 eggs**
- **1½ cups milk**
- **1 tablespoon snipped fresh basil or 1 teaspoon dried basil, crushed**
- **4 cups torn whole wheat English muffins or dry French bread**
- **1½ cups fresh or frozen whole kernel corn**
- **1 cup shredded reduced-fat cheddar cheese or Monterey Jack cheese with jalapeño pepper (4 ounces)**
- **Thin tomato wedges (optional)**

Exchanges: 2 Starch, 1½ Medium-Fat Meat

1 In a small bowl soak the dried tomatoes in enough hot water to cover for 10 minutes; drain.

2 Meanwhile, in a medium bowl beat together eggs, milk, and basil; set aside. In a 2-quart square baking dish toss together drained tomatoes, torn English muffins, corn, and cheese.

3 Carefully pour egg mixture evenly over the muffin mixture. Bake in a 375° oven about 30 minutes or until a knife inserted near center comes out clean. Cool slightly. If desired, serve on top of tomato wedges.

Note: You'll need about 5 cups fresh bread cubes to make 4 cups dry cubes. Cut bread into ½-inch slices; cut into cubes. Spread in a single layer in a shallow baking pan. Bake in a 300°F oven for 10 to 15 minutes or until dry, stirring twice; cool. (Bread will continue to dry and crisp as it cools.) Or let bread cubes stand, loosely covered, at room temperature for 8 to 12 hours.

Nutrition Facts per serving: 268 cal., 9 g total fat (4 g sat. fat), 160 mg chol., 393 mg sodium, 31 g carbo., 3 g fiber, 17 g pro.
Daily Values: 10% vit. A, 7% vit. C, 30% calcium, 11% iron

Dairy Differences

While different dairy liquids cause slight texture changes in foods, the biggest differences are the fat and calories they'll contribute to your recipe. One cup of whole milk has 150 calories and 8 grams of fat. The same amount of 2 percent milk contains 120 calories and 5 grams of fat; 1 percent has 100 calories, 2.5 grams of fat; and skim or fat-free milk has just 80 calories and no fat. An equal amount of half-and-half has 320 calories and 32 grams of fat, and light cream has a whopping 480 calories and 48 grams of fat in 1 cup.

oven entrées

crustless cheese QUICHE

By omitting the pastry crust from this healthful quiche recipe, you can cut 9 grams of fat and 141 calories per serving. The feta and cheddar cheeses lend tangy flavor and smooth texture.

Prep: 20 minutes
Bake: 40 minutes
Stand: 5 minutes
Oven: 350°F
Makes: 8 servings

Nonstick cooking spray

1 **cup refrigerated or frozen egg product, thawed**

⅓ **cup whole wheat pastry flour**

¼ **teaspoon black pepper**

⅛ **teaspoon salt**

1½ **cups low-fat cottage cheese (12 ounces), drained**

1 **10-ounce package frozen chopped broccoli, cooked and drained**

1 **cup crumbled feta cheese (4 ounces)**

1 **cup shredded reduced-fat cheddar cheese (4 ounces)**

Exchanges: ½ Other Carbo., 2 Lean Meat

1 Lightly coat a 9-inch pie plate with nonstick cooking spray; set aside.

2 In a medium bowl combine egg product, flour, pepper, and salt. Stir in cottage cheese, broccoli, feta cheese, and cheddar cheese. Spoon into prepared pie plate.

3 Bake in a 350° oven for 40 to 45 minutes or until a knife inserted near center comes out clean. Cool on a wire rack for 5 to 10 minutes before serving.

Nutrition Facts per serving: 158 cal., 6 g total fat (4 g sat. fat), 26 mg chol., 531 mg sodium, 8 g carbo., 1 g fiber, 16 g pro.
Daily Values: 23% vit. A, 24% vit. C, 23% calcium, 6% iron

oven entrées

desserts
& TREATS

Even in the healthiest of diets, you crave a little something sweet. A small bite of chocolate or some berries with smooth, luscious cream are sometimes all you need. And now, with an array of sugar substitutes available, low-sugar and sugar-free desserts are even easier to make.

Mocha Soufflé, *recipe page 229*

chocolate BREAD PUDDING

And you thought bread pudding couldn't get any better. Go ahead and dip into this light but luxurious finale.

Prep: 15 minutes
Bake: 15 minutes
Cool: 10 minutes
Oven: 350°F
Makes: 2 servings

Nonstick cooking spray

1 **cup firm-texture white bread cubes (from about 1¼ slices of Italian or sourdough bread)**

2 **tablespoons miniature semisweet chocolate pieces**

2 **tablespoons sugar**

⅓ **cup fat-free milk**

3 **tablespoons refrigerated or frozen egg product, thawed, or 1 egg**

½ **teaspoon finely shredded orange peel or tangerine peel**

¼ **teaspoon vanilla**

Sifted powdered sugar or fat-free whipped dessert topping (optional)

Exchanges: 2 Other Carbo., ½ Fat

1 Lightly coat two 6-ounce soufflé dishes or custard cups with nonstick cooking spray. Divide bread cubes between dishes.

2 Combine chocolate, sugar, and milk in a small saucepan. Stir over low heat until the chocolate melts; remove from heat. Beat smooth with a wire whisk, if necessary.

3 Place egg product in a small bowl; gradually stir in the chocolate mixture. Add orange peel and vanilla. Pour mixture over bread in the dishes. Press lightly with back of spoon to thoroughly moisten bread. (If desired, cover and refrigerate desserts for 1 to 2 hours before baking. Uncover before baking.)

4 Bake in a 350° oven for 15 to 20 minutes or until the tops appear firm and a knife inserted near centers comes out clean. Cool about 10 minutes; serve warm. If desired, top with powdered sugar.

Nutrition Facts per serving: 163 cal., 4 g total fat (0 g sat. fat), 1 mg chol., 125 mg sodium, 29 g carbo., 0 g fiber, 5 g pro.
Daily Values: 13% vit. A, 1% vit. C, 6% calcium, 7% iron

desserts & treats

mocha SOUFFLÉ

The classic combination of cocoa powder and coffee flavors this light-as-air soufflé.

Prep: 40 minutes
Bake: 15 minutes
Oven: 375°F
Makes: 4 servings

- 4   **egg whites**
- 3   **tablespoons sugar**
- 2   **tablespoons unsweetened cocoa powder**
- 4   **teaspoons cornstarch**
- 1   **teaspoon instant coffee crystals**
- ⅔   **cup evaporated fat-free milk**
- 2   **teaspoons vanilla**
- ¼   **teaspoon cream of tartar**

Exchanges: ½ Milk, 1 Other Carbo., ½ Very Lean Meat, ½ Fat

1 Allow egg whites to stand at room temperature for 30 minutes.

2 Meanwhile, in a small saucepan combine sugar, cocoa powder, cornstarch, and coffee crystals. Stir in milk all at once. Cook and stir over medium heat until bubbly. Remove from heat. Stir in vanilla. Pour into a small bowl. Cover surface of mixture with plastic wrap. Set aside.

3 In a medium bowl beat egg whites and cream of tartar with an electric mixer on medium speed until stiff peaks form (tips stand straight). Fold about one-fourth of the beaten egg whites into chocolate mixture to lighten. Fold in remaining beaten egg whites. Gently pour into 4 ungreased 1-cup soufflé dishes. Place soufflé dishes in a shallow baking pan.

4 Bake in a 375° oven for 15 to 20 minutes or until a knife inserted near centers comes out clean. Serve immediately.

Nutrition Facts per serving: 136 cal., 4 g total fat (2 g sat. fat), 12 mg chol., 100 mg sodium, 18 g carbo., 0 g fiber, 7 g pro.
Daily Values: 2% vit. A, 1% vit. C, 14% calcium, 3% iron

desserts & treats

chocolate chip COOKIES

With this reduced-sugar recipe there's no need to deprive yourself or your family of this beloved snack.

Prep: 25 minutes
Bake: 8 minutes per batch
Oven: 375°F
Makes: about 40 cookies

½ **cup shortening**

½ **cup butter, softened**

¾ **cup no-calorie, heat-stable granular sugar substitute**

½ **cup packed brown sugar**

½ **teaspoon baking soda**

  Dash salt

2 **eggs**

2 **teaspoons vanilla**

2¼ **cups all-purpose flour**

6 **ounces bittersweet chocolate, coarsely chopped**

Exchanges: 1 Other Carbo., 1½ Fat

❶ In a large mixing bowl beat shortening and butter with an electric mixer on medium to high speed for 30 seconds. Add sugar substitute, brown sugar, baking soda, and salt. Beat until combined, scraping sides of bowl occasionally. Beat in eggs and vanilla until combined. Beat in as much of the flour as you can with the mixer. Stir in any remaining flour. Stir in chocolate.

❷ Drop dough by rounded teaspoons 2 inches apart onto an ungreased cookie sheet. Bake in a 375° oven about 8 minutes or until edges are lightly browned. Transfer cookies to a wire rack; cool.

Nutrition Facts per cookie: 106 cal., 7 g total fat (3 g sat. fat), 17 mg chol., 49 mg sodium, 11 g carbo., 1 g fiber, 1 g pro.
Daily Values: 3% vit. A, 1% vit. C, 2% calcium, 4% iron

desserts & treats

cocoa SNICKERDOODLES

This is a deliciously lightened version of the familiar old-fashioned cookies with the crinkled tops.

Prep: 25 minutes
Chill: 1 hour
Bake: 10 minutes per batch
Oven: 375°F
Makes: about 48 cookies

⅓ **cup butter, softened**

1 **cup sugar**

1 **teaspoon baking powder**

½ **teaspoon ground nutmeg**

¼ **teaspoon baking soda**

⅓ **cup fat-free dairy sour cream**

1 **slightly beaten egg**

1 **teaspoon vanilla**

2 **cups all-purpose flour**

  Nonstick cooking spray

2 **tablespoons sugar**

1½ **teaspoons unsweetened cocoa powder**

Exchanges: 1 Fat

❶ In a large bowl beat butter with an electric mixer on medium to high speed for 30 seconds. Add the 1 cup sugar, the baking powder, nutmeg, and baking soda; beat until combined. Beat in sour cream, egg, and vanilla until combined. Beat in as much of the flour as you can with the mixer. Stir in any remaining flour with a wooden spoon. Cover and refrigerate for 1 to 2 hours or until dough is easy to handle.

❷ Lightly coat a cookie sheet with nonstick cooking spray; set aside. In a small bowl combine the 2 tablespoons sugar and the cocoa powder. Shape dough into 1-inch balls. Roll balls in cocoa mixture to coat. Place balls 2 inches apart on the prepared cookie sheet.

❸ Bake in a 375° oven for 10 to 11 minutes or until edges are golden brown. Transfer cookies to a wire rack; cool.

Nutrition Facts per cookie: 51 cal., 1 g total fat (1 g sat. fat), 8 mg chol., 30 mg sodium, 9 g carbo., 0 g fiber, 1 g pro.
Daily Values: 1% vit. A, 1% calcium, 1% iron

desserts & treats

devil's FOOD COOKIES

These chocolate lovers' delights have only 2 grams of fat and 12 carbs. Use them to satisfy your next craving.

Prep: 15 minutes
Bake: 7 minutes per batch
Cool: 1 minute per batch
Oven: 350°F
Makes: about 24 cookies

Nonstick cooking spray

1½ **cups all-purpose flour**

⅓ **cup unsweetened cocoa powder**

1 **teaspoon baking soda**

⅛ **teaspoon salt**

¼ **cup butter, softened**

⅔ **cup packed brown sugar**

½ **cup buttermilk or sour milk***

¼ **cup refrigerated or frozen egg product, thawed, or 2 egg whites**

1 **teaspoon vanilla**

1 **tablespoon sifted powdered sugar**

Exchanges: 1 Other Carbo., ½ Fat

❶ Lightly coat a cookie sheet with nonstick cooking spray; set aside. In a small bowl stir together flour, cocoa powder, baking soda, and salt; set aside.

❷ In a medium mixing bowl beat butter with an electric mixer on medium to high speed for 30 seconds. Add brown sugar. Beat until combined, scraping sides of bowl occasionally. Beat in buttermilk, egg product, and vanilla until combined. Beat in as much of the flour mixture as you can with the mixer. Stir in any remaining flour mixture with a wooden spoon.

❸ Drop dough by rounded tablespoons onto prepared cookie sheet. Bake in a 350° oven for 7 to 9 minutes or until nearly firm. Cool on cookie sheet for 1 minute. Transfer cookies to a wire rack; cool. Sprinkle cookies with powdered sugar.

*Note: To make ½ cup sour milk, place 1½ teaspoons lemon juice or vinegar in a glass measuring cup. Add enough fat-free milk to make ½ cup total liquid; stir. Let stand 5 minutes before using.

Nutrition Facts per cookie: 73 cal., 2 g total fat (1 g sat. fat), 5 mg chol., 99 mg sodium, 12 g carbo., 1 g fiber, 1 g pro.
Daily Values: 2% vit. A, 2% calcium, 4% iron

Don't Deprive Yourself

Often healthy eating is associated with the elimination of favorite foods. These tend to be the foods we think of as treats or extras—desserts and munchies—and typically foods with less nutritional value. But going cold turkey may not be the best plan. Eliminating favorite foods leads to feelings of deprivation, which lead to binge eating. Instead find ways to make the treats fit your diet, whether that means adjusting recipes or eating these foods in smaller amounts and less frequently. The result is healthier eating without depriving yourself of your favorite foods—a much more realistic way to succeed.

yo-yos

Like the toy, this goodie has two outsides with something in between: in this case, chocolate and sorbet. Play with different flavor options.

Prep: 30 minutes
Freeze: 1 hour
Makes: 12 cookie sandwiches

¼ **cup semisweet chocolate pieces**

¼ **teaspoon shortening**

24 **amaretti cookies (4.6 ounces total) or vanilla wafers**

⅓ **cup mango, orange, lemon, or raspberry sorbet**

Exchanges: 1½ Fat

1 In a heavy small saucepan heat chocolate pieces and shortening over low heat just until melted. Cool slightly. Using a narrow metal spatula, spread about 1 teaspoon chocolate mixture on the flat side of half of the cookies. Place coated cookies, chocolate side up, on a wire rack until chocolate mixture is set.

2 Using a melon baller, place a small scoop of sorbet (about 1 rounded teaspoon) on top of chocolate side of each coated cookie. Dip the melon baller into water between scoops to make the scoops come out neatly. Top sorbet with another cookie to make a sandwich. Cover and freeze for 1 to 4 hours.

Nutrition Facts per cookie sandwich: 71 cal., 2 g total fat (0 g sat. fat), 6 mg chol., 7 mg sodium, 12 g carbo., 0 g fiber, 1 g pro.
Daily Values: 1% vit. C, 1% iron

desserts & treats

chocolate CHEESECAKE BARS

Chocolate polka-dotted tops and chocolaty crusts complement a creamy vanilla foundation.

Prep: 30 minutes
Bake: 20 minutes
Cool: 1 hour
Chill: 2 hours
Oven: 350°F
Makes: 32 bars

- **2 cups finely crushed chocolate wafers (about 36) or chocolate graham crackers (about 24 squares)**
- **3 tablespoons butter, melted**
- **2 tablespoons water**
- **2 8-ounce packages reduced-fat cream cheese (Neufchâtel), softened**
- **1 cup fat-free ricotta cheese**
- **¾ cup no-calorie, heat-stable granular sugar substitute**
- **2 tablespoons sugar**
- **2 tablespoons all-purpose flour**
- **¼ cup fat-free milk**
- **2 teaspoons vanilla**
- **3 slightly beaten eggs**
- **¼ cup miniature semisweet chocolate pieces**

Exchanges: ½ Other Carbo., 1 Fat

❶ Line a 13×9×2-inch baking pan with foil, extending foil over edges of pan. Grease the foil; set pan aside. For crust, in a medium bowl combine crushed wafers, melted butter, and water. Press crumb mixture evenly into the bottom of prepared baking pan; set aside.

❷ For filling, in a large mixing bowl beat cream cheese, ricotta cheese, sugar substitute, sugar, and flour with an electric mixer on low speed until smooth. Beat in milk and vanilla. Stir in eggs just until combined. Pour cream cheese mixture over the crust, spreading evenly. Sprinkle with chocolate pieces.

❸ Bake in a 350° oven for 20 to 25 minutes or until top is set. Cool in pan on a wire rack. Cover and chill for at least 2 hours before serving. Use foil to lift cheesecake from pan. Cut into bars.

Nutrition Facts per bar: 105 cal., 6 g total fat (3 g sat. fat), 32 mg chol., 128 mg sodium, 10 g carbo., 0 g fiber, 4 g pro.
Daily Values: 5% vit. A, 1% vit. C, 7% calcium, 5% iron

desserts & treats

vanilla BEAN BISCOTTI

The extra effort it takes to use the vanilla bean is handsomely rewarded in flavor. Easier to make than you think, these cookie sticks are a great accompaniment to a dish of fresh fruit or a steaming cup of coffee.

Prep: 30 minutes
Bake: 45 minutes
Cool: 15 minutes
Oven: 325°F
Makes: 48 cookies

1 vanilla bean, split, or
    2 teaspoons vanilla extract
3 cups all-purpose flour
1 tablespoon baking powder
¼ teaspoon salt
3 eggs
¾ cup sugar
½ cup butter, melted and cooled

Exchanges: ½ Other Carbo., ½ Fat

❶ Grease a very large cookie sheet; set aside. Scrape seeds from vanilla bean, if using; set seeds aside.

❷ In a medium bowl combine flour, baking powder, and salt; set aside. In a large mixing bowl beat eggs with an electric mixer on high speed for 1 minute. Gradually beat in sugar, beating on high speed for 1 minute. Beat in butter and vanilla seeds or vanilla extract on low speed until combined. Beat in as much of the flour mixture as you can with the mixer. Stir in any remaining flour mixture with a wooden spoon.

❸ Divide dough into thirds. On a lightly floured surface, shape each portion into a 14×1½-inch log. Place logs 2½ inches apart on the prepared cookie sheet.

❹ Bake in a 325° oven for 25 minutes or until firm and lightly browned. Cool on cookie sheet on a wire rack for 15 minutes.

❺ Transfer each log to a large cutting board. With a serrated knife, gently cut each log diagonally into ½-inch slices. Arrange slices cut side down on the cookie sheet.

❻ Bake slices for 10 minutes. Turn slices and bake 10 minutes more or until crisp and lightly browned. Cool on the cookie sheet on a wire rack.

Nutrition Facts per cookie: 63 cal., 2 g total fat (1 g sat. fat), 19 mg chol., 62 mg sodium, 9 g carbo., 0 g fiber, 1 g pro.
Daily Values: 2% vit. A, 2% calcium, 2% iron

desserts & treats

date BARS

To lessen the temptation to eat more than you should from this big batch, wrap and freeze half of the bars after they're baked and cooled.

Prep: 25 minutes
Bake: 15 minutes
Oven: 350°F
Makes: about 24 bars

½ **cup boiling water**

⅓ **cup snipped pitted whole dates**

Nonstick cooking spray

½ **cup all-purpose flour**

½ **teaspoon baking powder**

¼ **teaspoon ground cinnamon**

⅛ **teaspoon baking soda**

1 **egg**

⅓ **cup packed brown sugar**

⅓ **cup evaporated fat-free milk**

2 **tablespoons finely chopped walnuts, toasted**

1 **teaspoon sifted powdered sugar**

Exchanges: ½ Other Carbo.

1 In a small bowl combine the boiling water and dates. Cover and let stand for 10 minutes. Drain.

2 Coat an 8×8×2-inch baking pan with nonstick cooking spray; set aside. In a small bowl combine flour, baking powder, cinnamon, and baking soda; set aside.

3 In a medium mixing bowl beat egg with an electric mixer on high speed until frothy. Add brown sugar; beat until combined. Stir in evaporated milk and drained dates.

4 Add flour mixture to egg mixture, stirring with a wooden spoon until combined. Stir in nuts. Pour batter into prepared baking pan.

5 Bake in a 350° oven about 15 minutes or until a wooden toothpick inserted near center comes out clean. Cool in pan on a wire rack. Sprinkle with powdered sugar. Cut into bars.

Nutrition Facts per bar: 40 cal., 1 g total fat (0 g sat. fat), 9 mg chol., 21 mg sodium, 8 g carbo., 0 g fiber, 1 g pro.
Daily Values: 2% calcium, 1% iron

Dried Fruits

Years ago the only dried fruits you would find in stores were raisins, prunes, and dates. Today you can find everything from dried cherries and cranberries to dried apples and mangoes. Use dried fruit to flavor baked goods, salads, oatmeal, and more. With the wide variety of choices, the possibilities are endless. Use a light hand: The drying process causes the sugars to become much more concentrated, and you don't want to go overboard. Keep your portions small.

desserts & treats

carrot SNACK CAKE

Usually you find carrot cake under a slathering of cream cheese frosting. Here powdered sugar steps in, cutting back on fat and calories.

Prep: 15 minutes
Bake: 30 minutes
Oven: 350°F
Makes: 12 servings

Nonstick cooking spray
1 **cup all-purpose flour**
¾ **cup granulated sugar**
1½ **teaspoons apple pie spice**
½ **teaspoon baking powder**
½ **teaspoon baking soda**
⅛ **teaspoon salt**
1 **cup finely shredded carrot**
⅓ **cup cooking oil**
¼ **cup low-fat milk**
3 **egg whites**
1 **teaspoon sifted powdered sugar**
   Fresh raspberries (optional)

Exchanges: 1½ Other Carbo., 1 Fat

1 Lightly coat an 8×8×2-inch baking pan with nonstick cooking spray. Set aside.

2 In a large bowl combine flour, granulated sugar, apple pie spice, baking powder, baking soda, and salt. Add carrot, oil, and milk. Stir to moisten. In a medium mixing bowl beat egg whites with an electric mixer on medium to high speed until stiff peaks form (tips stand straight). Fold egg whites into carrot mixture.

3 Pour batter into the prepared pan. Bake in a 350° oven for 30 to 35 minutes or until a wooden toothpick inserted near center comes out clean. Cool completely in pan on a wire rack.

4 To serve, sprinkle with powdered sugar and, if desired, garnish with raspberries.

Nutrition Facts per serving: 147 cal., 6 g total fat (1 g sat. fat), 0 mg chol., 114 mg sodium, 21 g carbo., 1 g fiber, 2 g pro.
Daily Values: 57% vit. A, 2% vit. C, 3% calcium, 4% iron

autumn APPLE FRITTERS

Whether you enjoy them for dessert or as a snack, these crispy no-fuss fritters hit the spot.

Start to Finish: 20 minutes
Makes: 12 fritters

- **2 medium tart cooking apples (such as Jonathan or Granny Smith)**
- **⅔ cup all-purpose flour**
- **1 tablespoon powdered sugar**
- **½ teaspoon finely shredded lemon peel**
- **¼ teaspoon baking powder**
- **1 egg**
- **½ cup milk**
- **1 teaspoon cooking oil**
  Shortening or cooking oil for deep-fat frying
  Powdered sugar (optional)

Exchanges: ½ Other Carbo., 1 Fat

1 Core apples and cut each crosswise into 6 rings. In a medium bowl combine flour, the 1 tablespoon powdered sugar, the lemon peel, and baking powder.

2 In a bowl use a wire whisk to combine egg, milk, and the 1 teaspoon cooking oil. Add egg mixture all at once to flour mixture; beat until smooth.

3 Using a fork, dip apple rings into batter; drain off excess batter. Fry 2 or 3 rings at a time in deep hot fat (365°F) about 2 minutes or until golden, turning once with a slotted spoon. Drain on paper towels. Repeat with remaining apple rings. If desired, sprinkle fritters with additional powdered sugar. Cool on wire racks.

Nutrition Facts per fritter: 91 cal., 5 g total fat (1 g sat. fat), 19 mg chol., 19 mg sodium, 9 g carbo., 1 g fiber, 2 g pro.
Daily Values: 1% vit. A, 3% vit. C, 2% calcium, 2% iron

desserts & treats

cannoli fruit TARTS

A spin on the traditional cannoli, these phyllo tarts feature the coveted ricotta filling.

Start to Finish: 15 minutes
Makes: 15 servings

⅔ **cup fat-free ricotta cheese**

**Sugar substitute to equal
   2 tablespoons sugar**

½ **teaspoon vanilla**

⅛ **teaspoon ground cinnamon**

2 **tablespoons miniature
   semisweet chocolate pieces**

1 **2.1-ounce package mini
   phyllo tart shells (15)**

15 **small strawberry halves or
   small raspberries**

Exchanges: ½ Other Carbo.

① In a small bowl stir together ricotta, sugar substitute, vanilla, and cinnamon. Stir in chocolate pieces. Divide ricotta mixture among tart shells. Top with fruit. Serve immediately or chill up to 2 hours before serving.

Nutrition Facts per serving: 45 cal., 2 g total fat (0 g sat. fat), 1 mg chol., 32 mg sodium, 5 g carbo., 0 g fiber, 2 g pro.
Daily Values: 1% vit. A, 6% vit. C, 5% calcium, 2% iron

desserts & treats

tiramisu CUPS

This lightened version of the popular Italian-inspired dessert is a snap to make at home.

Prep: 20 minutes
Chill: 1 hour
Makes: 4 servings

½ of a 3-ounce package
   ladyfingers, cubed
   (12 halves)

¼ cup espresso or strong coffee

¼ of an 8-ounce package
   reduced-fat cream cheese
   (Neufchâtel), softened

½ cup light dairy sour cream

   Sugar substitute to equal
   3 tablespoons sugar

1 teaspoon vanilla

½ teaspoon unsweetened cocoa
   powder

Exchanges: ½ Starch, ½ Medium-Fat Meat, 1 Fat

❶ Divide half of the ladyfinger cubes among four 4- to 6-ounce dessert dishes. Drizzle ladyfinger cubes with half of the espresso. Set aside.

❷ In a medium bowl stir cream cheese to soften. Stir in sour cream, sugar substitute, and vanilla. (Beat smooth with a wire whisk, if necessary.) Spoon half of the cream cheese mixture over ladyfinger cubes. Add remaining ladyfinger cubes and drizzle with remaining espresso. Cover and chill for 1 to 24 hours. Just before serving, top with remaining cream cheese mixture and sprinkle with cocoa powder.

Nutrition Facts per serving: 124 cal., 8 g total fat (5 g sat. fat), 61 mg chol., 85 mg sodium, 9 g carbo., 0 g fiber, 3 g pro.
Daily Values: 9% vit. A, 3% vit. C, 7% calcium, 5% iron

desserts & treats

247

mixed berry TRIFLE CAKES

Good things happen when the English trifle meets the all-American shortcake. Use any berries you like in this beautiful, bountiful dessert, but a combination of two or three kinds is best.

Start to Finish: 20 minutes
Makes: 8 servings

- **2 4.5-ounce packages individual shortcake cups (8 cups)**
- **2 tablespoons sugar-free apricot preserves**
- **2 tablespoons orange juice**
- **1 6-ounce carton vanilla fat-free yogurt with sweetener**
- **½ teaspoon vanilla**
- **¼ of an 8-ounce container frozen light whipped dessert topping, thawed**
- **1½ cups mixed fresh berries such as sliced strawberries, blueberries, raspberries, and/or blackberries**

Exchanges: 2 Other Carbo.

1 Arrange shortcake cups on a serving platter; set aside. In a small bowl stir together preserves and orange juice. Spoon some of the mixture over each shortcake cup. In another small bowl stir together yogurt and vanilla. Fold in whipped topping. Spoon yogurt mixture onto cake over preserves mixture. Top with berries.

Nutrition Facts per serving: 153 cal., 3 g total fat (1 g sat. fat), 15 mg chol., 13 mg sodium, 28 g carbo., 1 g fiber, 2 g pro.
Daily Values: 1% vit. A, 21% vit. C, 4% calcium, 3% iron

More Flavor

Fat-free, sugar-free yogurts are great multipurpose ingredients in healthy cooking. In addition to the flavor they provide, they add creaminess and moisture to recipes, both of which can be lost when fat is taken out. And, without much extra calories or fat, these yogurts add a protein and calcium boost. Vanilla and plain yogurts are neutral and mix well with any recipe, but why not get creative? Try a berry-flavor yogurt in this trifle recipe or coffee-flavor yogurt in a chocolate-based recipe.

desserts & treats

honey-ricotta CHEESECAKE

With a graham cracker crust, sweet honey filling, and mild lemon undertones, this dessert will satisfy any cheesecake lover's craving.

Prep: 30 minutes
Bake: 35 minutes
Cool: 1¾ hours
Chill: 4 hours
Oven: 350°F
Makes: 16 servings

Butter

⅓ **cup finely crushed graham crackers**

2 **8-ounce packages reduced-fat cream cheese (Neufchâtel), softened**

1 **cup fat-free ricotta cheese**

¾ **cup no-calorie, heat-stable granular sugar substitute**

2 **tablespoons honey**

2 **tablespoons all-purpose flour**

¼ **cup fat-free milk**

1 **teaspoon vanilla**

3 **slightly beaten eggs**

1 **teaspoon finely shredded lemon peel**

Exchanges: ½ Starch, 1 Medium-Fat Meat, ½ Fat

1 Generously butter the bottom and sides of an 8-inch springform pan. Sprinkle crushed graham crackers on bottom of pan; set aside.

2 For filling, in a large mixing bowl beat cream cheese, ricotta cheese, sugar substitute, honey, and flour with an electric mixer on low speed until smooth. Beat in milk and vanilla. Stir in eggs and lemon peel just until combined.

3 Pour filling into the prepared pan. Bake in a 350° oven for 35 to 40 minutes or until center appears nearly set when cake is gently shaken.

4 Cool in pan on a wire rack for 15 minutes. Using a small sharp knife, loosen the cheesecake from sides of pan; cool for 30 minutes more. Remove the sides of the pan; cool cheesecake completely on rack. Cover and chill at least 4 hours before serving.

Nutrition Facts per serving: 130 cal., 8 g total fat (5 g sat. fat), 64 mg chol., 179 mg sodium, 7 g carbo., 0 g fiber, 7 g pro.
Daily Values: 11% vit. A, 3% vit. C, 12% calcium, 4% iron

desserts & treats

249

berry CHEESECAKE DESSERT

This is cheesecake done the easy way. Just blend, chill, sprinkle, and serve.

Prep: 20 minutes
Chill: 4 hours
Makes: 4 servings

½ **of an 8-ounce tub (about ½ cup) fat-free cream cheese**

½ **cup low-fat ricotta cheese**

Low-calorie powdered sweetener equal to 3 tablespoons sugar, or 3 tablespoons sugar

½ **teaspoon finely shredded orange peel or lemon peel**

1 **tablespoon orange juice**

3 **cups sliced strawberries, raspberries, and/or blueberries**

4 **gingersnaps or chocolate wafers, broken**

Exchanges: 1 Fruit, 1 Lean Meat

1 In a blender container or food processor bowl combine cream cheese, ricotta cheese, powdered sweetener, orange peel, and orange juice. Cover and blend or process until smooth. Cover and chill for 4 to 24 hours.

2 To serve, layer fruit and cream cheese mixture among 4 dessert dishes. Sprinkle with broken cookies.

Nutrition Facts per serving: 115 cal., 2 g total fat (1 g sat. fat), 9 mg chol., 61 mg sodium, 17 g carbo., 2 g fiber, 8 g pro.
Daily Values: 11% vit. A, 109% vit. C, 12% calcium, 4% iron

desserts & treats

lemon torte WITH BERRIES

Put summer's bounty to good use. Raspberry and lemon make a naturally refreshing pair.

Prep: 25 minutes
Bake: 10 minutes
Chill: 5 hours
Oven: 350°F
Makes: 12 servings

1 **4-serving-size package low-calorie lemon-flavor gelatin**

½ **cup boiling water**

¼ **of a 12-ounce can (⅓ cup) frozen lemonade concentrate, thawed**

1 **12-ounce can evaporated fat-free milk**

1 **cup crushed graham crackers**

¼ **cup butter, melted**

1 **tablespoon sugar**

1 **cup fresh raspberries**

1 In a large bowl stir together lemon gelatin and the boiling water until gelatin dissolves. Stir in thawed lemonade concentrate and evaporated fat-free milk. Cover and chill for 1 to 1½ hours or until mixture mounds when spooned.

2 Meanwhile, for crust, in a small mixing bowl combine graham crackers, butter, and sugar. Press the mixture onto the bottom of an 8-inch springform pan. Bake in a 350° oven for 10 minutes. Cool in pan on a wire rack.

3 Beat gelatin mixture with an electric mixer on medium to high speed for 5 minutes or until almost doubled in volume. Pour gelatin mixture into crust-lined pan. Cover and chill for 4 to 24 hours or until firm.

4 To serve, loosen torte from sides of pan using a sharp knife; remove sides of pan. Cut torte into wedges and spoon raspberries on top.

Nutrition Facts per serving: 117 cal., 5 g total fat (3 g sat. fat), 12 mg chol., 131 mg sodium, 15 g carbo., 1 g fiber, 3 g pro.
Daily Values: 6% vit. A, 7% vit. C, 9% calcium, 3% iron

desserts & treats

cran-raspberry ICE

Refreshing is the word that best describes this berry-colored ice. Beating the mixture once during freezing lightens the texture and makes it easier to scoop.

Prep: 30 minutes
Stand: 15 minutes
Freeze: 10 hours
Makes: 8 (½-cup) servings

3 individual-size raspberry-flavor herbal tea bags

3 cups boiling water

1 11-ounce can frozen light cranberry-raspberry juice concentrate

2 teaspoons lemon juice

Exchanges: ½ Other Carbo.

1 In a medium bowl steep tea bags in boiling water for 5 minutes. Remove and discard tea bags. Stir juice concentrate and lemon juice into tea mixture.

2 Transfer mixture to a nonmetal freezer container. Cover and freeze for 4 to 6 hours or until almost firm, stirring after 2 hours. Break mixture into small chunks; transfer to a chilled mixing bowl. Beat with an electric mixer until fluffy but not melted. Return to container. Cover and freeze for 6 hours or until firm.

3 To serve, let mixture stand at room temperature for 10 minutes. Scrape the ice mixture into individual serving dishes.

Nutrition Facts per serving: 35 cal., 0 g total fat (0 g sat. fat), 0 mg chol., 6 mg sodium, 9 g carbo., 0 g fiber, 0 g pro.
Daily Values: 1% vit. C

A Spot of Tea

It seems researchers are continually coming up with new benefits to drinking tea. Tea can help prevent or delay cancer and reduces one's risk of heart disease and stroke. Unfortunately, not all teas offer these benefits. Herbal teas are actually combinations of several plants and therefore aren't actually teas at all. While they provide a variety of great flavors, herbal teas probably don't impart any of the health benefits associated with tea. When drinking to your health, stick to black, green, and oolong teas.

desserts & treats

special OCCASIONS

Birthdays, Christmas, and other celebrations are a time to indulge in your favorite foods. But if you're a diabetic, these typically high-fat, high-sugar foods probably aren't part of your diet. The recipes in this chapter change all that. They include the favorite foods you love in lower-fat, lower-sugar versions. There are even treats for kids' parties, like cupcakes and punch!

Birthday Cake with Frosting, *recipe page 276*

holiday cherry CHUTNEY

This thick, tart-sweet fruit mixture deserves a place on your holiday menu. Try it with slices of ham or turkey.

special occasions

Prep: 10 minutes
Cook: 15 minutes
Chill: 4 hours
Makes: 8 (2-tablespoon) servings

⅔ **cup light cranberry juice cocktail**

⅓ **cup no-calorie, heat-stable granular sugar substitute**

2 **tablespoons packed brown sugar**

1½ **cups fresh cranberries**

½ **cup dried tart or sweet cherries**

⅛ **teaspoon ground allspice**

Dash salt

Exchanges: 1 Fruit

① In a medium saucepan combine cranberry juice, sugar substitute, and brown sugar; stir to dissolve sugar. Add cranberries, dried cherries, allspice, and salt. Bring to boiling; reduce heat. Simmer, uncovered, for 15 minutes or until mixture thickens (the mixture will thicken further upon chilling). Transfer to a bowl. Cover and chill for 4 hours or up to 3 days.

Nutrition Facts per serving: 55 cal., 0 g total fat (0 g sat. fat), 0 mg chol., 23 mg sodium, 14 g carbo., 1 g fiber, 0 g pro.
Daily Values: 2% vit. A, 17% vit. C, 2% calcium, 3% iron

Winter Berries

Cranberries pack a real nutritional punch. A half-cup of raw berries has only 25 calories and 7 grams of carbohydrates. They've been shown to possibly play a role in preventing heart disease and some cancers, and they may slow down the development of ulcers and gum disease. And, after years of folklore, it seems as though cranberry juice really can help prevent urinary tract infections.

fennel-herb BREAD STUFFING

Whole grain bread yields stuffing that's moist but not mushy. Aromatic fennel and tender vegetables take it to flavorful heights.

Prep: 35 minutes
Bake: 40 minutes
Oven: 300°F/325°F
Makes: 12 to 14 servings

- 8 cups whole grain bread cubes (about 9 slices)
- 1 medium fennel bulb with tops
- 1 cup chopped carrot
- 1 cup chopped onion
- 2 cloves garlic, minced
- 2 tablespoons olive oil
- 1 teaspoon dried Italian seasoning, crushed
- ¼ teaspoon black pepper
- ⅛ teaspoon salt
- 1 to 1½ cups reduced-sodium chicken broth

Exchanges: ½ Vegetable, 1 Starch

1 Spread bread cubes in a large shallow roasting pan. Bake in a 300° oven for 10 to 15 minutes or until bread cubes are dry, stirring twice. Cool. Increase oven to 325°.

2 Remove green leafy tops from fennel; snip enough of the tops to make 1 to 2 tablespoons. Set aside. Cut off and discard upper stalks. Remove any wilted outer layers and cut a thin slice from the fennel base. Cut fennel bulb into wedges, removing the core. Coarsely chop fennel.

3 In a large skillet cook chopped fennel bulb, carrot, onion, and garlic in hot oil over medium heat until tender, stirring occasionally. Stir in snipped fennel tops, Italian seasoning, pepper, and salt. Place fennel mixture in a very large bowl. Stir in bread cubes. Drizzle with enough broth to moisten; toss gently to coat. Transfer mixture to a 2-quart casserole. Bake, covered, in the 325° oven for 20 minutes. Uncover; bake about 20 minutes more or until heated through.

Nutrition Facts per serving: 94 cal., 3 g total fat 0 mg chol., 212 mg sodium, 17 g carbo., 3 g fiber, 4 g pro.
Daily Values: 52% vit. A, 7% vit. C, 12% calcium, 12% iron

turkey and VEGETABLE BAKE

Rice and vegetables win an encore for the last of the holiday turkey. This creamy main dish gives leftovers a good name.

Prep: 35 minutes
Bake: 30 minutes
Stand: 15 minutes
Oven: 350°F
Makes: 6 servings

- 2 **cups sliced fresh mushrooms**
- ¾ **cup chopped red or yellow sweet pepper**
- ½ **cup chopped onion**
- 2 **cloves garlic, minced**
- 2 **tablespoons butter or margarine**
- ¼ **cup all-purpose flour**
- ¾ **teaspoon salt**
- ½ **teaspoon dried thyme, crushed**
- ¼ **teaspoon black pepper**
- 2 **cups fat-free milk**
- 1 **10-ounce package frozen chopped spinach, thawed and well drained**
- 2 **cups cooked brown or white rice**
- 2 **cups chopped cooked turkey or chicken**
- ½ **cup finely shredded Parmesan cheese (2 ounces)**

Exchanges: ½ Milk, 1 Vegetable, 1 Starch, 2 Lean Meat, ½ Fat

1 In a 12-inch skillet cook and stir mushrooms, sweet pepper, onion, and garlic in hot butter over medium heat until tender. Stir in flour, salt, thyme, and black pepper. Add milk all at once; cook and stir until thickened and bubbly. Stir in spinach, rice, turkey, and ¼ cup of the Parmesan cheese.

2 Spoon mixture into a 2-quart rectangular baking dish. Sprinkle with remaining Parmesan cheese. Bake, covered, in a 350° oven for 20 minutes. Uncover and bake about 10 minutes more or until heated through. Let stand 15 minutes before serving.

Nutrition Facts per serving: 297 cal., 10 g total fat (5 g sat. fat), 53 mg chol., 602 mg sodium, 28 g carbo., 3 g fiber, 24 g pro.
Daily Values: 165% vit. A, 59% vit. C, 26% calcium, 11% iron

apricot-almond COFFEE CAKE

Welcome guests to a weekend brunch buffet that includes this moist, fruity coffee cake.

Prep: 15 minutes
Bake: 25 minutes
Cool: 10 minutes
Oven: 350°F
Makes: 10 servings

Nonstick cooking spray

1½ **cups all-purpose flour**

1 **teaspoon baking powder**

¼ **teaspoon salt**

¼ **teaspoon ground cinnamon**

⅛ **teaspoon ground ginger**

1 **slightly beaten egg**

½ **cup snipped dried apricots**

½ **cup fat-free milk**

¼ **cup no-calorie, heat-stable granular sugar substitute**

¼ **cup unsweetened applesauce**

3 **tablespoons butter, melted**

2 **tablespoons honey**

1 **teaspoon vanilla**

2 **tablespoons reduced-sugar apricot preserves, melted**

2 **tablespoons toasted sliced almonds**

Exchanges: 1½ Other Carbo., 1 Fat

1 Lightly coat an 8×1½-inch round baking pan with nonstick cooking spray; set aside. In a medium bowl stir together flour, baking powder, salt, cinnamon, and ginger.

2 In a medium bowl combine egg and apricots. Stir in milk, sugar substitute, applesauce, melted butter, honey, and vanilla. Add fruit mixture all at once to flour mixture; stir to combine. Pour batter into the prepared baking pan.

3 Bake in a 350° oven for 25 to 30 minutes or until a toothpick inserted near center comes out clean. Cool in pan on a wire rack for 10 minutes. Cut up any large pieces of fruit in preserves; spoon over cake. Sprinkle with toasted almonds. Serve warm.

Nutrition Facts per serving: 157 cal., 5 g total fat (3 g sat. fat), 31 mg chol., 150 mg sodium, 24 g carbo., 1 g fiber, 3 g pro.
Daily Values: 10% vit. A, 7% vit. C, 7% calcium, 8% iron

cranberry-pecan MUFFINS

The dynamic duo of orange peel and cranberries leaves a memorable impression. Serve these tender muffins warm at a holiday brunch.

Prep: 20 minutes
Bake: 12 minutes
Oven: 400°F
Makes: 12 muffins

1¾ **cups all-purpose flour**

2 **teaspoons baking powder**

¼ **teaspoon salt**

¼ **teaspoon ground cinnamon**

1 **slightly beaten egg**

¾ **cup fat-free milk**

½ **cup no-calorie, heat-stable granular sugar substitute**

¼ **cup sugar**

3 **tablespoons cooking oil**

1 **teaspoon finely shredded orange peel**

¾ **cup coarsely chopped cranberries**

¼ **cup chopped pecans, toasted**

Exchanges: 1½ Other Carbo., 1 Fat

1 Grease twelve 2½-inch muffin cups; set aside. In a medium bowl stir together flour, baking powder, salt, and cinnamon. Make a well in center of the flour mixture; set aside.

2 In another medium bowl combine egg, milk, sugar substitute, sugar, oil, and orange peel. Add milk mixture all at once to flour mixture. Stir just until moistened (batter should be lumpy). Gently stir in cranberries and pecans.

3 Spoon batter into prepared muffin cups, filling each about two-thirds full. Bake in a 400° oven for 12 to 15 minutes or until muffins are lightly golden and a wooden toothpick inserted in centers comes out clean. Cool in muffin cups on wire rack for 5 minutes. Remove from muffin cups; serve warm.

Nutrition Facts per muffin: 146 cal., 6 g total fat (1 g sat. fat), 18 mg chol., 130 mg sodium, 21 g carbo., 1 g fiber, 3 g pro.
Daily Values: 3% vit. A, 4% vit. C, 9% calcium, 8% iron

special occasions

apple CRANBERRY CRISP

As tasty as it is simple to fix, this down-home recipe will remind you of Grandma's old-fashioned autumn dessert.

Prep: 15 minutes
Bake: 30 minutes
Oven: 375°F
Makes: 6 servings

- **5 cups thinly sliced peeled apples**
- **1 cup cranberries**
- **2 tablespoons granulated sugar**
- **½ teaspoon apple pie spice or ground cinnamon**
- **½ cup quick-cooking rolled oats**
- **3 tablespoons packed brown sugar**
- **2 tablespoons all-purpose flour**
- **½ teaspoon apple pie spice or ground cinnamon**
- **2 tablespoons butter**

Exchanges: 1 Fruit, 1½ Other Carbo., ½ Fat

1 In a 2-quart baking dish combine apples and cranberries. Stir together granulated sugar and ½ teaspoon apple pie spice. Sprinkle over fruit mixture in dish; toss to coat.

2 In a small bowl combine oats, brown sugar, flour, and ½ teaspoon apple pie spice. Cut in butter until crumbly. Sprinkle oat mixture evenly over apple mixture.

3 Bake in a 375° oven for 30 to 35 minutes or until apples are tender. Serve warm.

Nutrition Facts per serving: 189 cal., 5 g total fat (3 g sat. fat), 11 mg chol., 45 mg sodium, 37 g carbo., 4 g fiber, 2 g pro.
Daily Values: 4% vit. A, 10% vit. C, 2% calcium, 5% iron

special occasions

maple-nut BAKED APPLES

These apples are pleasers alone or topped with frozen yogurt.

Prep: 15 minutes
Bake: 25 minutes
Oven: 350°F
Makes: 4 servings

- **2 medium cooking apples, such as Rome Beauty, Granny Smith, or Jonathan**
- **3 tablespoons water**
- **3 tablespoons sugar-free maple-flavor syrup with no-calorie, heat-stable granular sugar substitute**
- **¼ cup snipped dried figs, snipped pitted whole dates, raisins, or mixed dried fruit bits**
- **¼ teaspoon apple pie spice or ground cinnamon**
- **2 tablespoons chopped toasted pecans or walnuts**
- **Low-fat vanilla frozen yogurt (optional)**

Exchanges: 1 Fruit, ½ Other Carbo.

1 Core apples; peel a strip from the top of each. In a 2-quart square baking dish stir together the water and 2 tablespoons of the maple-flavor syrup. Add apples to dish. In a small bowl combine dried fruit, remaining 1 tablespoon syrup, and apple pie spice; spoon into center of apples. Cover dish with foil; fold back one corner of foil to vent. Bake in a 350° oven for 25 to 30 minutes or until the apples are tender, spooning syrup mixture over apples once halfway through baking.

2 To serve, halve warm apples lengthwise. Transfer apple halves to dessert dishes. Spoon some of the cooking liquid over apples. Sprinkle with nuts. If desired, top with a small scoop of frozen yogurt.

Nutrition Facts per serving: 103 cal., 3 g total fat (1 g sat. fat), 0 mg chol., 21 mg sodium, 22 g carbo., 4 g fiber, 1 g pro.
Daily Values: 1% vit. A, 6% vit. C, 3% calcium, 3% iron

Healthy Holiday Eating

The challenge of healthy eating grows more difficult during the holidays when high-fat, sugar-laden foods are everywhere. Keeping the principles of a healthy lifestyle at the forefront is especially important. In addition to sticking with your exercise routine, continue to eat scheduled meals. Eating regularly keeps you from getting hungry and makes it easier to say no. When faced with something you can't or don't want to say no to, find a way to make it fit into your meal plan. Try eating a small amount with a meal or eating just a little bit less of everything to make room for the extra calories.

pumpkin PIE

The tender pastry, pleasant sweetness, and piquant spices are enough to make you forget that you're watching what you eat.

Prep: 30 minutes
Bake: 45 minutes
Oven: 375°F
Makes: 8 servings

- 1 **recipe Easy Oil Pastry**
- 1 **15-ounce can pumpkin**
- ⅓ **cup no-calorie, heat-stable granular sugar substitute**
- 2 **tablespoons honey**
- 1 **teaspoon ground cinnamon**
- ½ **teaspoon ground ginger**
- ¼ **teaspoon ground nutmeg**
- 2 **slightly beaten eggs**
- 1 **teaspoon vanilla**
- ¾ **cup fat-free milk**

Exchanges: 1 ½ Starch, 1 ½ Fat

❶ Prepare Easy Oil Pastry. Press dough firmly onto bottom and up sides of a 9-inch pie plate.

❷ For filling, in a medium bowl combine pumpkin, sugar substitute, honey, cinnamon, ginger, and nutmeg. Add eggs and vanilla. Beat lightly with a fork just until combined. Gradually add milk; stir until combined.

❸ Place the pastry-lined pie plate on the oven rack. Carefully pour filling into pastry shell.

❹ To prevent overbrowning, cover edge of the pie with foil. Bake in a 375° oven for 25 minutes. Remove foil. Bake 20 to 25 minutes more or until a knife inserted near center comes out clean (edges of filling may crack slightly). Cool on a wire rack. Cover and refrigerate within 2 hours.

Easy Oil Pastry: In a medium bowl stir together 1¼ cups all-purpose flour and ¼ teaspoon salt. Add ¼ cup cooking oil and 3 tablespoons fat-free milk all at once to flour mixture. Stir lightly with a fork. Form into a ball.

Nutrition Facts per serving: 201 cal., 9 g total fat (2 g sat. fat), 54 mg chol., 108 mg sodium, 26 g carbo., 2 g fiber, 5 g pro.
Daily Values: 239% vit. A, 7% vit. C, 9% calcium, 14% iron

special occasions

pumpkin CHEESECAKE

A blend of low-fat ricotta cheese and fat-free cream cheese keeps this cheesecake light. Sensible portions keep carb counts within reach of diabetics.

Prep: 25 minutes
Chill: 4 hours
Makes: 12 servings

- ¾ **cup finely crushed graham crackers**
- 2 **tablespoons butter, melted**
- 1 **15-ounce carton low-fat ricotta cheese**
- 1 **8-ounce tub fat-free cream cheese**
- 1 **cup canned pumpkin**
- ½ **cup fat-free milk**
- 1 **envelope unflavored gelatin**
- ½ **cup orange juice**
- 2 **teaspoons finely shredded orange peel**
- ⅓ **cup granulated sugar**
- ⅓ **cup packed brown sugar**
- 2 **teaspoons vanilla**
- 1 **teaspoon pumpkin pie spice**
  Light whipped dessert topping (optional)
  Pumpkin pie spice (optional)

Exchanges: 1½ Starch, 1 Lean Meat

1 For crust, in a medium bowl stir together crushed graham crackers and melted butter until crackers are moistened. Press mixture onto bottom of a 9-inch springform pan. Refrigerate while preparing filling.

2 For filling, in a food processor bowl or blender container combine half of the ricotta cheese, half of the cream cheese, half of the pumpkin, and half of the milk. Cover and process or blend until smooth. Transfer to a large bowl. Repeat with remaining ricotta, cream cheese, pumpkin, and milk.

3 In a small saucepan sprinkle gelatin over orange juice; let stand for 5 minutes. Cook and stir over low heat until gelatin is dissolved. Stir into pumpkin mixture. Stir in orange peel, granulated sugar, brown sugar, vanilla, and pumpkin pie spice. Pour mixture into chilled crust. Cover and chill for at least 4 hours or until firm.

4 To serve, using a small sharp knife, loosen crust from sides of pan; remove sides of pan. Cut into wedges. If desired, garnish with whipped topping and sprinkle with additional pumpkin pie spice.

Nutrition Facts per serving: 160 cal., 4 g total fat (2 g sat. fat), 15 mg chol., 116 mg sodium, 22 g carbo., 1 g fiber, 10 g pro.
Daily Values: 93% vit. A, 11% vit. C, 26% calcium, 4% iron

pumpkin BREAD

Plan to bake this bread a day before you want to serve it. Like most quick breads it slices best if wrapped and stored overnight.

special occasions

Prep: 15 minutes
Bake: 65 minutes
Oven: 350°F
Makes: 1 loaf (16 servings)

- 2 cups all-purpose flour
- ¾ cup no-calorie, heat-stable granular sugar substitute
- 1 tablespoon baking powder
- 1½ teaspoons ground cinnamon
- ¼ teaspoon baking soda
- ¼ teaspoon salt
- ¼ teaspoon ground nutmeg
- ¼ teaspoon ground ginger or ⅛ teaspoon ground cloves
- 2 beaten eggs
- 1 cup canned pumpkin
- 1 cup fat-free milk
- ⅓ cup cooking oil
- ¼ cup packed brown sugar
- 1 teaspoon vanilla

Exchanges: 1½ Starch, ½ Fat

1 Grease the bottom and ½ inch up the sides of an 8×4×2 inch loaf pan; set aside.

2 In a large bowl combine flour, sugar substitute, baking powder, cinnamon, baking soda, salt, nutmeg, and ginger. In a medium bowl stir together eggs, pumpkin, milk, oil, brown sugar, and vanilla. Add egg mixture all at once to flour mixture. Stir just until moistened.

3 Spoon batter into prepared pan. Bake in a 350° oven for 65 to 70 minutes or until a wooden toothpick inserted near center comes out clean. Cool in pan on a wire rack for 10 minutes. Remove loaf from pan. Cool completely on a wire rack. For easier slicing, wrap and store overnight.

Nutrition Facts per serving: 135 cal., 5 g total fat (1 g sat. fat), 27 mg chol., 150 mg sodium, 19 g carbo., 1 g fiber, 3 g pro.
Daily Values: 71% vit. A, 4% vit. C, 10% calcium, 9% iron

chocolate CREAM CHEESE PIE

Like cheesecake? Crave chocolate? Put them together to form a luscious union.

Prep: 20 minutes
Chill: 4 hours
Makes: 8 servings

- **1 4-serving-size package fat-free, sugar-free instant chocolate pudding mix**
- **1¾ cups fat-free milk**
- **1 teaspoon vanilla**
- **½ of an 8-ounce package reduced-fat cream cheese (Neufchâtel), softened**
- **½ of an 8-ounce container frozen light whipped dessert topping, thawed**
- **1 6-ounce chocolate-flavor crumb pie shell**
- **1 cup fresh raspberries**
- **1 tablespoon grated semisweet chocolate**

Exchanges: 2 Other Carbo., 1½ Fat

1 In a medium bowl prepare pudding mix according to package directions using the 1¾ cups milk. Stir in vanilla; set aside.

2 In a large microwave-safe mixing bowl microwave cream cheese, uncovered, on 100 percent power (high) for 15 seconds; stir. Microwave on high for 15 seconds more. Beat cream cheese with an electric mixer on medium speed for 15 seconds. Add half of the pudding mixture; beat until smooth. Add remaining pudding mixture; beat until smooth. Fold in half of the whipped topping. Spread mixture in pie shell. Chill for 4 hours or until set. (Cover and chill for longer storage up to 24 hours.)

3 Top individual servings with remaining whipped topping, raspberries, and grated chocolate.

Nutrition Facts per serving: 228 cal., 10 g total fat (5 g sat. fat), 12 mg chol., 350 mg sodium, 27 g carbo., 2 g fiber, 5 g pro.
Daily Values: 6% vit. A, 7% vit. C, 8% calcium, 5% iron

Choosing Chocolate

Everyone has a favorite kind of chocolate. The varying amounts of chocolate liquor are the basis for the categorizations. Dark chocolate, which may be bittersweet or semisweet, contains the most. Milk chocolate is a mixture of milk powder, sugar, and flavorings and a smaller amount of chocolate liquor mixed with cocoa butter. White chocolate contains no chocolate liquor, and, for this reason, many don't consider it chocolate. Recent research claims chocolate contains powerful antioxidants that can protect against heart disease. The higher the chocolate liquor content in the product, the more antioxidant power.

special occasions

sugar cookie CUTOUTS

Edible egg paint bakes right onto the cutouts for hassle-free decorating. The range of paste food coloring available means your color options are almost limitless.

Prep: 45 minutes
Bake: 6 minutes per batch
Oven: 375°F
Makes: about 36 cookies

⅔ **cup butter, softened**

½ **cup no-calorie, heat-stable granular sugar substitute**

¼ **cup sugar**

1 **teaspoon baking powder**

¼ **teaspoon salt**

1 **egg**

2 **teaspoons vanilla**

2 **cups all-purpose flour**

1 **to 2 egg yolks**

Few drops water

Paste food coloring

Exchanges: ½ Other Carbo., ½ Fat

① In a large mixing bowl beat butter with an electric mixer on medium to high speed for 30 seconds. Add sugar substitute, sugar, baking powder, and salt. Beat until combined, scraping sides of bowl occasionally. Beat in egg and vanilla until combined. Beat in as much of the flour as you can with the mixer. Stir in any remaining flour with a wooden spoon. Divide dough in half. If necessary, cover and chill dough about 30 minutes or until easy to handle.

② On a lightly floured surface, roll half the dough at a time until ⅛ inch thick. Using a 2½-inch cookie cutter, cut into desired shapes. Place cutouts 1 inch apart on an ungreased cookie sheet.

③ For egg paint, in a small bowl stir together egg yolk and water. Divide mixture among several small bowls. Mix a little paste food coloring into each. Use a small clean watercolor paintbrush to paint various colors onto unbaked cutout cookies. Clean the brush between colors using plain water. Put only a small amount of paint on the brush. If the egg paint thickens while you're working with it, stir in a little water, a drop at a time. If using more than one color on a cookie, leave a narrow strip of cookie between painted areas so the colors don't run together.

④ Bake in a 375° oven for 6 to 7 minutes or until edges are firm and bottoms are very lightly browned. Transfer cookies to a wire rack; cool.

Nutrition Facts per cookie: 68 cal., 4 g total fat (2 g sat. fat), 21 mg chol., 66 mg sodium, 7 g carbo., 0 g fiber, 1 g pro.
Daily Values: 4% vit. A, 1% vit. C, 2% calcium, 3% iron

special occasions

gossamer spice COOKIES

The word gossamer refers to something light and delicate and aptly describes these crisp, paper-thin cookies of northern European descent.

Prep: 45 minutes
Chill: 1 hour
Bake: 5 minutes per batch
Oven: 375°F
Makes: about 66 cookies

1⅓ **cups all-purpose flour**
½ **teaspoon ground ginger**
½ **teaspoon apple pie spice**
¼ **teaspoon ground cloves**
¼ **teaspoon ground cardamom**
⅛ **teaspoon cayenne pepper**
⅓ **cup butter, softened**
⅓ **cup mild-flavor molasses**
¼ **cup packed dark brown sugar**

Exchanges: ½ Other Carbo.

1 In a medium bowl stir together flour, ginger, apple pie spice, cloves, cardamom, and cayenne pepper; set flour mixture aside.

2 In a large mixing bowl beat butter with an electric mixer on medium speed for 30 seconds. Add molasses and brown sugar. Beat until combined, scraping sides of bowl occasionally. Beat in flour mixture until just combined. Divide dough in half. Cover and chill dough about 1 hour or until easy to handle.

3 On a lightly floured surface, roll half of the dough at a time until ¹⁄₁₆ inch thick. Using a floured 2-inch round scalloped cookie cutter, cut out dough. Place cutouts 1 inch apart on an ungreased cookie sheet.

4 Bake in a 375° oven for 5 to 6 minutes or until edges are lightly browned. Transfer cookies to a wire rack; cool.

To store: Place in layers separated by waxed paper in an airtight container; cover. Store at room temperature for up to 3 days or freeze for up to 3 months.

Nutrition Facts per 2 cookies: 50 cal., 2 g total fat (1 g sat. fat), 5 mg chol., 22 mg sodium, 8 g carbo., 1 g pro.
Daily Values: 2% vit. A, 1% calcium, 2% iron

special occasions

chocolate-mint COOKIES

Kids eagerly accept these fudgy treats as an after-school snack along with a cold glass of milk.

Prep: 30 minutes
Bake: 9 minutes per batch
Freeze: 30 minutes
Oven: 350°F
Makes: about 36 cookies

1⅓ **cups all-purpose flour**

1 **cup no-calorie, heat-stable granular sugar substitute**

1½ **teaspoons baking powder**

¼ **teaspoon salt**

1 **cup semisweet chocolate pieces**

⅓ **cup butter, softened**

2 **eggs**

1½ **teaspoons vanilla**

¼ **teaspoon mint extract**

Sifted powdered sugar (optional)

Exchanges: ½ Other Carbo., ½ Fat

1 In a bowl combine flour, sugar substitute, baking powder, and salt; set aside.

2 In a small saucepan heat chocolate pieces over low heat until melted, stirring constantly.

3 In a large mixing bowl beat butter with an electric mixer on high speed for 1 minute. Beat in melted chocolate, eggs, vanilla, and mint extract.

4 Gradually beat in flour mixture. Wrap dough in plastic wrap. Freeze for 30 minutes or until firm enough to shape into balls. Shape dough into 1-inch balls. Place balls about 1½ inches apart on an ungreased cookie sheet. Bake in a 350° oven for 9 to 11 minutes or until tops are cracked. Transfer cookies to a wire rack; cool.

5 If desired, dust cookies lightly with sifted powdered sugar before serving. Store up to 2 days at room temperature. Freeze for longer storage.

Nutrition Facts per cookie: 63 cal., 4 g total fat (2 g sat. fat), 17 mg chol., 56 mg sodium, 7 g carbo., 0 g fiber, 1 g pro.
Daily Values: 3% vit. A, 1% vit. C, 3% calcium, 4% iron

marbled CUPCAKES

These little cakes love to party! Let the holiday, birthday party theme, or school colors (for a graduation party) dictate the cake and frosting colors.

Prep: 30 minutes
Stand: 30 minutes
Bake: 15 minutes
Oven: 350°F
Makes: 18 cupcakes

4 egg whites

2 cups all-purpose flour

1¼ cups no-calorie, heat-stable granular sugar substitute

1½ teaspoons baking powder

½ teaspoon baking soda

⅛ teaspoon salt

½ cup butter, softened

½ cup sugar

2 teaspoons vanilla

1⅓ cups buttermilk or sour milk*

1 4-serving-size package sugar-free lemon-, orange-, or strawberry-flavor gelatin

Few drops food coloring (optional)

1 8-ounce container frozen light whipped dessert topping, thawed

Exchanges: 1½ Other Carbo., 1 Fat

1 Allow egg whites to stand at room temperature for 30 minutes. Meanwhile, grease and lightly flour eighteen 2½-inch muffin cups or line with paper or foil bake cups; set aside. In a medium bowl stir together flour, sugar substitute, baking powder, baking soda, and salt; set aside.

2 In a large mixing bowl beat butter with an electric mixer on medium to high speed for 30 seconds. Add sugar and vanilla; beat until combined. Add egg whites, 1 at a time, beating well after each addition. Add flour mixture and buttermilk alternately to beaten mixture, beating on low speed after each addition just until combined. Place half of the batter in a medium bowl; stir in desired gelatin. Spoon some plain and some flavored batter into each muffin cup, filling each cup about half full. Use a knife to swirl batter.

3 Bake in a 350° oven about 15 minutes or until a wooden toothpick inserted near the centers comes out clean. Cool in pans on wire racks for 5 minutes. Carefully loosen and remove cupcakes from muffin cups. Cool on wire racks.

4 For frosting, if desired, fold food coloring into whipped topping. Pipe or spread topping on cupcakes.

***Note:** To make 1⅓ cups sour milk, place 4 teaspoons lemon juice or vinegar in a 2-cup glass measuring cup. Add enough fat-free milk to make 1⅓ cups total liquid; stir. Let stand 5 minutes before using.

Nutrition Facts per cupcake: 168 cal., 7 g total fat (5 g sat. fat), 15 mg chol., 187 mg sodium, 21 g carbo., 0 g fiber, 3 g pro.
Daily Values: 8% vit. A, 4% vit. C, 8% calcium, 7% iron

special occasions

birthday cake WITH FROSTING

You'll get a slightly whiter cake if you use shortening instead of butter to prepare this moist, dense treat.

Prep: 40 minutes
Stand: 30 minutes
Bake: 20 minutes
Cool: 1 hour
Oven: 350°F
Makes: 16 servings

4 egg whites

2 cups all-purpose flour

1¼ cups no-calorie, heat-stable granular sugar substitute

1½ teaspoons baking powder

½ teaspoon baking soda

⅛ teaspoon salt

½ cup shortening or butter, softened

½ cup sugar

2 teaspoons vanilla

1⅓ cups buttermilk or sour milk*

1 4-serving-size package fat-free, sugar-free instant white chocolate pudding mix

1 cup fat-free milk

1 8-ounce container frozen light whipped dessert topping, thawed

Exchanges: 1½ Other Carbo., 1½ Fat

1 Allow egg whites to stand at room temperature for 30 minutes. Meanwhile, lightly grease bottoms of two 9×1½-inch or 8×1½-inch round cake pans. Line bottoms of pans with waxed paper. Grease and lightly flour bottoms and sides of pans. Set aside. In a medium bowl stir together flour, sugar substitute, baking powder, baking soda, and salt; set aside.

2 In a large mixing bowl beat shortening with an electric mixer on medium to high speed for 30 seconds. Add sugar and vanilla; beat until combined. Add egg whites, 1 at a time, beating well after each addition. Add flour mixture and buttermilk alternately to beaten mixture, beating on low speed after each addition just until combined. Spread batter in prepared pans.

3 Bake in a 350° oven for 20 to 25 minutes for 9-inch pans, 25 to 30 minutes for 8-inch pans, or until a wooden toothpick inserted near centers comes out clean. Cool cakes in pans on wire racks for 10 minutes. Remove cakes from pans; peel off waxed paper. Cool thoroughly on racks.

4 For frosting, in a medium bowl prepare pudding mix according to package directions using the 1 cup milk. Fold in whipped topping. Immediately spread between cake layers and over top and sides of cake. Refrigerate until serving time.

*Note: To make 1⅓ cups sour milk, place 4 teaspoons lemon juice or vinegar in a 2-cup glass measuring cup. Add enough fat-free milk to make 1⅓ cups total liquid; stir. Let stand 5 minutes before using.

Nutrition Facts per serving: 199 cal., 8 g total fat (3 g sat. fat), 1 mg chol., 222 mg sodium, 26 g carbo., 1 g fiber, 4 g pro.
Daily Values: 5% vit. A, 4% vit. C, 11% calcium, 9% iron

brownie fruit PIZZA

Honor the birthday child or say "Happy Valentine's Day" with wedges of this chocolaty fruit pizza.

special occasions

Prep: 20 minutes
Bake: 15 minutes
Chill: 1 hour
Oven: 350°F
Makes: 12 servings

- 1 10¼-ounce package fudge brownie mix
- ¼ cup unsweetened applesauce
- 1 4-serving-size package fat-free, sugar-free instant chocolate fudge or chocolate pudding mix
- 1 cup fat-free milk
- 1 teaspoon vanilla
- 1 cup sliced banana
- 1 cup sliced fresh strawberries

Exchanges: 2 Other Carbo.

1 Grease the bottom of a 10-inch springform pan; set aside. Prepare brownie mix according to package directions, except substitute the ¼ cup unsweetened applesauce for cooking oil. Spread batter in prepared pan. Bake in a 350° oven for 15 minutes or until sides begin to pull away from pan. Cool completely on a wire rack. Remove sides of pan.

2 Prepare pudding mix according to package directions, using the 1 cup milk and adding the vanilla with the milk. Cover and chill at least 1 hour.

3 Spread pudding mixture over cooled brownie crust. Arrange fruit on pudding. Cut into wedges and serve immediately.

Nutrition Facts per serving: 141 cal., 2 g total fat (1 g sat. fat), 18 mg chol., 216 mg sodium, 28 g carbo., 2 g fiber, 3 g pro.
Daily Values: 2% vit. A, 14% vit. C, 4% calcium, 7% iron

Fitting In Fruits

Fruits are loaded with vitamins and minerals and they're a good source of fiber. Although the sugar they contain is natural, it can still send your blood sugar up. To get the benefits of fruit without the problems, always eat it with a meal instead of by itself. Limit your intake of juice (100 percent fruit juice only) to 4 to 6 ounces per day and drink it with a meal.

white chocolate PARFAITS

Make these parfaits with blueberries and strawberries for a festive red, white, and blue dessert at a Fourth of July party. Guests will love the contrast of satiny pudding with crisp cookies and fresh berries.

Start to Finish: 20 minutes
Makes: 6 servings

- **1 4-serving-size package fat-free, sugar-free instant white chocolate pudding mix**
- **2 cups fat-free milk**
- **1 teaspoon vanilla**
- **6 chocolate wafers or shortbread cookies, broken into small pieces**
- **½ of an 8-ounce container frozen light whipped dessert topping, thawed**
- **1½ cups fresh blueberries, raspberries, and/or sliced strawberries**

Exchanges: ½ Fruit, 1 Other Carbo., ½ Fat

1 In a medium mixing bowl prepare pudding mix according to package directions using the 2 cups milk. Stir in vanilla. Divide pudding mixture among 6 parfait glasses or dessert dishes. Sprinkle with cookie pieces. Top with whipped topping and berries. Serve immediately.

Nutrition Facts per serving: 139 cal., 3 g total fat (3 g sat. fat), 2 mg chol., 309 mg sodium, 22 g carbo., 2 g fiber, 4 g pro.
Daily Values: 4% vit. A, 20% vit. C, 11% calcium, 5% iron

sparkling BERRY LEMONADE

These ice cubes require more prep work—but not much, and they're well worth it. They cool, flavor, and garnish all at the same time—great for a kids' party or summertime cooler.

Prep: 15 minutes
Freeze: 4 hours
Makes: 8 (6-ounce) servings

- 1 envelope or tub low-calorie lemonade-flavor soft drink mix (enough to make 2 quarts)
- 5 cups water
- 8 medium strawberries, hulled and quartered
- 1 envelope or tub low-calorie cherry- or raspberry-flavor soft drink mix (enough to make 2 quarts)
- 1 1-liter bottle club soda, chilled

Exchanges: Free

1. In a 2-quart pitcher stir together lemonade drink mix and the water. Place 1 strawberry quarter in each of 32 compartments of ice cube trays; fill with 3 cups of the lemonade mixture. Freeze about 4 hours or until solid.

2. Stir cherry or raspberry drink mix into remaining lemonade mixture in pitcher. Cover and chill until serving time.

3. To serve, slowly pour club soda into lemonade mixture in pitcher. Put 4 ice cubes in each of 8 glasses. Pour lemonade mixture into each glass.

Nutrition Facts per serving: 4 cal., 0 g total fat (0 g sat. fat), 0 mg chol., 31 mg sodium, 1 g carbo., 0 g fiber, 0 g pro.
Daily Values: 31% vit. C, 1% calcium

special occasions

279

index

tips

metric information

The charts on this page provide a guide for converting measurements from the U.S. customary system, which is used throughout this book, to the metric system.

Product Differences: Most of the ingredients called for in the recipes in this book are available in most countries. However, some are known by different names. Here are some common American ingredients and their possible counterparts:

- Sugar (white) is granulated, fine granulated, or castor sugar.
- Powdered sugar is icing sugar.
- All-purpose flour is enriched, bleached or unbleached white household flour. When self-rising flour is used in place of all-purpose flour in a recipe that calls for leavening, omit the leavening agent (baking soda or baking powder) and salt.
- Light-colored corn syrup is golden syrup.
- Cornstarch is cornflour.
- Baking soda is bicarbonate of soda.
- Vanilla or vanilla extract is vanilla essence.
- Green, red, or yellow sweet peppers are capsicums or bell peppers.
- Golden raisins are sultanas.

Volume and Weight: The United States traditionally uses cup measures for liquid and solid ingredients. The chart below shows the approximate imperial and metric equivalents. If you are accustomed to weighing solid ingredients, the following approximate equivalents will be helpful.

- 1 cup butter, castor sugar, or rice = 8 ounces = ½ pound = 250 grams
- 1 cup flour = 4 ounces = ¼ pound = 125 grams
- 1 cup icing sugar = 5 ounces = 150 grams

Canadian and U.S. volume for a cup measure is 8 fluid ounces (237 ml), but the standard metric equivalent is 250 ml.

1 British imperial cup is 10 fluid ounces.

In Australia, 1 tablespoon equals 20 ml, and there are 4 teaspoons in the Australian tablespoon.

Spoon measures are used for smaller amounts of ingredients. Although the size of the tablespoon varies slightly in different countries, for practical purposes and for recipes in this book, a straight substitution is all that's necessary. Measurements made using cups or spoons always should be level unless stated otherwise.

common weight range replacements

Imperial / U.S.	Metric
½ ounce	15 g
1 ounce	25 g or 30 g
4 ounces (¼ pound)	115 g or 125 g
8 ounces (½ pound)	225 g or 250 g
16 ounces (1 pound)	450 g or 500 g
1¼ pounds	625 g
1½ pounds	750 g
2 pounds or 2¼ pounds	1,000 g or 1 Kg

oven temperature equivalents

Fahrenheit Setting	Celsius Setting*	Gas Setting
300°F	150°C	Gas Mark 2 (very low)
325°F	160°C	Gas Mark 3 (low)
350°F	180°C	Gas Mark 4 (moderate)
375°F	190°C	Gas Mark 5 (moderate)
400°F	200°C	Gas Mark 6 (hot)
425°F	220°C	Gas Mark 7 (hot)
450°F	230°C	Gas Mark 8 (very hot)
475°F	240°C	Gas Mark 9 (very hot)
500°F	260°C	Gas Mark 10 (extremely hot)
Broil	Broil	Grill

*Electric and gas ovens may be calibrated using celsius. However, for an electric oven, increase celsius setting 10 to 20 degrees when cooking above 160°C. For convection or forced- air ovens (gas or electric) lower the temperature setting 25°F/10°C when cooking at all heat levels.

baking pan sizes

Imperial / U.S.	Metric
9×1½-inch round cake pan	22- or 23×4-cm (1.5 L)
9×1½-inch pie plate	22- or 23×4-cm (1 L)
8×8×2-inch square cake pan	20×5-cm (2 L)
9×9×2-inch square cake pan	22- or 23×4.5-cm (2.5 L)
11×7×1½-inch baking pan	28×17×4-cm (2 L)
2-quart rectangular baking pan	30×19×4.5-cm (3 L)
13×9×2-inch baking pan	34×22×4.5-cm (3.5 L)
15×10×1-inch jelly roll pan	40×25×2-cm
9×5×3-inch loaf pan	23×13×8-cm (2 L)
2-quart casserole	2 L

U.S. / standard metric equivalents

⅛ teaspoon = 0.5 ml	
¼ teaspoon = 1 ml	
½ teaspoon = 2 ml	
1 teaspoon = 5 ml	
1 tablespoon = 15 ml	
2 tablespoons = 25 ml	
¼ cup = 2 fluid ounces = 50 ml	
⅓ cup = 3 fluid ounces = 75 ml	
½ cup = 4 fluid ounces = 125 ml	
⅔ cup = 5 fluid ounces = 150 ml	
¾ cup = 6 fluid ounces = 175 ml	
1 cup = 8 fluid ounces = 250 ml	
2 cups = 1 pint = 500 ml	
1 quart = 1 litre	